KEYS TO
LIBERAL ARTS
SUCCESS

HOWARD E. FIGLER, PH.D.

CAROL CARTER • JOYCE BISHOP • SARAH LYMAN KRAVITS

Prentice
Hall

Upper Saddle River, New Jersey
Columbus, Ohio

Library of Congress Cataloging-in-Publication Data

Keys to liberal arts success / Howard E. Figler .... [et al.].
   p. cm.
   Includes bibliographical references and index.
   ISBN 0-13-030483-2
   1. Education, Humanistic. 2. College student orientation. 3. Study skills. I. Figler,
Howard E.

LC1021 .K49 2002
378'.012—dc21   2001036932

Vice President and Publisher: Jeffery W. Johnston
Senior Acquisitions Editor: Sande Johnson
Assistant Editor: Cecilia Johnson
Production Editor: Holcomb Hathaway
Design Coordinator: Diane C. Lorenzo
Cover Designer: Melissa Cullen
Cover Art: Artville
Production Manager: Pamela D. Bennett
Director of Marketing: Ann Davis
Director of Advertising: Kevin Flanagan
Marketing Manager: Christina Quadhamer
Marketing Assistant: Barbara Koontz

This book was set in Sabon by Aerocraft Charter Art Service. It was printed and bound
by R. R. Donnelley & Sons Company. The cover was printed by Phoenix Color Corp.

Pearson Education Ltd., *London*
Pearson Education Australia Pty. Limited, *Sydney*
Pearson Education Singapore Pte. Ltd.
Pearson Education North Asia Ltd., *Hong Kong*
Pearson Education Canada, Ltd., *Toronto*
Pearson Educación de Mexico, S.A. de C.V.
Pearson Education–Japan, *Tokyo*
Pearson Education Malaysia Pte. Ltd.
Pearson Education, *Upper Saddle River, New Jersey*

10 9 8 7 6 5 4 3 2 1
ISBN 0-13-030483-2

This book is dedicated to all of the faculty members and administrators at liberal arts colleges who work so diligently to maintain the integrity and spirit of the liberal education. These educators, and their students, are the "keepers of the flame."

—HOWARD FIGLER

Contents

2 LIBERAL ARTS COURSES   33

LEARNING ACROSS THE SPECTRUM

GOAL SETTING AND TIME MANAGEMENT   91

MAPPING YOUR COURSE

CRITICAL AND CREATIVE THINKING   113

TAPPING THE POWER OF YOUR MIND

7 READING AND STUDYING   143

MAXIMIZING WRITTEN RESOURCES

8 NOTE TAKING AND WRITING   173

HARNESSING THE POWER OF WORDS AND IDEAS

LISTENING, MEMORY, AND TEST TAKING   205

TAKING IN, RETAINING, AND DEMONSTRATING KNOWLEDGE

ADVANTAGES FOR LIBERAL ARTS GRADUATES   229

SUCCEEDING IN THE JOB MARKET

LIBERAL ARTS GRADUATES DO "GOOD WORK"   249

SEEKING BETTERMENT OF COMMUNITY AND SELF

Foreword

What place does a liberal arts education have in our fast-paced, high-tech society? Some wonder about the practical aspects of the liberal arts and question their relevance in an era of globalization, reengineering, and information overload. To the contrary, it is precisely the increasing complexity of issues and unprecedented rate of change that require a broad base of knowledge and a creative outlook. It seems to me that the time has never been more ripe nor the reasons more compelling to embrace the liberal arts as a framework from which to clarify personal values, launch a career, and address matters of global significance.

> To avoid the fatal flaws of the tragic Shakespearean heroes. . .
>
> To uncover and communicate the social implications of a business policy. . .
>
> To appreciate cultural nuances in a local economy. . .
>
> To understand the interpersonal dynamics inherent in teamwork. . .
>
> To give a voice to pressing matters of health and environment. . .

This is the grounding a liberal education provides for a successful career and a fully experienced life in a complex world.

Outfitted to climb the mountain of information and tackle the bottom line, liberal arts graduates are equipped, also, to enter the arena of human and ethical issues. Such issues are inherent in each new advancement from e-commerce to biotechnology. With willing students, a liberal arts education enlivens all of the senses, fostering curiosity and a passion for learning. It will ignite and nurture a search for meaning and discovery that will continue beyond the classrooms into the boardrooms and corporate suites, sports arenas and arts communities, and neighborhoods and governments.

Admittedly, securing the first professional position after graduation can present a challenge for liberal arts graduates. Once inside organizations, however, they advance admirably as they gain experience and apply their learning to workplace challenges. Seeing the big picture, communicating persuasively, applying analytical-thinking skills, and building relationships are liberal arts qualities highly coveted by potential employers.

Despite all of the noble reasons to value a liberal arts education, the knowledge of how best to apply and benefit from it exists primarily on an intuitive level. The elusive nature of the liberal arts is sadly discouraging to its students and graduates who seek to fully comprehend and articulate the contributions of a liberal education on a personal level and on the world stage.

Enter *Keys to Liberal Arts Success* to clearly and concisely spell out exactly how to get the most out of a liberal arts education, while earning the degree and after graduation. Over the years, the name of Howard Figler has become synonymous with the advancement of liberal arts. Although an accomplished career counselor, published author, and popular presenter on a wide variety of career-related topics, his unequivocal endorsement of liberal arts has held fast and remained a passion throughout his career.

I was introduced to Howard's work in the 1980s through his book *PATH: A Career Workbook for Liberal Arts Students*. This one-of-a-kind resource was extraordinarily valuable in my first career counseling position helping liberal arts students find their way.

Howard's enthusiastic lessons on the liberal arts have stuck with me over the years, from my diverse clientele at Career Development Services to current conversations with business people from around the globe. Through my Careers Q&A column featured on the *Wall Street Journal's* on-line career site (www.careerjournal.com), the evidence mounts that the world is packed with successful professionals in every arena whose higher education began with the liberal arts.

Still, many graduates find that it is they who have to build the bridge from their liberal arts education to their potential employers. Although their careers will be advanced and their lives enriched from their education, it will be incumbent on them to make their case and to make the connections. Howard Figler offers valuable insights to liberal arts students and graduates on how to do just that.

Keys to Liberal Arts Success provides suggestions on courses to take and promotional strategies to secure meaningful work. Howard's writing is clear and compelling in this inspiring book that beautifully blends the philosophy and the pragmatism of a liberal education. As serious as the subject is, the book is just plain fun and engaging.

The frame of reference that liberal arts graduates have to draw upon spans the history of civilization, the rhythms of nature, the beauty of art, and the wisdom of great philosophers. On your personal journey through work and life would you want to fortify yourself with anything less? Can our society and its institutions afford anything less from its community of workers and leaders?

Now more than ever "liberal arts is the course for life," and *Keys to Liberal Arts Success* is the gem of a book to help you make the most of it.

Deb Koen
Columnist, www.careerjournal.com
Author of *Career Choice, Change, and Challenge*
Vice-President, Career Development Services, Rochester, NY

Preface

This book was written to answer several persistent questions heard from liberal arts students around the country. Here are these questions and how this book will help you respond to them:

1 Why Should I Study Liberal Arts Rather Than a More "Vocationally Oriented" Curriculum?

A liberal education offers both career benefits and personal benefits. It allows you to have the best of both worlds—an appropriate education for the fast-changing, diverse world of work that exists today, and a breadth of learning that attunes you to the issues of life that affect everyone, regardless of their career aspirations or personal goals.

2 What Kinds of Liberal Arts Courses Should I Take?

This book gives you insights about the skills to look for in your liberal arts courses that will have a lasting benefit in your career. These skills are not found in course titles as much as they are between the lines of the syllabus. It's up to you to investigate courses beforehand to see which ones will maximize these valuable skills.

3 How Should I Choose My Liberal Arts Major?

Most students have an erroneous understanding of how their liberal arts majors relate to career opportunities. This book clears up the question of major and careers and helps you to see that your possibilities are far broader than you may think.

4 What Advantages Can I Anticipate in the Job Market as a Liberal Arts Graduate?

There are numerous ways in which your liberal education will help you progress in your work and adapt successfully to the rapidly changing and unpredictable world of jobs and entrepreneuring. This book will enhance your confidence in approaching your career, regardless of the kind of work you may want to do.

5 How Do I Find Social Value in My Career—"Good Work"?

Not many liberal arts students ask this question, but it comes up frequently after graduation, so it is useful to address it now. This book will show how your liberal education makes it possible for you to find many opportunities for "Good Work."

This book will help you to understand what may seem to be a paradox—that nonvocational courses, liberal arts, can enable you to progress greatly in the world of work. This is because liberal arts courses go above and beyond the mere acquisition of information or technical skills. They enable you to learn intellectual skills and adopt a creative perspective that you can apply to any new body of knowledge or set of problems. Even more importantly, you learn to reflect on the impact on humanity of the decisions you make in your work. You're not a mere technician. You're an actor on the stage of life.

—Howard Figler

Acknowledgments

My appreciation for liberal education has been a cumulative experience of 8 years as a college and university student, 20 years as a professional in colleges and universities, and 10 years in the business world. As a counselor, administrator, teacher, speaker, and author during these working years, I have observed the broad and pervasive successes of liberal arts graduates in the world of work. Therefore, I would like to acknowledge: All of the professors and students who have enabled me to gain an ever-deepening respect for the beauty and value of liberal learning; and all of the business and nonprofit leaders who have taught me the importance of liberal learning in their enterprises.

I have a special affection for the liberal education that I experienced as an undergraduate student at Emory University. In addition, I felt much like a "student" of liberal education during the 12 years that I served as director of the counseling and career center at Dickinson College. Faculty and students at Dickinson provided inspiring examples of the liberal arts at work in people's lives.

I would like to acknowledge with much gratitude the Career Center directors who made possible the profiles of liberal arts graduates in this book—Sharon Plew of Azusa Pacific University, Maureen Beck of Loyola Marymount University, Gloria Myklebust of Claremont McKenna College, Lynn Pearson of Whittier College, and Marcie Kirk-Holland of the University of California at Davis.

I am grateful to reviewer Scott Strausberger of Moravian College for his constructive suggestions regarding the manuscript. My editor at Prentice Hall, Sande Johnson, has been a tower of good cheer and support. She guided me through the various stages of this book with a keen eye for the organization of the overall book and the abundant good sense to tone down the excesses of my writing.

Jeff McIlroy first planted the seed of my thinking about writing this book, and I am most thankful to him for his encouragement. In the later stages of consideration, Carol Carter was a source of timely and helpful support.

—*Howard Figler*

About the Authors

Howard Figler, Ph.D., was Director of the Career and Counseling Center at Dickinson College for 12 years and Director of the Career Center at the University of Texas at Austin for 8 years. For the past 26 years, he has been a nationally known speaker, consultant, and workshop leader for numerous professional associations, businesses, nonprofit and government agencies, and colleges and universities. He has been head of Howard Figler, Ph.D. Associates since 1990. He is the  co-author of *The Career Counselor's Handbook* (with Richard Bolles), three editions of the best-selling book *The Complete Job-Search Handbook,* three editions of *PATH: A Career Workbook for Liberal Arts Students,* and *Liberal Education and Careers Today.* He holds a Ph.D. from Florida State University, an M.B.A. from New York University, and a B.A. from Emory University. Please write to Howard at **hefigler@pacbell.net.**

Carol Carter is Vice President, Director of Student Services for the College Learning Network. She has also been Director of Faculty Development at Prentice Hall for the last six years. She has written *Majoring in the Rest of Your Life: Career Secrets for College Students* and *Majoring in High*  *School.* She has also coauthored *Keys to Preparing for College, Keys to College Studying, The Career Tool Kit, Keys to Career Success, Keys to Study Skills, Keys to Thinking and Learning,* and *Keys to Success.* She has taught welfare to work classes, team taught in the La Familia Scholars Program at the Community College of Denver, and has conducted numerous workshops for students and faculty around the country. She is the host of the Keys to Lifelong Learning Telecourse, a 26-episode telecourse to help students at a distance prepare for college, career, and life success. In addition to working with students of all ages, Carol thrives on foreign travel and culture; she has been fortunate enough to have been a guest in 40 foreign countries. Please visit her Web site and write her at **www.caroljcarter.com.**

Joyce Bishop holds a Ph.D. in psychology and has taught for more than 20 years, receiving a number of honors, including Teacher of the Year for 1995 and 2000. For five years she has been voted "favorite teacher" by the student body and Honor Society at Golden West College, Huntington Beach, CA, where she has taught since 1987 and is a tenured professor. She has worked with a federal grant to  establish Learning Communities and Workplace Learning in her district, and has developed workshops and trained faculty in cooperative learning, active learning, multiple intelligences, workplace relevancy, learning styles, authentic assessment, team building, and the development of learning communities. She is currently teaching on-line and multimedia classes, and training other faculty to teach on-line in her district and region of 21 colleges. She also coauthored *Keys to College Studying, Keys to Success, Keys to Thinking and Learning,* and *Keys to Study Skills.* Joyce is the lead academic of the Keys to Lifelong Learning Telecourse, distributed by Dallas Telelearning.

Sarah Lyman Kravits comes from a family of educators and has long cultivated an interest in educational development. She coauthored *Keys to College Studying, The Career Tool Kit, Keys to Success, Keys to Thinking and Learning,* and *Keys to Study Skills* and has served as  Program Director for LifeSkills, Inc., a nonprofit organization that aims to further the career and personal development of high school students. In that capacity she helped to formulate both curricular and organizational elements of the program, working closely with instructors as well as members of the business community. She has also given faculty workshops in critical thinking, based on the Thinktrix critical-thinking system. Sarah holds a B.A. in English and drama from the University of Virginia, where she was a Jefferson Scholar, and an M.F.A. from Catholic University.

Introduction

by Howard Figler

How many people have you heard say: "You can't do anything with a liberal arts degree"? These people completely miss the evidence all around them, that liberal arts graduates are successfully employed across the entire spectrum of the world of work, and often they are CEOs of companies, heads of organizations, owners of businesses, leaders of government, and prominent in the professions. Those who do not become leaders are almost always successful and often highly satisfied with their work.

There is a great gulf between people's low expectations of liberal arts graduates and their abundant success. Generation after generation of liberal arts students have to explain to their parents and friends just why they're enrolling in such a "worthless" educational program. The graduates do not have opportunities to meet or talk with the freshmen, and the cycle starts all over again. Many people have a narrow view of the purposes served by higher education. They see college only as "vocational training." They evaluate every course in terms of its surface relationship to the "job market." If a course doesn't look as though it is obvious "vocational training," it is considered of little value.

Liberal arts courses serve different purposes. They exist to develop general mental faculties, generic learning skills, and perspectives on life. The appreciation for such values has diminished as students increasingly seek "job-related" courses. Colleges themselves are largely to blame for this reductionist view of higher education. Colleges and universities "sell" themselves as purveyors of vocational curricula. The broader and deeper purposes of higher learning are often left choking in the dust.

LIBERAL ARTS IS OFTEN MORE IMPORTANT THAN TECHNICAL TRAINING

Liberal arts curricula help a person's career far more than is commonly believed. I have been a career counselor for 30 years and have seen the qualities that lead to success and satisfaction in the world of work. These qualities are mental facility, versatility, understanding people, communication skills, higher values, and a spiritual involvement in one's work. Liberal education fosters these qualities, even though students, parents, and the general public may not notice that it's happening.

Many businesses . . . now want graduates with a liberal arts degree because they're often better able to adapt, solve problems, and think critically in an ever-changing economy.

"The more rapidly that technology in the workplace changes, the greater the premium for the skills a liberal arts graduate brings to the job market," says Joe Stone, Dean of the University of Oregon's College of Arts and Sciences. "One might think that as we become more technologically oriented, the training has to be narrowed to specific technical skills. But the exact opposite is true. A technical skill learned in college might become obsolete in a year or two.

"It's more common now to see an English major take a few computer classes, then get hired by a small Web publishing business or a software company," Stone says.[1]

Graduates of technical programs have a slight edge in getting their first jobs, but after that a liberal education graduate adapts better to the changing demands of the workplace. Liberal arts students are accustomed to studying 10 or 12 widely diverse areas of knowledge over only a year's time—from philosophy to physics to art history; they can, therefore, move from one project to another on the job with relative ease.

I studied as a liberal arts undergraduate at Emory University and had a dim awareness of the liberal education being provided for me. I liked the literature, philosophy, sociology, history, and religion courses but I didn't know why. I wondered which of these courses would help me survive in the world of work. I majored in economics for all the wrong reasons—to get "vocational training" and have a chance of being acceptable to the business world. I really thought I was a poor candidate for business, but I did not know of anything else to do. Doctoring and lawyering were too unpleasant for me to contemplate. I was scared of both of them because I knew I had no talent for either.

Inside you there's an artist you don't know about. Say yes quickly, if you know, if you've known it from before the beginning of the universe.

JALAI UD-DIN RUMI

My "age of enlightenment" regarding liberal arts came 10 years after graduation from Emory, beginning in 1970, when I was hired as a college counselor by Dickinson College, a superb liberal arts college in Carlisle, PA. Through 12 years of exposure to the faculty, students, alumni, and administrators, I came to appreciate the depth and perspectives of liberal learning. I saw that learning was approached as something more powerful, enduring, and richly human than mere preparation for the world of work. In fact, the faculty disavowed "job preparation" in the strongest terms.

They knew, and I gradually learned, that mental acuity, breadth of content, and the skills of learning would be many times more beneficial to their students than any "technical training" might be. Amidst calls from the market for "job preparation programs," the Dickinson faculty held firm. Other quality liberal arts colleges did likewise. The market proved them right. Colleges that upheld the substance and merits of liberal arts were rewarded with high enrollments. Surveys of Dickinson graduates showed them to be successfully employed. Alumni questionnaires revealed that they were highly pleased with their learning at Dickinson, and they believed this learning contributed greatly to their career success.

REASONS FOR THIS BOOK

I am writing this book for at least three reasons: First, to encourage you to develop the academic and study skills that are so central in a liberal education. You will benefit from these "habits of mind" and careful thinking all your life—in both your career and personal involvements. Second, to affirm that liberal arts graduates have strong prospects in the world of work. The more you embrace the substance of liberal education, and the skills that accrue, the more effective and satisfied you'll be in your jobs and careers. Finally, to state my belief that liberal arts graduates will be better citizens, neighbors, spouses, and friends, to the extent that they absorb the lessons and understandings of humanity that are so widely available in liberal education. Liberal arts graduates tend to be more likely to reflect on their behavior, learn from it, and have a broader perspective of how their lives fit with everyone else's on the planet.

The better a person understands her place in the world, the interconnections between concepts and phenomena, and the consequences of her behavior, the better she will do in her work. The broader and deeper her thinking, the more valuable she will be to an employer. The more she reads values into her work project, the better she will understand the effects of her company's products on its customers. Employers look for people who have the "vision" that liberal arts promotes.

Liberal arts is a muddle in the minds of many people who approach higher education. Those whose parents have liberal arts degrees have some positive idea of what to expect, but first-generation students are often completely mystified by it. The colleges themselves often confuse matters. They push their "vocational" majors because they're easier to "sell" and attract students, while they let the liberal arts courses just sit like a vast unspecified blob in their catalogs. In a consumerist culture that wants simple labels on everything (e.g., majors), the subtleties of liberal arts can be difficult to "sell."

Nonetheless, liberal arts proves itself in the job market. Go to the Alumni Office of your college or university, get names of alumni, call these graduates, and ask what their liberal education did for them. Read quotes of the liberal arts graduates in this book. Find liberal arts graduates in your neighborhood and ask them how their learning helped their careers.

We encourage you to take advantage of all that a liberal education can give you. Simply enrolling in liberal arts courses is not enough. Clever students can find ways to slide by, though it's harder in liberal arts because they make you write, think, and speak up. You have to want the best that liberal arts has to offer. Jump on those courses that work your mind like a jungle gym.

If you challenge yourself with the best professors, the courses that have the perspectives that are newest to you, and the courses that require you to improve your weaker skills, you will be the big winner. Liberal arts will evoke your finest creativity and call upon mental resources you didn't know you had.

HOW TO READ THE PROFILES OF THE LIBERAL ARTS GRADUATES IN THIS BOOK

This book includes many profiles of recent liberal arts graduates. In each of these profiles, the graduate describes his or her role in the world of work and offers observations about how liberal arts has affected his or her career. As you read these statements and perhaps identify with some of these graduates concerning your own career aspirations, please keep the following factors in mind.

They Are Young

None of these liberal arts graduates has been out of college more than 10 years. Some of them have only been out a year or two, many only three or four years. We chose to focus on the more recent graduates because we wanted to keep the gap between your age and their age fairly small. All are happy in their work and all have jobs with significant responsibilities. But, you haven't seen anything yet. They're just getting started. Each of these graduates will achieve far more of both traditional and nontraditional "success" in the years ahead because it's widely known that typical "liberal arts skills" (e.g., writing, managing complex problems, working well with people) are more valued as individuals take on greater responsibility and advance in their organizations.

They Have Jobs Across the Spectrum of the World of Work

A wide variety of jobs are represented in this small sample—lawyer, teacher, business consultants, financial administrators and counselors, fund-raiser, entrepreneur, the high-tech world, recruiter, writer, fountain designer, detective, and many others.

This makes the point, oft-stated by the graduates, that liberal arts people have the capability of doing almost anything. If we had offered a sample of 100 liberal arts graduates, you would have seen an even broader variety of areas represented in the world of work.

Many Jobs Are Learned On-the-Job

Many of the graduates make it clear that they knew little or nothing about their jobs when they first arrived. They were hired because of their general learning skills. From "knew little or nothing," they acquired knowledge of the job and quickly assimilated what they needed to know to become capable performers. Thus, any lack of prior "training" they may have worried about was not an issue.

Many of Their Comments Reinforce Each Other

Many of the graduates make similar comments—"I use my writing skills all the time," "critical thinking has been important for me," "I analyze problems, just like I did in college," "I appreciate getting to study diverse cultures; it helps me on the job," "I have to think out of the box, and liberal arts taught me that."

Hearing these comments from numerous graduates is fair evidence that liberal arts degree holders are having many similar and positive experiences in the world of work. They remind us that liberal education has a base of common skills and an inner core of encouraging the ability to learn with breadth and versatility.

They Are Adapting to the Flexible Marketplace

No matter how rapidly the pace of change revs up in the job market, liberal arts graduates are keeping up with it and adapting to the new jobs, new industries, and new problems. None of the graduates profiled complained about getting swamped by the changes or trying to avoid them. All seemed eager to go with the flow, take on new responsibilities, and learn new concepts whenever necessary.

Liberal Arts

Many students wonder how liberal education relates to the world of work and how the value of a liberal education compares to "vocational" majors. A liberal arts curriculum has many enduring benefits with respect both to careers and your personal and intellectual development.

Dear Ann Landers: I thought that this was pretty funny and that you might want to share it with your readers:

The graduate with an engineering degree asks: "Why does it work?" The graduate with an accounting degree asks: "How much will it cost?" The graduate with a liberal arts degree asks: "Do you want fries with that?"[1]

This Ann Landers column reflects what many people believe about those who graduate with a liberal arts degree—that it is useless and will lead to menial employment. In reality, liberal arts graduates' career prospects are vastly better than those in this "humorous" view.

In this chapter, you will explore answers to the following questions:

- What are the broad purposes of a liberal education?
- What are some of the unique benefits of a liberal education?
- Why is it a shortsighted view to look on a liberal education as an "investment"?
- What benefits of a liberal education appeal most to you?
- What does it mean when we say that a liberal arts graduate is "well rounded"?
- Why do all students need some liberal education?
- What is emotional intelligence, how does it relate to liberal education, and why is it important to your career?
- What is the importance of laughing in your work and life?

Students declare liberal arts majors for a variety of reasons. In fact, almost a half-million students completed liberal arts degrees in 1999 as did similar numbers in previous years.[2] Even in this age of computers, more college students study English.

> According to the National Center for Educational Statistics, computer science and informational technology accounted for only 2 percent of all bachelor's degrees awarded in 1995–1996. More than twice as many earned degrees in English language and literature. . . . The number of college degrees given in humanities and social sciences has been rising steadily since the mid-1980s. . . . Computer science grads peaked in 1986, at a level almost twice what it is today.[3]

This chapter will focus on the value that students find in liberal education, including the development of career potential.

The real university is a state of mind.

ROBERT PIRSIG, *ZEN AND THE ART OF MOTORCYCLE MAINTENANCE*

HAT IS A LIBERAL ARTS PROGRAM?

You may be uncertain what a *liberal arts* program involves. It's a broad program that encompasses a number of courses, many of which may be required for you to complete your degree. Having "required" courses may already sound distasteful, but bear with us.

> We must be the change we wish to see in the world.
>
> GANDHI

The liberal arts program includes both arts and sciences courses that offer a great breadth and depth of knowledge to help you succeed in college and in every step of your career, regardless of what area of employment you may choose.

Following are some of the values of liberal arts courses that will benefit you in your academic and personal pursuit of excellence.

1. *You will learn how to learn.* Liberal arts gives you the confidence to tackle ANY area of knowledge. In college and a job marketplace that are continually changing, you will find this confidence comes in handy. Time and again in your work, you'll encounter subjects that are new to you; your general learning skills will pay off handsomely.

2. *You will learn how to write.* The best thing that ever happened to me in college was the D that I received on my first paper in English Composition. Until then, I thought my writing was pretty hot stuff. After that D, and the notations that littered my paper like confetti, my liberal education began.

3. *You will discover the interconnectedness of all knowledge.* Though liberal arts courses are divided into compartments, the liberal arts approach emphasizes that there are fibers of connection between all areas of knowledge. For example, the water supply feature of the environment involves biology, chemistry, the politics of water distribution, the sociology of water use, the spiritual aspects of water rituals, and religious rites that revolve around water. Your ability to see interconnections in your work will enable you to see creative solutions to complex problems.

4. *You will look at your actions in terms of the effect they have on others and on the world.* Liberal arts teaches that one's actions are part of the cosmos, that energy you expend on anything has a place in the "big picture." Behavior has consequences. Whether now in a part-time capacity or after you graduate, you will discover that work is not merely earning a living. It's leaving your mark on people and things. Work is an opportunity to touch the lives of others, to participate in the great experiments known as America, humanity, and the life of the spirit.

Thus, you will examine your work in terms of its deepest possible meanings. This gives your work a sense of exhilaration. Sound a little lofty? Why not dream? Cure a disease? Build an enterprise? Write a book? Start a movement? Liberal arts encourages you to see the possible.

5. *Liberal arts fosters your communication skills.* Because ideas are always in the air when studying liberal arts, you will, by necessity, become a communicator. Professors will insist that you write your ideas clearly and the liberal arts environment will encourage you to speak up—both in class and out. Your growing ability to speak and write will pay great dividends in your career because most career progress rides on the flying carpet of effective communication.

6. *Liberal arts makes you unafraid of being ignorant.* Liberal education teaches you that research skills are your right arm. Today's ignorance becomes tomorrow's knowledge when you are accustomed to being a learner. You begin by acknowledging what you don't know, and then you figure out how to get the information that you need. Liberal arts teaches that whatever you need to know, it can be found. So, no matter how deep or profound your ignorance, it's a starting place and you won't be there for long.

7. *Liberal arts students come to regard learning as a joy in itself.* Isn't learning a dull thing that happens in libraries and who wants to spend their life there? Isn't "learning as a joy in itself" something that the author of the college catalog and the college president would like to believe, but "come on—give us a break"?
The pleasure of learning will grow on you. At first, you may not feel it. Give it a chance to take hold. Step back from looking at college as "what's it gonna get me?" Instead, think "How are my mind and spirit changing as a result of these experiences?"

8. *Liberal arts gives you a growing appreciation for the stunning array of human differences in this world.* Study other cultures, tune into the differing beliefs that people have, observe the rituals that are so foreign to us. Get a close-up look at Hindus and what they believe, how they dress, how they view marriage, and their philosophy of "the good life." No two societies are alike. We're not all Americans on this globe and history did not begin the day we were born.

What does this have to do with being a successful student? Everything. The United States is populated by dozens of different cultures. Most businesses have connections with other countries. Your neighbors, taxi drivers, store owners, and business colleagues increasingly have cultural backgrounds different from your own. Learning how to appreciate each other's differences will better enable you to enjoy working together now and in the future, and will serve to strengthen your common goals.

The liberal education philosophy requires that we study and reflect on our place in the cosmos, that learning must be as broad and interconnected as possible. If we don't contemplate what it means to be human, why we are here, what we are doing, and how people relate to each other, we have not done anything.

This broad approach to learning works in your favor when you seek employment or enter the working world as an entrepreneur. The greatest prosperity comes to those who can adapt smoothly to changing conditions (e.g., job market), can tune into the differences in other subcultures and cultures (e.g., anthropology sensitizes you to the corporate culture), and can absorb new areas of knowledge quickly.

I believe that businesses should go back to basics in recruiting, should forget about business schools and recruit the best liberal arts students we can find. What is desperately needed in an increasingly complex world dominated by technicians is the skepticism and sense of history that a liberal arts education provides.

FELIX ROHATYN

If I had it to do over again, I would not have majored in journalism. I would have chosen history or English, or political science as preparation for a journalism career. After all, news is history the next day.

CONNIE CHUNG

It is essential that the student acquire an understanding of and a lively feeling for values. He must acquire a vivid sense of the beautiful and the morally good. Otherwise he—with his specialized knowledge—more closely resembles a well-trained dog than a harmoniously developed person.

ALBERT EINSTEIN

HY AM I A LIBERAL ARTS MAJOR?

The poem on the following pages, "I Tell Them I'm a Liberal Arts Major,"[4] was written by Carol Jin Evans, then a student at Metropolitan State College in Denver, majoring in English. "I was angry when I wrote that poem. I had a feeling about my education that went far beyond the commercial aspects of it," said Evans. She recognized that her liberal education was giving her something completely different and far better than "vocational training."

It bothers me to hear people ask a liberal arts graduate, "What are you going to DO with it?" As though a liberal education were a commodity, like potatoes or rice. When Evans writes, "I'm going to sneak it away from my family gathered for my commencement and roam the high desert making love to it," she expresses both the beauty and despair of liberal arts learning; it's a lover of the highest sensibility, but others may fail to acknowledge or understand it.

When I hear liberal arts being kicked around, I muse that seldom has there been such a vast ocean of difference between what people believe

---

I Tell Them I'm a Liberal Arts Major

And then, of course, they say: how quaint; and what are you
going to do with that?
What am I going to do with it?
As though these four phenomenal years were an object I could cart away
from college—
a bachelor's degree across my back like an ermine jacket,
or my education hung from a ceiling on a string.
What am I going to do with it?
Well, I thought perhaps I'd put it in a cage
to see if it multiplies or does tricks or something
so I could enter it in a circus
and realize a sound dollar-for-dollar return
on my investment.
Then, too, I am exploring the possibility of
whipping it out like folding chair
at V.F.W. parades and Kiwanis picnics.
I might have it shipped and drive through Italy.
Or sand it down and sail it.
What am I going to do with it?
I'll tell you one thing:
I'm probably never going to plant sod around it.

(continued)

such a degree is worth (often cited as "worthless") and the substantial rewards, both financial and personal, that are experienced by liberal arts degree holders. Liberal arts graduates do exceedingly well in their careers, and they value the scope and richness of their education. Yet, the general public still sniffs at the degree and wonders why people pursue it. Most of us have friends and neighbors who are liberal arts graduates, but we don't know it. We often fail to make the connection between their successes and their undergraduate study.

I Tell Them I'm a Liberal Arts Major, continued

You see, I'm making it a definitive work:
repapering parts of my soul
that can never be toured by my friends;
wine glass balanced in one hand,
warning guests to watch the beam
that hits people on the head
when they go downstairs to see the den.
You don't understand—
I'm using every breath to tread water
in all-night swimming competitions
with Hegel, Marx, and Wittgenstein;
I am a reckless diver fondling the bottom of civilization
for ropes of pearls;
I am whispering late into the night on a river bank with Zola;
I am stopping often, soaking wet and exhausted, to weep
at the Bastille.
What am I going to do with it?
I'm going to sneak it away from my family
gathered for my commencement
and roam the high desert
making love to it.

—*Carol Jin Evans, Metropolitan State College*

When Evans writes, "Well, I thought perhaps I'd put it in a cage to see if it multiplies or does tricks or something so I could enter it in a circus and realize a sound dollar-for-dollar return on my investment," she uses sarcasm to expose the small-minded commercialism of people who want their degrees to "pay off" immediately. Evans' "circus" metaphor is not accidental. We want our educations to make us trained animals.

WHY REACH BEYOND YOURSELF?

We live in an intensely consumerist culture. We value our education in terms of what it can buy us. It is hard to rise above that level when advertising counsels, implores, and manipulates us to buy, buy, buy. Look around your room and in your closet. How many of those items do you use or need? If you're still thinking of when you're going to buy your first BMW or Porsche, you may want to skip this section and read elsewhere.

As producers (we) bemoan the grinding pace of (our) jobs. As consumers, (we) demand 59-cent tacos, $199 coast-to-coast flights, instantaneous delivery, a never-ending cavalcade of new products and . . . The protesters at the World Trade Organization were chasing the wrong culprit. It's not faceless corporations that are responsible for capitalism's sometimes rapacious instincts. It's us. A chicken in every pot has become two SUVs in every garage. American consumers have rewritten the Bill of Rights: life, liberty and more cheap stuff.

GARY HAMEL[5]

Why liberal arts? This course of study enriches who you are as a student, a community participant, or a professional. More importantly, it helps you envision your career as a "work," a body of creativity and effort designed to accomplish more than just earning a living. If you view your job merely as something to be tolerated, you'll get the drudgery and feelings of "slavery" that go with it.

The money is always there, but the pockets change; it is not in the same pockets after a change; and that is all there is to say about money.

GERTRUDE STEIN

Why liberal arts? Why live? To do a work that means something. To have a burning desire to accomplish something. To "leave a scratch on the wall." To touch the lives of others. To do something better than it has been done before. To be excited to talk with your spouse and family about your work.

Liberal arts—what are you going to DO with it? You'll do whatever you most want to do. You'll do what strikes you as a mountain worth climbing. You'll do anything you want because your versatile skills allow you to learn new material, form new working relationships, and conceive new solutions to problems.

Those who worry about what to DO with a college degree have the view of a technician, who needs to see an obvious, simple connection between college "training" and a job. A technician does not have the perspective to recognize that a broad education allows you to choose from the entire rainbow of possibilities.

Furthermore, education stimulates your search for what is much deeper than career advancement—the Good.

The highest objective of knowledge is the essential nature of the Good, from which everything that is good and right derives its value for us.

PLATO

WHY IS LIBERAL EDUCATION RIGHT FOR YOU?

Living as we do in the age of product promotion, it seems appropriate to "advertise" for liberal education. Which of the following motivations speak to you as you embark on your liberal arts journey?

- Want to be so adaptable that today's pace of change will never bother you, it will only make you better?
- Want to see "the big picture" so that America's best businesses will want to hire you?
- Want to invent a profitable business that brings delight to people's lives?
- Want to tap the depths of your being?
- Want to be able to support yourself the way you like to live because your well of financial creativity will never run dry?
- Want to develop your mind so that it knows no boundaries?
- Want to have a career that reaches beyond yourself?

Get your red-hot liberal arts education while you can! Businesses want it! Your soul wants it! YOU want it! Sign up now!!

The population from which all our production and consumption arises is highly oriented toward humanistic drives—the enjoyment of music, art, cinema, and politics, for
example. Nothing kills sales more than dull products. People lead with their senses.
We love to touch, feel, listen, and see. Our fundamental activity is communication.
Scholastically, these senses are in the domain of liberal arts.

TOM JACKSON6

Here are a few more perspectives that are characteristic of a liberal
arts curriculum and the people who study it.

The Knowledge of the World Is in Books

Ever watch liberal arts graduates in a bookstore? They think it's a candy
store. They want to buy everything in sight. They run their fingers gently
along the spine or cover of a book, just to get the feel of it—we're talking
about love here. It could be a poem by a Romantic poet: "Ode to a
Bookstore." The graduate picks up a book, opens it, starts reading it, fon-
dles it, adds it to the stack of possible "buys" and moves on to the next
one—browses through it—looks good. Hey, they *all* look good! The liberal artser just knows there's something in every book that she needs to
learn—if she can just find time to read all of them.

Books capture and collect the wisdom of the world. Whatever perspective one needs, it's in a book somewhere. If there's a question you're
trying to answer, a few well-chosen books will help. If there's a new field
you want to know all about, books will get you up-to-speed. If you want
to get lost in a new world of information, insight, perspectives, or stories,
a book is the place for you.

Liberal arts graduates don't necessarily respect all books equally. But
they know that if one doesn't have the insight or information they seek,
another one will. They know that when someone has something of importance to say, sooner or later he'll put it in a book.

Books are the vessels that carry and preserve a civilization. If you
think books are just what fill shelves, by the time you've graduated, you'll
choose your home near a library or a bookstore, or both.

The Liberal Arts Graduate Is Well-Rounded

This is the most frequent description of the merits of a liberal education.
Are we sculptures that have had our rough edges scraped off? Are we well-
fed? Do we have a little of this and a little of that, adding up to a big ball
of clay that represents nothing?

People who say we're "well-rounded" are really searching for words such as versatile, multi-dimensional, able to adopt many different viewpoints, and knowledgeable in a wide variety of areas. Jack of all . . . . and master of none? Better than that. Well-roundedness indicates that the graduate is capable of being comfortable in any of numerous disciplines. By implying a circle, it means that the graduate is accessible from any direction. No matter which way he faces, he's in the right position.

A well-rounded graduate is comfortable with any problem and can deal with people whose knowledge bases are different from her own. Parachute the liberal arts person into any unfamiliar location and she will adapt, become familiar with the culture, and begin to acquire the knowledge necessary to be useful.

Most of all, well-roundedness implies versatility, the ability to address many different tasks and see many sides of a problem. Well-roundedness is valuable to any employer. We can put you in Brazil or Ethiopia—new culture, new religion, new ecology—and you'll figure out how to make yourself useful.

Everyone Views Things Differently

Empathy is the skill that binds us together, the ability to see the world the way the other person sees it. Liberal education fosters empathy. What is history, French, philosophy, or sociology but a difference of viewpoints? You and your roommate may not initially see eye-to-eye. He's Chinese. You're South American. He's an athlete. You're a nature bug. He wants to make money. You want to save the world. Can you coexist? Liberal arts encourages you to recognize and honor your differences.

People Want to Be Loved, Appreciated, and Respected

All liberal arts graduates are humanists at heart. Under the veneer of commerce, daily activity, even wars, all human beings want to love and be loved. Liberal education teaches us that the human drive to be loved, appreciated, and respected is fundamental. It reminds us that we are social and spiritual beings.

Making Money Is a Reflection of Your Beliefs

How we choose to make money tells a lot about what we believe in. Work occupies 50 to 70 percent of our waking hours, so it represents our day-to-day philosophy of how to live. How do you approach your job? Bitterly? Numbly? Or with spirit? With laughter?

LIBERAL ARTS GRADUATE IN THE REAL WORLD: CASE 1

Letitia was a music major who migrated to liberal arts. She had decided not to be a performing violinist, but still wanted to stay involved with music. She was extremely disappointed that her dream of a performing career had not been realized. In fact, she felt as though her entire identity had been ripped away. Though few who seriously study music become successful performers, Letitia had believed all along that she was one of those few, and now the dream was fading.

Though Letitia enjoyed her liberal arts courses, any hope she had of joining the working world seemed dim. Music and philosophy. What does one *do* with those? Especially if you're not going to make it as a musician, and you have no interest in teaching philosophy. "What happens to all the other music and philosophy graduates?" she wondered, and then, "Maybe I don't want to know the answer to that."

Letitia graduated and did the only thing that made sense to her—she began looking for employment in the world of music. She hounded music stores and finally got a job as a salesperson at a store that specialized in pianos—Steinway grand pianos. So, Letitia sold and sold, and enjoyed it because she was around beautiful music and could bring music into others' lives.

A few years passed and she became a part-owner of the store. Eventually, she bought out the older, original owners. And then disaster struck. Two things happened in rapid succession—a flood in the store destroyed several of the pianos, and the market for Steinways dropped precipitously.

"People are not buying enough of our Steinways to keep us going. We must either come up with a new market or we're gone." Letitia considered expanding to include a new line of pianos in addition to Steinway, but she was resistant. "Everybody I know in this business tells me that Steinway is what the teachers want, what the students want, and what the concert halls want. Every concert I see has a Steinway. Every reputable teacher has a Steinway. Every concertizer aspires to play on a Steinway."

Checking with other pianos stores, Letitia was surprised to find Yamahas and other non-Steinways selling reasonably well, but she could not believe that the professional market she serviced would find anything but Steinway acceptable.

Then, while worrying about the future of her business, Letitia thought of something she had heard in a philosophy course, and had also heard her college roommate, a physics major, talk about: the Heisenberg "Uncertainty Principle."

What does this have to do with a piano store? The "Uncertainty Principle" can be paraphrased something like this: "Every observation is affected by the observer." In other words—and this has turned scholarly research on its collective ear—all research is suspect because the investigator gathers data with his own ideas about how it will turn out, or worse yet, how he *wants* it to turn out. What does this have to do with Letitia's business dilemma?

Letitia realized that her "data," the opinions of her fellow music professionals, teachers, and students, were biased by the fact that her music clients all adored Steinways. Their lives were enmeshed with the Steinway piano. They did not *want* the Steinway to have a falling market share.

But, Letitia reasoned, "Could there be a new generation of piano teachers and students who are not nearly as attached to the Steinway, who feel good music can be produced on other pianos, and who want to pay less?" Letitia realized that her data had been biased and that a new non-Steinway market was waiting to be tapped. She had needed a little nudge from her liberal arts background to help her see the light.

Liberal arts pops up in strange places. Just when you think you cannot solve your real-world problem, an idea or a concept from past liberal learning slides into your head and you see the problem and its possible solution in a new way.

WHY OBTAIN A HIGHER EDUCATION?

Why take four years to complete college, when there are fortunes to be made and mountains to climb? Time's a-wasting. Why sit in a chair and study at a desk for four years?

Many entrepreneurs skipped college on their way to the bank. Some would say that liberal arts and college courses are just for eggheads or people who want to impress each other at parties.

Some people can make a good case for self-education, or for no education beyond high school. College is not for everyone. Some prefer to be completely in charge of all their learning.

However, people have been gathering in learning communities for thousands of years. There must be something about learning from and with others that is appealing and beneficial. I suspect that most people would not educate themselves as well as they would be educated by a planned curriculum. If you accept that group learning may be for you, here are some of the chief benefits you can expect. You are far more likely to derive these benefits from a liberal education because the approaches of liberal arts courses emphasize these benefits.

1. A Sense of Awe and Wonder

Sure, you wonder what you're doing in college in the first place. Maybe mom and dad sent you here, and that's all you know. You wonder why college could be even half as important as your parents think it is.

In a liberal arts curriculum, you develop a sense of awe and wonder about the world and humanity. A profound respect for all that is living and how everything fits together. Awe that there is so much to learn and how magnificently it all intertwines. Wonder that human beings are so resilient and creative. Awe in the face of human complexity. Wonder at what greater forces and spirits exist that we cannot see or hear.

2. You Can Learn Anything

Liberal arts throws so many different ideas, tasks, and viewpoints at you that you're overwhelmed at first. It feels like trying to catch raindrops. Gradually, you come to appreciate your ability to learn a vast array of different subjects. Eventually, you say to yourself, "I can learn it."

3. A Sense of Your Place in the World

It is possible to recognize how many other people there are besides yourself and, at the same time, believe you were put here for a reason. Your uniqueness—the combination of talents and drives that characterizes only you—will allow you to make a place for yourself. Liberal arts brings you the world as your study vehicle, and then encourages you to ask, "Where am I in all this?"

4. A View of What It Is to Be Human

The human condition. Why we suffer. What brings us joy. How we influence each other. What distinguishes humans from other forms of life? What is free will? How does your will interact with people and forces that impact you? Human differences and human commonalities.

5. The Pleasure of Learning

Liberal arts emphasizes that learning itself is prized more than "using" learning to gain material ends. Understanding your life and your world are goals in themselves.

"The best thing for being sad," replied Merlin, beginning to huff and blow, "is to learn something. That is the only thing that never fails. You may grow old and trembling in your anatomy, you may miss your only love, you may see the world around you devastated by evil lunatics, or your honor trampled in the sewer of baser minds. There is only one thing for it then—to learn . . . That is the only thing the mind can never exhaust, never alienate, never be tortured by, never fear or distrust, and never dream of regretting . . ."

TERRENCE H. WHITE, *THE ONCE AND FUTURE KING*

6. A Stimulated Curiosity

Higher education encourages your deeper curiousity. Liberal arts graduates are enticed by opportunities to explore, research, and discover new ideas, new phenomena, and new viewpoints.

7. To Become an Interesting Person

It's been said that a liberal arts graduate is one with whom you would not be bored if you sat together for a 12-hour train ride. Being a good conversationalist is not a small thing. You learn more by being interesting and accessible. Learning begets learning begets more learning.

Technology . . . the knack of so arranging the world that we don't have to experience it.

MAX FRISCH

8. The Ability to Look Beyond Today's Technology

It seems we are entering the age of cyberspace, where all is accessible on the Internet, everybody is networked to each other, and every human convenience is at our fingertips. Perhaps computer technology will continue to pervade our lives, just as the telephone, the automobile, and the airplane have become fixtures in modern existence.

Nonetheless, liberal education teaches you to step back from emerging technology, and ask, "What is this doing to us? What may happen to our lives as a result? Is there such a thing as too much technology? What lines should be drawn in the sand?" Liberal arts recognizes that so-called "progress" is not necessarily good, and it may not be inevitable. Some believe technological change cannot be stopped. Just because we invent it, does that mean we have to use it? Is it going to be "technology whether we like it or not"? Or do we have choices?

9. Learning to Ask "Why?"

Just because it can be done doesn't mean it should be done. Ultimately, the "Why?" questions are what our lives are about. Liberal arts insists that those questions be asked, debated, reconsidered, and applied to decisions about human affairs.

D O YOU NEED A HIGHER EDUCATION?

You're at least 18 years old, you've already been sitting in school for 12 or more years, and you question whether the benefits outlined here are worth the effort. Why not just slide by, take the courses that get you through as fast as possible, have as much fun as you can, and leave all that educational stuff for the intellectuals? Who needs awe and wonder when you can have parties, easy courses, and good times with your friends?

There is no need to give up good times, friends, or getting out of your study chair. They can coexist with the learning benefits of higher education. It doesn't have to be an either–or situation.

Why should you get as much as possible from your liberal education? The benefits of higher education described in this book are precisely the ones you need most in the world of work. They are not just for intellectuals. They're for everyone. The attributes that will enable you to soar in the world of work are exactly those that liberal arts gives you—curiosity, seeing the "big picture" (awe and wonder), love of learning, examining how technology affects human beings, conversational ability, and a deeper sense of your humanity. Ask anyone who hires college graduates what they look for and they will cite the qualities discussed here, as well as communication skills and other skills that will be identified later.

You need what liberal arts has to offer. The more you embrace the qualities noted here, the more you'll prosper. Liberal arts is the best chance you'll ever have to sharpen your learning and communication skills and develop a habitual "big picture" way of looking at things. In a fast-paced world of work where technology changes overnight, the person who has nimble learning skills will get ahead every time. Liberal arts is the most challenging set of "rope courses for the mind" that you ever saw. You need them. Your friends need them. Everyone in the business world and elsewhere needs them.

In the future there will be more and more concentration in the academic system on vocationally oriented education. What will be in scarcest supply will be individuals who have well-rounded preparation and a foundation to move through the different career demands of the future. That preparation comes best from learning that includes the ability to communicate well in writing as well as verbally, a perspective on the past that comes from history, a broad exposure to literature, a knowledge of science and mathematics, and a taste of the artistic. That preparation comes from a core of liberal arts education. . . . Spend the college years engaged in the preparation that will not come on the job.

BOB TREADWAY[7]

WHAT IS EMOTIONAL INTELLIGENCE?

Daniel Goleman has written several books about "emotional intelligence."[8] It's worth calling attention to this area of human functioning because it is widely underappreciated. Emotional intelligence has much to do with success, perhaps even more than you think. Furthermore, conventional intelligence—IQ, cognitive intelligence—has a connection to success that may surprise you.

Let's refer to "IQ" as a generic label for general, cognitive intelligence, what people think of as "being smart." "General intelligence" is often identified with what people score on IQ tests, the Scholastic Aptitude Test, and other general ability tests. The surprising fact is that seldom has anyone found more than a weak positive correlation between such aptitude tests and career success. In a review of Thomas Stanley's book, *The Millionaire Mind,* by Chad Roedemeier, Stanley is quoted as declaring that "I find no correlation between SAT scores, grade-point averages and economic achievement. None."[9] In *The Millionaire Mind,* Stanley notes that only 20 percent of millionaires attribute their financial success to their IQs.[10]

Yes, that's right, smart people don't succeed any more often than those of average IQ. The same is true of people who make high grades in college. They don't succeed any more often than those who earn average grades.

So, what's going on here? Is there a conspiracy against intelligence? Is it the same reason that the brightest people (e.g., Adlai Stevenson, Bill Bradley) tend not to get elected President?

We frequently see straight A students who can't make the cut. A pathetic preoccupation with marks seems to clog the entryway for other experiences.

DR. ROBERT K. ARMSTRONG, *MANAGER, COLLEGE RELATIONS, E.I. DUPONT DE NEMOURS*

It turns out that what's measured by IQ and aptitude tests is only a small part of what enables individuals to be successful. A much bigger part is their ability to relate effectively, warmly, productively, and persuasively

REAL WORLD PERSPECTIVE

Jennifer Wong, *Claremont McKenna College, 1990,*
Majors: Literature and Psychology

I have a close-up perspective of liberal arts because I work in the Admissions Department of Claremont McKenna College. I've been an admissions officer at three colleges—St. Mary's in Moraga, California, Sarah Lawrence, and Claremont McKenna.

My first job after graduation was in sales and marketing for a local publisher. I changed to my first admissions job at St. Mary's because the publishing job was a poor fit for me. I was working for a math textbook publisher. While I had no problem mastering the math knowledge needed for the job, I had no great love for the products I was selling and marketing. One of my college friends was working in admissions for Harvey Mudd College and suggested that I explore that field.

I saw college admissions work as an opportunity to introduce students to the liberal arts experience.

I grew up in Berkeley thinking it was normal. I recognize that every high school student views his or her hometown as "the way things are." Liberal arts helps you to see that there are a thousand different perspectives. There is no single version of "normal."

As an admissions officer, I encounter high school students who are confused about the meaning of a liberal education. I explain it to them so that they may consider enrolling, and then I observe their progress during the four years of learning. I see how liberal arts impacts them.

I took several literature courses involving Picaro characters (outside the mainstream of society). I think that by reading and analyzing picaresque characters, I developed an attraction to such characters and a sense of how they might fit in and be good for society. When I work with prospective students, I am often drawn to the quirky kids and may act as their advocate in the admissions process.

(continued)

To me, the liberal arts experience is a chance to take a lot of different courses and realize that very little is black and white; there's always the stuff in the middle that's gray. There's never one right way to do or think about anything.

It's the skills you get out of a liberal education that matter, such as communication and problem solving. The social skills you learn at party conversations are very important too. Community pressure and support help students to become more articulate because you're more intimately accountable to each other.

I'll tell you the value of a liberal education. Was there an Internet start-up major when I enrolled in college? No. Yet many of my fellow graduates are employed by those companies now. Becoming a good communicator and problem solver, being analytical, thinking on your feet; this is what has enabled the international studies, literature, and other majors to succeed in high tech and everywhere else.

Everything in this world is connected, and part of a liberal arts education is seeing those connections. Highly successful people see outside the traditional boxes.

I GREW UP IN BERKELEY, THINKING IT WAS NORMAL.

In a business school or other vocational program, the boundaries of thought are pretty clearly defined; in a liberal arts school they're not. The interconnections between disparate things are emphasized and embraced.

A liberal arts graduate usually has a lot of social consciousness. People from liberal arts colleges are ultimately those who are more thoughtful and more concerned about what's going on in this world.

Larger universities have noticed the merits of the liberal arts approach in small colleges and are trying to incorporate them. The trend in large universities has been toward honors colleges (small colleges within large universities).

with the widest possible range of people. These aspects are what we now know as "emotional intelligence." IQ measures certain limited kinds of intelligence, but it misses those qualities that are more predictive of success in the real world. People who succeed are those who have an abundance of "emotional skills." You can call them people skills, social skills, emotional skills, common sense, or being skilled in the ways of the world. These are the qualities that make a difference.

No one ever accused President Eisenhower of being dumb because he finished near the bottom of his West Point class. Nor was President Truman castigated because he didn't have a college degree. Both Eisenhower and Truman had enormous common sense, managerial ability, compassion, and understanding of human nature that made them successful Presidents.

DAN K. THOMASSON[11]

When I was an adolescent, I had the idea that if you could succeed in school and make good grades, things would fall into place. I didn't know there was such a thing as "emotional intelligence"; I just thought I was shy, inarticulate, unpersuasive, and likely to remain so for the rest of my life. In a way, "emotional" and "intelligent" seemed like opposite words. Being intelligent sounded like being cool and detached, whereas being emotional sounded like screaming all over the place. Only lately have we discovered that the two words go together.

Because many people, especially men, believe that being "emotional" is being weak, "emotional intelligence" is still often identified with women; men often resist the very idea. That profoundly misguided view will slow the acceptance of emotional IQ. But the good news is that emotional intelligence can be learned, and that men and women who are open to such learning will enhance their lives and their career prospects.

There are lots of brilliant people who can't relate with others. We replace that kind of person every day.

ROBERT LOPRESTO, *SENIOR PARTNER, KORN/FERRY INTERNATIONAL*

Emotional IQ and Liberal Arts

What does emotional IQ have to do with liberal education? They may seem to be different concepts because liberal education emphasizes the development of your cognitive abilities. And, we already know that grades are unrelated to emotional development or career success.

Following are some suggestions on how you can apply your liberal education in ways that will enhance your emotional IQ.

1. *Take courses that require oral presentations.* You'll become accustomed to voicing your viewpoint and having give-and-take with others. Life in the career world is like that. Speaking out requires you to manage your emotions. What if someone intensely disagrees with you? How do you handle it? How do you control yourself yet still support your emotionally felt viewpoint? What if someone criticizes you behind your back? What do you do about it without blowing up or being vindictive? How do you handle criticism in general? What if someone deliberately misrepresents your viewpoint? How do you manage your emotions?

2. *Socialize with your fellow students outside class.* Some students hide in study rooms to avoid contact with people because the books are more friendly and less threatening. They miss many opportunities for emotional development. Being active includes discussing class topics, participating in college activities, and generally being part of informal exchanges whenever you can. Some may regard "bull sessions" as wasting time, but they are not. Social interchange is how business gets done. When everyone is talking at once, what do you do? How do you get yourself heard?

3. *Develop friendships.* Friendships are connections with others that call on many features of emotional intelligence—loyalty, trustworthiness, empathy, compassion, and the ability to be accommodating. A constructive friendship is characterized by all of those qualities and more. There are many superficial friendships, where disloyalty and lack of compassion are present. You don't need these. They are not evidence of emotional intelligence.

4. *Develop your awareness of "emotional intelligence" and how to improve it.* Many people may understand emotional IQ at a rudimentary level, but they don't believe it can be learned. They may say, "Well, some have it and others don't. I'm just not a people person."

Violence in our society is the direct result of poor emotional intelligence—people who choose not to manage their emotions for peaceful results. They turn to angry, physical responses instead.

Learn to see emotional intelligence (or the lack of it) at work in your everyday existence. When the guy in the grocery checkout line takes a slight bump from a shopping cart as a personal affront, there's low emotional intelligence at work. When a woman sees two people arguing angrily, smiles at them, and asks if she can help in some way, she may help to defuse the conflict.

REAL WORLD PERSPECTIVE

James Schermerhorn, *UC–Davis, 1996,*
Major: International Relations; Minor: Rhetoric, Concentration in German

I majored in international relations while completing my degree at the University of California–Davis in 1996. The road I traveled to Davis had some twists and turns. I dropped out of high school and made F's in junior college even though my father and mother were educated at Stanford and Radcliffe, respectively. I was a handful.

I had dyslexia and a serious distaste for school during those years. I encourage dyslexic students to seek help from their schools and I encourage the schools to look out for such students and help them. This is a personal goal of mine. If you're dyslexic, it's not your fault and you deserve help.

I went to work as a salesman and cold-caller and was training to earn my stock broker's license when I decided to give college another shot. I said to myself, "I'm going to pick the toughest thing I can find in higher education and if I can do it, that will be a sign that I'm meant to complete a college degree."

What I chose was a 10-week immersion course in German at the University of California–Berkeley. That meant I spoke only German every day and night. I passed the course, enrolled full-time at the College of Marin, then later transferred to Davis to complete my degree.

I had a two-month internship in Moscow, Russia, during my junior year in 1995. I was the marketing coordinator for Russian-American Marketing Services. I assisted in the creative brainstorming process, proposal writing, and presentations in the Moscow office for Russian/American joint ventures. Results: three proposals written, three presentations given, one account won.

During my early years at the College of Marin, I waited tables at Alessia, an upscale restaurant in Ross, California. That job taught me a lot about people. It felt Shakespearean. Every new table of people was a different stage on which I would perform. I figured out what they wanted and gave it to them.

What I liked about my liberal education was that it taught me to have different perspectives. Studying other cultures taught me that everyone sees a situation differently.

(continued)

For example, I've done some work with Dutch people. I learned that although Americans think of a "hub" as the center of a wheel or a metaphor for the central point of a nexus of information, the Dutch think of "hub" as a small box with nothing inside. So, in Holland I could not use "hub" as a metaphor for the center of a computer-based system.

My first job after graduating from UCD was as marketing coordinator for an architecture firm, The Design Partnership. It was a temporary job from my perspective, because I was doing it until I found something specifically using my interests in international relations. I did it full-time for a year. I helped the principals of the firm figure out how to market their products because I had a sense for selling and marketing.

I took a temporary job because I wanted time to think about what I *really* wanted to do. I chose to have time working for me rather than against me.

STUDYING OTHER CULTURES TAUGHT ME THAT EVERYONE SEES A SITUATION DIFFERENTLY.

I then decided to start my own enterprise, and I called my business Forward Thinking. I served as a consultant to various businesses that needed help with marketing and organizing their operations. A chief operations officer is considered a salesperson because he is selling his ideas about how the company should be run.

One of the projects I worked on included dealing with delegates from Chiapas, Mexico, where I applied my sensitivity to other cultures by learning how the Catholic influence affected people in that region.

Forward Thinking business clients included a spin-off venture from ECG/McGraw Hill and CINEMATRIX, Inc. Among other events and projects, I acted as a project director for The Bug House, a Walt Disney/Pixar production.

In 1998, I co-founded WeaselSoft, an Internet gaming company. I worked in the gaming industry until 1999 when I joined Mediasurface, a London-based software company. I was hired as the first Alliance Partner Manager for North America and my job was to create business-to-business alliances with large consulting firms in the high tech arena. *(continued)*

Mediasurface is my dream job. When I joined them, they consisted of an eclectic group of 33 programmers and entrepreneurs working in a converted tannery in London.

Recently I accepted a promotion to help open new offices in the European, Middle Eastern, and African regions (EMEA). I train employees on our product and company culture and help them set up business contacts with U.S. service/technology companies that wish to expand into the EMEA region.

Liberal arts very much encourages one to be an entrepreneur. The skills needed to do my job include a broad conceptual knowledge of Internet technology, very strong communication skills, and a strong knowledge of different business cultures of various countries.

My liberal education helped me in many ways. It taught me to step back and look at the big picture. I saw two things: First, it was the end of a cycle for large organizations. I did not want to work for Oracle or some other large company. The action was going to be in small start-ups. Second, as a part of the MTV generation, I saw that people were responding to visual design. It was the demand for images that inspired the Internet. The design of user interface is crucial. Liberal arts helped me to appreciate that.

Liberal arts was a Renaissance education for me. I got a wide smorgasbord of learning. If I had studied simply business, I would never have been exposed to people like Wittgenstein, Goethe, Rousseau, and many others. For example, I learned from Wittgenstein that you can look at language from entirely opposite points of view. He turned his own philosophy of language completely inside out halfway through his scholarly life.

I learned that cultural boundaries are only about a foot high, but you have to learn to step over them rather than trip over them.

When you have a broader world view, it is far easier to learn the specifics of a culture or a particular project because you accept that the differences between people are both necessary and appropriate.

A liberal arts graduate can learn any set of skills and is therefore more valuable in a wide variety of work settings.

A liberal arts curriculum is not designed to deliberately enhance your emotional IQ, but it can do so indirectly. In addition to the previous recommendations, you should create your own opportunities for building your emotional smarts. Here are a few suggestions:

- Design class projects that require you to interview people, interact with them, and gain their cooperation. The more you put yourself in the thick of human interaction, the more your emotional IQ is likely to grow. Like any set of skills, emotional IQ skills improve the most through practice, through the bumps and bruises of making mistakes and correcting them.

- Get jobs during college that require you to encounter other people. Engage people with differing opinions and varying needs. Sometimes, the more conflict, the better. Working in a busy restaurant where people are scrambling around, handling the many emotions of customers (e.g., pomposity, selfishness, drinking behavior), is a great forum for having to manage your emotions and be socially intelligent.

- Create your own small business venture. There's nothing like trying to get people to part with their money to discover where everyone's emotions are. Endeavoring to make money can bring out conflict between people. "Why are you doing it *that* way?" "Do it *my* way." Life in the pit is a good way to sharpen your emotional intelligence.

- Take an adventure vacation with a group of friends. Will you still be friends when it's over? We'll see. Yes, adventure trips are fun, but they also require people to do more cooperating than they want to. Consider the model of Outward Bound, which has been adapted and copied across the country. A group of people "expeditioning" is required to accomplish certain tasks "as a team." Teamwork is "emotional intelligence" personified. If there are 12 people in the group, then there are 12 ideas about how the group should proceed.

Shyness Is No Excuse for Lacking Emotional IQ

College gives you many opportunities to expand and improve your emotional IQ, but you'll have to seek them out. Being passive in your classes and retreating to quiet places is not the way to work on your social and emotional skills. Being shy is not a reason to avoid developing your emotional intelligence.

Shyness is not genetic. It's an interactive world out there. Careers are made through mixing with people. Your relationships and your ability to work in groups will be central to your career progress.

Little babies are not shy. If you're "shy," you learned it. And you can un-learn it. It takes practice, but the rewards are considerable—feeling more comfortable in social situations, being heard and respected on project teams, approaching people to talk with them, learning how you come across and how to do it better. These are lifetime skills, and they're all learnable.

HOW DO YOU ADAPT TO THE COLLEGE ENVIRONMENT?

Human beings are adaptive. We enter a new environment, and we figure out what we need to do to survive. After an early, uncomfortable transition, we settle into the new scene.

"Who are you?" said the caterpillar.

"I—I hardly know, Sir, just at present," Alice replied rather shyly. "At least I know who I was when I got up this morning, but I think I must have been changed several times since then."

—**LEWIS CARROLL**, *ALICE'S ADVENTURES IN WONDERLAND*

College is a big leap into the unknown. You're trying to succeed quickly. Parents and friends are "watching" your adjustment. You want to convince them everything's fine but this place is not what you expected. It's *always* different than you think it's going to be. Something's out of line. Certain students, professors, and others cause you discomfort, and problems happen.

The typical advice includes: you'll learn from your mistakes, hard work overcomes most everything, and learn to manage your time. So, what else is new? Is there anything original to say? You'll follow the conventional advice to the extent that you care to. Work as hard as feels right to you. Repeat your mistakes if you like. Maybe you have to make a mistake a few times before the lesson sinks in. Mismanage your time if you see fit. Don't necessarily copy the other guy, even if he's working like a madman. Find your pace and be comfortable with it. The hardest workers sometimes work too hard, and they're not always efficient. "Working smart" gets better results.

Here are a few pieces of less conventional advice that you may not have heard before and that may assist you in adapting to the college environment.

In the fight between you and the world, back the world.

Laughter is the sun that drives the winter from the human face.

Learn to Laugh

Laugh as a way of reacting to life; that is, laugh as a response to things that happen to you at college. When making the transition to college, you may have a tendency to be overly serious. Everybody's observing your progress and you're trying hard to show that you're being an adult about all this. Fix your gaze. Grit your teeth. Clench your fist. March forward into battle. You've got that grim, serious expression. You're taking college courses—life is for keeps now.

If you don't find your facial contortions funny, it's time to lighten up and laugh at them. In your determined march into the halls of academe, you will do a lot of funny things. Awkward sentences, mispronounced words in class, papers and books flying down the stairs, ideas misunderstood, and occasionally making a fool of yourself. When these things happen, laugh. There is a growing body of physical evidence that laughter is good for you.

Norman Cousins, in *Anatomy of an Illness*, used laughter to overcome a near-death illness some years ago. We've been learning ever since about the power of laughter. A good laugh sends healing oxygen barreling through your system. Twenty good laughs a day are positively rejuvenating, and they probably add years to your life.

Comedy illustrates that survival depends upon . . . (our) ability to accept
limitations rather than curse fate for limiting (us).

Of course, laughter begins with laughing at yourself. You are funny. We're all funny. Some people choose to ignore how funny they are, and their bodies suffer. When you do something goofy, recognize it as the inherent laughability of life.

[Regarding Peter Sellers as Inspector Clouseau:] "Sellers describes his technique as 'taking any given subject to an illogical conclusion' . . . [Discussing the Pink Panther movies,] Sellers offered comic meditations on his character's absolute incompetence. Clouseau's adventures repeated and repeated until they built to a crescendo of happy irrationality, while sensible people around him wrung their hands in despair."

If you do not laugh naturally, make sure you hang around plenty of people who laugh a lot. Not laughter that is snide, cynical, and essentially negative. Find people who enjoy themselves, who do not take themselves too seriously, and who create occasions to laugh with each other. Their behavior will be infectious for you. You'll learn to laugh from your exposure to them.

Researchers have discovered that laughter is physiologically contagious: "Our brains seem to be pre-wired to detect laughter and respond in kind . . . Specific neural circuits may be involved in detecting and generating this instinctual social behavior."[13]

Avoid Grade Mania

One half of students graduate in the lower half of the class. You may not think that's something to laugh at, but consider that grades mean almost nothing in the real world of business and other employment. Grades correlate little if at all with career success. Those in the lower half of the class do just as well as those in the top half. Grades are, however, important for getting into graduate and professional schools. So, are you bucking for graduate school? Did your older siblings make straight A's, and it's now up to you to uphold the family honor by making the Dean's List, and if you do less than that you'll suffer a loss of self-esteem? Is that what's troubling you?

You may want to get into graduate school, but if you make yourself a wreck over grades, you may set a pattern of self-defeating behavior that will follow you well into adulthood. Strive, but do not make yourself an anxiety machine. When people give you problems to be solved in the "real world," they don't ask what your grade average was. It is far more important to learn the content and skills of a college course than it is to make a grade. The content and skills will help you be successful in the long run.

Manage Difficulties

There will be bad moments. The occasional professor will seem impossible. Some students will be difficult to be around. Something will go wrong in your game plan. An extended bout with the flu. A 20-page paper you did not expect. Four tests on the same day.

There will be tough times. What to do to ward off the blues? Each week have something you do that is highly appealing to you. It can be a personal, out-of-class interest or it can be a course that you find enthralling. Your "happy thing to do" will serve as a reward for the trials of your week.

Serve Others

Being a college student can be a very "alone" experience. You spend hours and hours by yourself, poring over books, writing papers, and studying your notes. You get tired of being around yourself. The whole academic environment encourages you to be self-centered. "If I don't get it done, then who will?"

Self-centeredness can be a deafening experience. You do this, write that, study here, research there. And you report only to yourself. Even though you see students in classes every day, you may feel as though you're living on another planet. The lonesomeness of the long-suffering student. Solution?

Get involved in anything where you can give something of yourself to others. Volunteer to work at the youth center, give time at the campus radio station, help at a drug rehab center, write articles for the school paper, or work with a professor on a community project. Being involved outside your academic life reminds you that you're a member of the human race. Otherwise, you may spend the entire week, day and night, *in your head*.

Celebrate your adaptive abilities as a human being. As Alice said earlier, every day you're someone different, and yet you don't collapse under the weight of these changes. The ancient Chinese book of wisdom, *I Ching*, is about the inevitability of change. Liberal arts is about change because it teaches you that every location, culture, language, social setting, and physical environment gives you a new experience. A liberal arts curriculum gives you dozens of new teachers, courses, and viewpoints to adapt to.

Welcome the ebb and flow. Each change will make you more adaptable to the volley of new changes that come your way.

OW CAN THIS BOOK HELP YOU?

Liberal arts graduates are going to be hired (or start their own businesses) with or without this book. Why? Because, unless you wandered into higher education by accident and somehow stumbled to a degree by doing the absolute minimum, as a liberal arts graduate, you are likely to have these qualities:

1. You are well-educated.
2. You have high achievement motivation.
3. You have developed many skills that are attractive to employers. You can work with people, read quickly and with depth, you know how to analyze and solve problems, and you are ambitious enough to want to do a job well.

These are the very qualities that employers prize the most. They'll help you get hired in many places.

Successful job hunting for the liberal arts graduate is not just getting someone to hire you. Here's what you're looking for and what this book encourages you to do.

Don't Settle for Job Security

Go for situations that take full advantage of your talents, not just those that happen to be readily available. This means you must take risks, look at different options, perhaps wait a bit longer, and suffer some disappointments. So what? Trust those who have gone before you. It's worth the trouble.

Don't Take a Job That Undernourishes Your Spirit

Don't waste your career potential just taking a job as a salesperson of candy machines to supermarkets. Look for jobs where you feel the work is valuable and makes a difference to someone, the kind of job that you talk about with pride. Long after you have established your financial stability, it is your spiritual bank account that will matter most.

Don't Take a Job for Status Alone

Signing with a household-name corporation or entering a "respectable" profession may be nice to talk about to your family and friends, but it doesn't last if you chose that career only to look good to others. In the rush to get settled in the world of work, or to give your parents something to talk about, you may enter a field of work because it is handy or sounds good. Look closer. Does the job fit who you are as a person? Are you inspired by what goes on there? Or is it just a place to hang your hat and have a surface identity?

Don't Take a Job That Compromises Your Personal Values

You can only shut your eyes to questionable practices so long before you get headaches from seeing what goes on there. You wish you were someplace else. Take a good look at how prospective employers deal with people, both those they employ and their customers. Will you be pleased to tell others about your work or will you end up not wanting to defend practices that you don't agree with?

IBERAL ARTS GRADUATE IN THE REAL WORLD: CASE 2

Marvin got through his liberal education as best he could. He majored in English, so he could read his favorite novelists. He satisfied the other requirements without too many bruises, grudgingly learning to write and think his way through an assortment of courses. His parents thought he was a chronic malcontent because he didn't get excited about anything in the curriculum. "All those theories and philosophies are just wild ideas, just smoke in someone's head; all that matters is matter."

Marvin was a hands-on guy, building cabinets, building houses. He earned a living during college by constructing bookshelves for students in their dorm rooms. His parents wanted him to be "a professional," something like a doctor, lawyer, or architect, so they could be proud of him. They were pretty sure they would *not* be proud if he worked with his hands. The parents hauled their son from one career counselor to another in the hope that the light of "professionalism" would dawn on him. They reasoned that he was going through a phase and waited patiently for the transformation that would never come.

Marvin graduated and promptly started a business building decks, cabinets, and anything a homeowner wanted. He was happy. He was happy to have gotten free of the college classroom. He figured the liberal arts must have done something for him, but he was not sure what. It just felt like it was a "finishing school" to enable him to talk intelligently to people.

So, the business chugged along . . . until competition from the large lumber yards, heavy construction firms, and do-it-yourselfers cut into Marvin's bottom line. Contracts dropped, more competitors appeared, and profits dwindled. Marvin was beside himself. "How can this be? I do good work, but there are too many competitors out there. I'm getting eaten up."

Marvin perceived an opportunity to expand into the home-remodeling market. Few competitors had Marvin's range of skills. But it would cost money for re-tooling, and a heavy investment in a marketing campaign would be required. "Can I do it? Should I do it?"

Then, inexplicably, Marvin remembered a Philosophy of Religion course he had taken, and a concept known as "Pascal's Wager," which was about "betting" on whether or not God existed. Blaise Pascal was a renowned mathematician of the seventeenth century who participated in the discovery of the laws of probability. Pascal had had a religious conversion experience, and he proposed his wager as a way of encouraging people to believe in God. The reasoning was that, if you "bet" that God does exist, then your upside potential (salvation) makes the bet worthwhile. You have nothing to lose if He does not exist. However, if you bet that God does not exist and He does, your downside potential is enormous (eternal damnation).

How did this connect with Marvin's business predicament? He reasoned, "I can 'bet' that the remodeling market will help my business, and this has tremendous upside potential. If I bet that the new market does not exist, I may lose big-time."

Marvin borrowed from the bank, invested in the new market, and doubled the size of his business in two years.

Liberal arts students learn concepts that apply to their lives; they can be both ethereal and practical. In liberal education, everything relates to everything. Pascal's Wager in the rough-and-tumble marketplace is an example of that.

JOURNAL ENTRY

To record your thoughts, use a separate sheet or journal.

What did you hear about liberal arts before you came to college? Why did you decide to enroll in a liberal arts program? Now that you've read about it, what are your feelings about liberal education? Write about how you think liberal education will fit with what you want from college. Discuss how you believe liberal arts will help your career. Do you see points of connection or are you still unclear about it?

Liberal Arts Courses

LEARNING ACROSS THE SPECTRUM

A liberal arts student has a wide variety of choices when planning a course schedule. There are many electives from which to choose, and often courses having the same title can differ in terms of what the professor emphasizes. There are many ways to benefit from your course selection if you know what to look for.

It is useful to focus on the numerous skills you can develop during your college studies. These skills will help you continually in your personal life and your career. They can be obtained from a wide variety of courses. It's your job to research where in the college curriculum you can maximize the development of these skills.

The primary reason for taking a college course is that the content interests you, and you'll find that your interest in the subject matter will enhance the development of your skills. This chapter will highlight the skills that will be most useful to you in your life and career and that are most widely available in the liberal arts curriculum.

In this chapter, you will explore answers to the following questions:

- What kinds of key career skills should you look for in liberal arts courses?
- Why are language skills especially important for American students?
- What are some reasons you should take courses you dislike?
- What's good about taking courses that are far outside your major?
- Why are all your courses "career preparation"?

WHY BUILD YOUR WRITING SKILLS?

Words give shape and substance to your thoughts; they bring your feelings to life and create pictures of scattered and fragmented ideas. Writing forces you to make coherent sentences of your unshaped flashes of insight. It puts flesh on the bones of your ideas and allows you to capture images that dart to and fro in your mind.

Writing is a way of remembering what we already know.

ROBERT FROST

You will find it hard to avoid courses in a liberal arts curriculum that require you to write papers. Be happy that this is the case. Writing is the *sine qua non* of the liberal arts experience—there is no substitution.

With some effort, you could find courses where the teacher's writing demands are not too intense or even a few courses where there are no papers at all. This is not the way to pursue liberal arts. If you don't want any writing, find a curriculum far away from liberal arts—and regret it later.

Writing can make you sweat, but when you learn how to put words together in ways that speak to readers, you'll never have to fear writing a report, a letter, an article, or a memo.

Clear writing is clear thinking. Writing papers and getting them redlined is a military-like "boot camp" experience. You may dislike the papers and the professors when you're doing it, but you'll be grateful later. Writing forces you to translate your often-inarticulate opinions into sentences that make sense. It is wrenching. It makes your brain twist into a knot. But you think better when you're done. Instead of dodging the demands of writing, embrace them. Your professors' comments, corrections, grammatical cross-outs, and notations are all *pure gold*. You would have to pay thousands of dollars for this kind of feedback in the outside world. By that time, it is too late because you're already on the job.

Very few students come to college with perfect writing skills. Be grateful that your professors are helping you improve your writing. Take the courses where you know the required papers are numerous and the professor slices and dices your writing with a hyperactive pen. Writing help is a manyfold blessing. When a professor takes that kind of time *for you,* it means that she cares about helping you improve your writing.

If you can't spell and your grammar is poor, *do not* fall back on computer corrections such as spell check. Learn to spell and use correct grammar. Keep the dictionary by your side and use it. Looking up words and grammar rules may seem tedious. Get used to it. After a while, you'll be so proud you know what to do with an errant sentence that you'll tell your friends. Keep a copy of Strunk and White's *Elements of Style* nearby to check your grammar, syntax, and word usage. Spelling and grammar errors are like spinach on your teeth. They'll make you look ridiculous.

But, you protest, you're not aiming toward a career in writing. Why should you put all this emphasis on stringing sentences together? Because every job with any significant responsibility—*anywhere* in the world of work—requires people to write clearly. People want to know your thoughts. Whether you send them by e-mail, letter, or fax, your writing has to be easily readable or the reader will disregard it, and throw it away.

Good writing is a necessity. Although a certain amount of looseness in e-mail writing may be acceptable, typographical, spelling, and grammatical errors should be avoided. Readers may make judgments about your "loose" e-mail messages, and these judgments will work against you.

How will you know which are the good writing courses? Ask professors and other students. Find students who say, "Those papers are tough. She really marks them up. By the end of the course my writing was much better."

To make your writing as clear as possible and eliminate unnecessary verbiage, William Zinsser's *On Writing Well* is an excellent resource. Advice on how to develop your writing skills is covered in greater detail in Chapter 8.

REAL WORLD PERSPECTIVE

Adam Pava, *Whittier College, 1999, Majors: English and Creative Writing*

I graduated from Whittier College in 1999 with majors in English and Creative Writing. After graduation, I enrolled in the University of Southern California graduate program of television and film writing.

My goal is to have a steady day job writing comedy and working with funny people, and I hope to write a script for a film that makes it big. I'd also like to teach at a college like Whittier or a community college—a very noble profession.

As a kid of 10 or so, I would watch a sitcom and say, "I can think of something funnier than that." I'm going to write sample episodes for sitcoms—"Everybody Loves Raymond" and "Malcolm In The Middle"—and try to get them read.

The hours for comedy writing are difficult. As a writer you sit in a room with eight other writers and take apart a script that one of you wrote. You don't leave that room until every line is funny. Then, you show it to the producers and they say, "That isn't funny." So, you go back to the drawing board.

Making somebody laugh is one of the most rewarding feelings for me. It's a very unique, dynamic connection between a comedian and the audience. If someone is having a bad day, you can overturn it with a turn of a phrase. Or, more often the case, if someone is looking to have a fun time, you can fulfill that expectation. There is something quite powerful about having that ability.

My liberal education has helped me as a comedy writer. I feel that I have a major advantage over other students because all they studied as undergraduates was writing. I have a wide range of knowledge—Spanish, geology, history, political science—all of which actually help my writing.

(continued)

If other graduates have studied film, and they're making a movie, it's about the movie industry because that's all they know. I read about five screenplays and determined that I knew what I was doing. I didn't have to major in screenplay or take several courses to know what to do.

Some say a liberal education will help you only if you're playing "Jeopardy," but your whole life is playing "Jeopardy" . . . having a general sense of what's going on around you. The question is not how much do you know about writing, rather what are you going to write about? Liberal education gives you a lot to write about.

You know from the start that you're not going to be a liberal artist; but your wide range of knowledge gives you many choices about what you will do. Because you know so much about so many things, you have the upper hand.

Unless you have a passion for business or something that requires a vocational degree, liberal arts is a great choice because it allows you to see everything that's out there. You can go into business with a liberal arts degree—chances are you know more about the world than the person who has the MBA.

YOU KNOW FROM THE START THAT YOU'RE NOT GOING TO BE A "LIBERAL ARTIST."

Liberal arts gives you a sneak peek into many different disciplines. You get to explore many avenues without the pressure of having to choose one right away. At Whittier, I was able to take a broad range of courses, like philosophy, science, and religion, before eventually finding my niche in writing classes.

Even after I knew that I wanted to be a writer, the very nature of liberal education did not allow me to disconnect from other disciplines. That was really important for me because writing isn't a trade or a craft. You can't go to vocational school to learn how to write. Liberal arts gave me a context for my words.

WHY TAKE COURSES THAT REQUIRE ORAL PRESENTATIONS?

Employers continually emphasize "communication skills" as something that too many of their employees do not have. CEOs stress that speaking and writing skills are very important in their organizations, especially in leadership roles.

> The ability to express an idea is well nigh as important as the idea itself.
>
> BERNARD BARUCH

Although courses requiring written papers are everywhere in the liberal arts curriculum, speaking opportunities are harder to find. Only a few courses in public speaking are found in most curricula. Nonetheless, there are many liberal arts courses that call on students to answer questions and discuss issues in class. You should use your in-person research skills to find and enroll in as many of these courses as you can.

Speaking out in class is often not a student's favorite thing to do. You're vulnerable, you're exposed. It's easier to keep quiet. But some professors won't let you hide and that is good for you.

There is one fundamental way to become a better speaker, and that is to practice doing it. Making mistakes is a given. Being unsure of how your words are received is the price of admission. But the more you speak up, the better you'll become. Why should you put any emphasis on speaking in public when you're not going to be a public speaker? Because "public speaking" is not limited to making speeches. Whenever, in the business world or elsewhere in employment, you speak to any two or more people (e.g., in a meeting, giving a report, participating on a project team), you are, by definition, publicly speaking. It's your job to be good at it.

If you avoid speaking in college, you will tend to avoid it later. Every job, every career, and every self-owned business requires the individual to speak publicly. There are no exceptions.

Smaller courses more often require you to speak up, but do not limit yourself to these. Large classes are good places to practice your skills too, because the larger audience presents a different kind of "pressure."

Everyone has moments of anxiety when speaking in public. College classes and out-of-class activities give you many occasions to practice and become familiar with hearing the sound of your own voice.

The more "speaking" courses you take, the better. Hiding out in the classroom and looking for opportunities to sleep is not a classic way of learning.

Charlie once had a 10-minute oral presentation to do for his Abnormal Psychology class of 125 people. He was terrorized, frightened stiff, totally immobilized by the idea that he would "talk out loud" to his peers.

"The professor is probably trying to see who the 'abnormal' ones are by putting us through this torture test," Charlie thought. Charlie's name was called by the professor, he got up to speak and, for 60 agonizing seconds, nothing came out of his mouth. He was frozen. Then, ever so slowly, Charlie stammered a few words, stumbled through the talk, and bolted from the classroom. "I don't know how I got my voice, but I guess that was something I had to go through," he said.

WHY DEVELOP YOUR CRITICAL-THINKING SKILLS?

Critical thinking is at the core of any liberal arts curriculum—the ability to reason, adopt different perspectives, and examine an argument carefully from all sides. These skills can be found in any college course. Philosophy courses might be the most obvious, but art, music, Russian literature, science, mathematics, and others all call for critical thinking. If you hear students debating the merits of issues raised in class, ask what the course is about. It's likely the class encourages critical thinking.

The more debate of different perspectives you have in a course, the better that course is going to be. You want to adopt and try out the different sides as a matter of course because that's how you see things the ways others do.

There is a detailed discussion of critical thinking—what it is and how you can develop it—in Chapter 6.

WHY LEARN ANOTHER LANGUAGE?

What do you call a person who speaks two languages? Bilingual. Three languages? Trilingual. What do you call a person who speaks one language? An American.

Regardless of whether your college has a language requirement, you should give serious attention to the study of at least one foreign language.

In ethnocentric America, there is resistance to the study of other languages and cultures. It is important to study a foreign language because:

- People from other cultures like to be appreciated.

- There are many languages represented in the United States; it's been said, for example, that the United States is the second or third largest Spanish-speaking country in the world.

- Your appreciation of other cultures will deepen your understanding of people in general.

REAL WORLD PERSPECTIVE

Martha Alvarado, *Whittier College, 1999, Major: Philosophy*

I graduated from Whittier College in 1999 with a major in philosophy. I originally wanted to be a psychologist, a counselor, because problem solving and mediating was always my function in the family. But I hated psychology here—all the behavioral, physiological stuff. Then, my choice was between social work and philosophy; I picked philosophy because you could graduate in the shortest time.

I found benefits in philosophy that I did not expect. The ethics class changed my whole perception on how you know what you know.

My mom said, "I can't believe you're majoring in that. What are you going to do with that? I paid all this money for you to get your degree. What are you going to do when you get out?" But then she said, "Just graduate. I don't care what you do, just graduate."

When we'd go out together and see family friends, they'd ask what are you doing, and my mom would answer, "Oh, she's majoring in philosophy, she doesn't know what she's doing." But she didn't stop me, so I was getting to do what I wanted to do and that was the main thing.

While studying philosophy, my ideas began to change and I became an atheist. My mother said, "It's just a phase, you'll outgrow it."

I went to the philosophy department chair and said, "Let me ask you the question of all questions: What can I do with a philosophy degree?" He responded, "The study of philosophy is not just the study of dead people. It is how to learn critical thinking and analysis, how to learn reason and symbolic logic, how to write. You can go into business, law, management, teaching, and other fields."

I agreed with him. It sounded like I had options and from what I had experienced, it sounded as if it would prepare me to do anything I wanted to do. He took me from "you can't do anything with philosophy" to "you can do almost anything."

(continued)

I still believe what he said. I have to learn the technical aspects and details for a job, but being able to reason, analyze, and write will help me in any position.

What will eventually set you apart when the resumes have been tallied is your liberal arts personality. Everyone can eventually learn the skills needed for a specific job, by volunteering or work experience, but what will set you apart is your ability to communicate effectively, your open-mindedness, and your creativeness. I think you perfect many of these skills with all of the papers you have to write as a liberal arts major.

Even though a business major has more business courses on her transcript, it's my job to present myself in a way that the employer will see I can be an asset to their company. As a liberal arts graduate, I may do a better job of communicating my value to the company.

Presently, I am the job development coordinator for the CalWorks Program of East Los Angeles College, a program that helps people get jobs. We teach them how to package themselves for changing jobs and careers. Philosophy gave me the tools to think quickly on my feet and that has helped in this job.

OH, SHE'S MAJORING IN PHILOSOPHY; SHE DOESN'T KNOW WHAT SHE'S DOING.

I strongly recommend volunteer work as a means of discovering your interests and where you would like your career to be headed.

For former welfare recipients, low self-esteem and helplessness is pervasive. Change is slow, but as a few people develop a more positive attitude, it begins to catch on and others use them as role models and become more positive. It takes only a small number of people to change the world, so I like what I'm doing.

I don't really have a set timetable for when things will happen in my career. From the time that I started to get into philosophy, I've always felt that things sort of fall into place. I'm not really worried about where I'm headed. I figure it will just happen. If I just keep progressing and do what I enjoy, I'm going to fall into something that I like.

Do you want to do business with the French? It would be better to speak French and appreciate their culture. Want to understand Brazilians? You'd better learn Portuguese. Most cultures developed long before the American culture. It will be beneficial to the success of any venture if you're conversant with the culture where you want to do business.

When studying the language, you also study the society and learn to respect non-American ways. The "Ugly American" phrase of recent years didn't come about by accident. When you learn a language, you learn not to do things that alienate people of that country.

Tapping the center of the forehead with the forefinger is, in the Netherlands, a way of silently saying, 'He's crazy.'

Japanese and Korean parents train their children to avert the eyes and avoid eye contact. Direct eye contact is, to them, considered intimidating or may indicate sexual overtones.

Take care in France where the 'OK' gesture means 'zero' or 'worthless' . . . . In places like Brazil and Germany, it is the signal for a very private body orifice.

ROGER AXTELL[1]

Some colleges allow students to substitute computer science as a "language" instead of the real languages representing other societies and cultures. Computer science is not a language. It will deprive you of a golden opportunity to break out of your ethnocentric shell.

WHY ENROLL IN COURSES YOU DON'T LIKE?

There are some types of subject matter you might prefer to avoid because of a previous bad experience or because the subject matter sounds awful. Maybe you're trying to keep up your grade average and there's a course you think would ruin it. Make a list of the courses you are trying to avoid. If you avoid those subjects now, you'll probably try never to go near them for the rest of your life. Let's say it's mathematics you hate. You find a way to get through college without taking a math course. Then, you get a job and the boss gives you a company report you have to analyze and it has a lot of statistics in it. Whatever will you do? Go find a statistics text? Maybe. But you'll probably look for a way to dodge the assignment or ask for help from a friend. In other words, you're stuck. Now do you wish you had taken that math course?

Translations Gone Bad

Coors put its slogan, "Turn it loose," into Spanish, where it was read as "Suffer from diarrhea."

Scandinavian vacuum manufacturer Electrolux used the following in an American campaign: "Nothing sucks like an Electrolux."

An American T-shirt maker in Miami printed shirts for the Spanish market that promoted the Pope's visit. Instead of "I saw the Pope" (el Papa), the shirts read "I saw the potato" (la papa).

Frank Perdue's chicken slogan "It takes a strong man to make a tender chicken," was translated into Spanish as, "It takes an aroused man to make a chicken affectionate."

In Taiwan, the translation of the Pepsi slogan "Come alive with the Pepsi generation" came out as "Pepsi will bring your ancestors back from the dead."

Sign posted in a Beirut Hotel: Ladies are kindly requested not to have their babies in the cocktail bar.

In a Tel Aviv Hotel: If you wish breakfast, lift the telephone and our waitress will arrive. This will be enough to bring up your food.

In a Barcelona Travel Agency: Go Away.

In an Israeli Butcher Shop: I slaughter myself twice daily.

In a French Riviera Swimming Pool: Swimming is forbidden in the absence of a savior.

JENNIFER F. TAYLOR[2]

Liberal arts gives you a valuable opportunity to sample from different areas of knowledge, and try out different ways of thinking. You will take the courses you like, but it's the unpleasant ones that you really need. Will those "undesirable" subjects show up later in your life? Count on it. Those areas will appear in your work, no matter what job or career you enter. If you're a mortgage banker and you hate science, sooner or later there will be a big loan package that requires looking into water flow, air currents, wildlife, or plant life.

What's the real reason for taking courses you don't like? To develop your intellectual versatility. Don't be afraid of subject matter that is unfamiliar. Learn to be a learner. Perhaps those courses in philosophy, semiotics, or ecology sound unbearable. That's the best reason to take them. How will they benefit you?

REAL WORLD PERSPECTIVE

Liesel Collins, *Whittier College, 1998, Major: Economics*

I graduated from Whittier College in 1998 with a major in economics. I am presently an associate with Aon Consulting. Aon's accounts include corporate, government, and multi-employer clients. I analyze the value of a benefit package that a company is preparing to offer its employees. Employers use health care benefits and other salary extension plans to attract talented employees. I analyze their benefits within the marketplace to ensure they remain competitive within their industry.

At Whittier I wrote an extensive paper on health care in America. That assignment helped me realize the importance of my job today.

There is a certification in our field known as CEBS—Certified Employee Benefits Specialist. There are 10 exams to pass in order to be certified. I passed the first one and I am confident I will pass the rest.

My friends would tell me about their large class sizes at large universities, over 200 in some classes. I felt very fortunate to have the small classes at Whittier. At a liberal arts college, you receive much more personal attention than at a large university.

I believe my verbal and written communication skills will help me to advance and be effective in my company and career. I must be an effective verbal communicator in order to influence or motivate others and I must write clearly in order for my message to be understood.

I value Whittier's emphasis on writing skills. Without that commitment to writing, I would not have excelled in the discipline and would have lacked an

(continued)

If you take the most challenging courses and wrestle your way through them, the next time you encounter unfamiliar material, you'll dive into it. You'll become a fearless learner. That's what employers want because every project involves new ideas, new concepts, new thinking.

important skill in the marketplace. I recently took an entrance exam for graduate school and I achieved the highest possible score on the writing section of the exam.

I appreciated the language courses and other international courses I took because they exposed me to different people and different ways of thinking and being. I work for an international company and my appreciation of the diversity between cultures is important in my daily interactions with colleagues and clients. My liberal arts education has helped me be aware of different cultures, different viewpoints, and different ways of life beyond the United States.

AMERICANS NEED TO KNOW LANGUAGES OTHER THAN THEIR OWN.

I plan to take additional language courses so that I can become more knowledgeable about diverse cultures. This will help me in the global marketplace, and because I plan to stay in this field, a global perspective is important to me.

Many Europeans know English in addition to their own language and one or two other languages as well. Americans need to know languages other than their own.

I live in Los Angeles, where there are truly many diverse cultures, races, and beliefs. Although we may have different backgrounds, to succeed in our economy, we must be patient and understanding of others. I am thankful for Whittier's commitment to diversity and the requirement that I take a pair of courses in Asian, African, or Latin American studies. Without this requirement, I would not have been enriched by the eastern cultures.

If you take only those courses in college that come easily to you, you'll develop habits of avoidance. When the going looks as though it might get rough, avoid, avoid, avoid. This little habit will cost you on the job. When an employer gives you an assignment and you don't like the subject matter, or it looks difficult to you, you can't say, "Well, I just won't take that assignment." The task is yours. If you slog your way through the unpleasant material, you demonstrate your versatility and ability to persevere.

Instead of having 'answers' on a math test, they should just call them 'impressions,' and if you get a different 'impression,' so what, can't we all be brothers and sisters?

JACK HANDY, *DEEP THOUGHTS*

There will always be college subjects you find less interesting, harder to work through, and less appealing. Did you expect anything different? Broaden your intellectual capabilities as much as possible so that you can handle any situation that's thrown at you.

Harmon got a job as a stock brokerage trainee. He loved numbers, the whole business atmosphere, and everything financial. In college, he enjoyed the economics and math courses, but he hated science and had taken a low-level geology course to fulfill the minimum science requirements. Wouldn't you know it, the first big investment opportunity Harmon had to research involved heavy science: a company that creates landfills. Scientific issues abounded—ecological issues, toxicity of land dumps, the biochemistry of disposing of waste matter. If Harmon had taken a few of those environmental science courses, he'd have felt more comfortable with the topic. As it was, he nearly got fired for an ill-informed presentation to the firm's key officers.

Judy had a strong aversion to language courses. She staggered through Spanish by finding a teacher who was retiring and didn't care. After graduation, she got a job as a lobbyist and, sure enough, the first bill she had to research and follow was for a Spanish-speaking voter group. Judy signed up for Very Remedial Spanish at the local college and, while she was studying, she missed a chance to meet with local Spanish leaders.

WHY TAKE COURSES OUTSIDE YOUR MAJOR?

Many of the "I hate 'em" courses you take will be very different from those in your major. If you're going to be an English major, look at math and science. If chemistry is your love, look at philosophy and religion.

Courses very different from your major challenge you to have new perspectives on the world. As they say, "If all you have is a hammer, everything looks like a nail." Chemists see molecules. A philosophy major wonders if the molecules are real and how one knows what one knows. A sociology major wonders why certain groups of molecules are attracted to each other, and others are not. An English major knows that if you get close enough to the molecules, there's a human, compelling story in there somewhere.

Courses outside your major stretch you. You've been raised by a particular family, in a particular culture, in the United States. America is very centered on itself. Very parochial. You tend to believe what Americans believe. You need stretching.

Once you take 10 different courses in 10 different disciplines, it dawns on you that there are a great variety of ways to see life. This insight will take you a long way. It will help you to appreciate those views that are not the same as your own. For example, Americans frequently hug each other. By contrast, Muslims don't like to hug because they feel it unnecessarily encourages sexual feelings. If you missed the world religions course, you might never have known that. So, you pause before your next hug. A moment of reflection.

Some American Indians believe that spirits dwell in trees. That's where our popular expression and superstition "knock on wood" comes from. Knock the tree to keep the spirits at bay. Crazy stuff? Maybe, if you're a purely rational scientist. But, Native Americans have much to teach us about the spiritual life, including passionate rituals. Ever been to an Indian campfire ceremony? With thundering drums and dance, it is a heart-thumping communion with the natural world.

> The most beautiful and profound emotion that we can experience is the sensation of the mystical. It is the sower of all true science.
>
> **ALBERT EINSTEIN**

WHY ENROLL IN COURSES THAT CHALLENGE YOUR COMFORTABLE PERSPECTIVES?

Your opinions are as good as the next person's, right? Don't settle into your viewpoints too rigidly. Let's suppose you believe that medieval history was a wasteland. Nothing of value could possibly have happened then, you maintain. They didn't have flush toilets, they wrote on parchment, they prayed incessantly, and they lived in feudal seclusion. No intellectual life. No gated communities. No book clubs.

Take a course in medieval history. Find out what really went on then. Discover that algebra was invented by the Muslims. Learn that an Italian named Fibonacci invented a series of numbers that led to the number system that we take for granted today. Discover that, in many ways, people of the Middle Ages were more mystical than we are today. Mysticism is good. It puts us in touch with what our senses fail to tell us.

Skeptical about the culture of our Mexican neighbors? Uninterested? Not curious about how the Mexicans lived before white people showed up? Take a course in Mexican history. Treat yourself. Discover that the Mexicans' lives were so different from ours that we may have gone to war with them because we couldn't believe that we could coexist peacefully. Learn that Mexicans, like American Indians, have had a far richer spiritual life than our culture.

Do you live in a world of words? Are you most comfortable with reading and writing? Are you highly verbal and very happy operating in that mode? Take an art history course and a practical arts course, such as ceramics. See the world from visual perspectives. Get away from words for a while. Think in images. Learn to see what your images are telling you to pay attention to. Many believe that the purest and best thinking we do is intuitive, and intuition comes to us in pictures, not words.

The liberal arts catalog is a veritable grocery store of choices. There are many "basic food groups" in this store and your job is to build a balanced diet from them. Most liberal arts colleges have a core of "distribution requirements" that forces you to dive into many different disciplines. Take advantage of that "forced" breadth in your curriculum, and add to this breadth through your own choices of elective courses. From this range of courses, you will develop your intellectual muscles. After four years of courses from 15 or 20 different disciplines, you'll have the confidence to tackle *any* subject matter you may encounter in your work or your life.

They Probably Overlooked a Few of Those Liberal Arts Courses

"Do you want your pizza cut into four pieces or eight?"
"Just four. I'm not that hungry."

—Yogi Berra

"Nobody in football should be called a genius. A genius is a guy like Norman Einstein."

—Joe Theismann

DO YOU CONSIDER ALL OF YOUR COURSES AS "CAREER PREPARATION"?

Your development of a career goal can embody the questions of your personal philosophy: What is a good life? What is good? What is life about? Why am I here? Why should I do the right thing? What is the right thing?[3]

The search for meaning raises your career to higher levels. The best careers are filled with meaning—for you, for those you love, and for the people in your community, your country, and your world. With every choice you make, career and otherwise, you're making decisions about meaning.

All of your courses in college will contribute to your career goal, and to your search for meaning. Every course adds skills to your repertoire and layers to your understanding of the world. You don't market your major. You offer the world of work your entire package of skills and values. An employer wants the research skills you developed in history and psychology courses as much as she wants the analytical skills you developed in English and physics courses.

For every course you're considering, ask yourself these three questions:

1. What skills am I likely to acquire or improve as a result of this course?
2. How much am I excited about the subject matter?
3. How will this course build on my existing philosophy and help to challenge, enhance, or refine it?

JOURNAL ENTRY

To record your thoughts, use a separate sheet or journal.

What factors do you think of when you decide what college courses to take? How much you like the subject matter? Quality of the professor? Possible relevance to your career? Other factors? The liberal arts approach suggests that you study a variety of disciplines. What is a beneficial way to mix these different kinds of courses? You would not take all courses in your major. How would you spread out your interests in the curriculum? The catalog is like a grocery store. What combination of items will provide you the best possible education?

Your Liberal Arts Major

CHOOSING AND USING IT

The choice of major is an important one, but it does not necessarily determine your career path. The purpose of this chapter is to help you consider the factors involved in making the best possible choice of a major. The varying relationship between liberal arts majors and careers gives you many degrees of freedom in your choice.

Students can be obsessive about their choice of major. One's choice of major should be a joyful affirmation of learning, rather than a grim search for a meal ticket. Well over 50 percent of liberal arts graduates will work successfully in fields that are unrelated to their college majors.

Don't be intimidated by the more vocational majors, such as various forms of business. Liberal arts students can get all the business-related skills they need from a combination of liberal arts courses and out-of-class experiences (see the section in Chapter 10 titled "What Are The Ten Hottest Marketable Skills?").

In this chapter, you will explore answers to the following questions:

- What range of career choices is possible with a liberal arts major?
- How much access do liberal arts graduates have to high-tech jobs?
- What are some reasons it is good to be undecided about your liberal arts major?
- How do you answer those who ask: "What are you going to do with your liberal arts degree?"
- What factors should you consider in deciding whether to have a double major?

WHAT IS THE RELATION BETWEEN A MAJOR AND A CAREER?

Most students identify their majors with their career plans. However, the relation between major and career is more fluid than you might think, and this is especially true for liberal arts majors.

For certain technical majors, such as engineering, one's major is closely linked to career aspirations. People who aspire to be electrical engineers must definitely complete the required curriculum.

However, the relation between a liberal arts major and career options allows a greater degree of freedom.

- You can major in English, philosophy, French, art history, or any other liberal arts major and get jobs in the business world.
- You can major in economics and go into business, but there are many non-business careers you can do.
- You can become a journalist without majoring in journalism.
- You can major in sociology, religion, history, or biology and do many different kinds of work, including business or nonprofit work.
- You can take any liberal arts major and be hired for jobs in the field of computer science.
- You can be a lobbyist with a major other than political science or government.

If you're beginning to think: "Well, it looks as though I can do almost anything I want with a liberal arts degree," you're getting the idea.

Of course, there are many professions you cannot enter without an advanced degree, such as law, medicine, psychology, and architecture. Your liberal arts degree is suitable preparation for these fields of graduate and professional study. Many graduate and professional schools prefer liberal arts majors because of their superior general learning skills.

The biggest mistake that liberal arts students and graduates make regarding their career prospects is to believe that their majors *limit* their career choices. Many English majors mistakenly believe that their major qualifies them only for jobs in publishing, journalism, and other literary-related fields. Many psychology and sociology majors believe they're supposed to be looking only in the nonprofit or human services sector. Many philosophy and religion majors believe there's almost nothing for them because there are no job titles that have philosophy or religion stamped on them. Many science majors think that they must find jobs that are science-related. These are all unnecessary and mistaken limitations that graduates place on themselves.

"Liberal arts" can be a muddle in the minds of those students, and their parents, who approach higher education. The colleges themselves sometimes confuse matters. They promote their "vocational majors" because it is easier to attract students, while the liberal arts courses are merely mentioned in the catalogs. In a consumerist culture that wants labels on everything (e.g., majors), the subtleties of liberal arts can be difficult to "sell." So, do not limit your career thinking because of your major. For example, if you have a biology/botany major, that is good background for a job with a plant nursery. But if you don't have a biology major, go ahead and apply for such jobs anyway. You may get hired because of your interpersonal skills, your writing skills, or other skills.

Although having college courses that relate to a particular field of work is okay, it is often not necessary to have a major in a specific field before applying for related jobs. Perhaps the best example of this is the computer field. As Robert Schaffer notes in his excellent book *High Tech Jobs for Low-Tech People:*[1]

> I asked (a VP in a young software company) what skills he considers fundamental to success in the high-tech industry. (He said): "Excellence in communication. That means listening, writing, speaking . . . Listening is especially important because that implies a lot of social skills." (p. ix)

*   *   *

Consider the educational backgrounds of a few friends of mine who are happily working in the high-tech industry: fine arts, art history, fashion design, urban planning, English literature, French literature, history, theology, linguistics, music, psychology, economics, film making, philosophy. (p. 1)

*   *   *

A young (liberal arts graduate) observed: "I started the job knowing very little . . . I was clueless actually. I learned on the job, just picking it up on the fly, making it a point of doing some research every day." (p. 2)

*   *   *

And a woman whose Spanish language skills took her from work as a homemaker to an international high-tech job advised: "Definitely don't be afraid of high-tech. . . . If you can use a telephone, you can use a computer. If you can use a tape deck, you can use a computer." (p. 3)

*   *   *

(Another liberal arts graduate said): "I felt like a fraud at some time or another in half the jobs I've done. I was a teacher for grade school kids. I taught dance lessons. I did theater technical work. . . . I produced children's videos for about five years. I had studied biology and chemistry, and then I jumped around, did photography and all those other things. When I got to (the high-tech company), I realized that nobody knows everything about this stuff." (p. 4)

Thus, English, political science, Spanish, chemistry, music, sociology, fine arts, and *all* other liberal arts majors are welcome in the world of computer jobs. Why? Because computer firms recognize that liberal arts majors have abundant thinking skills, and thinking is what designing computer systems and software is all about. Hopefully this news is liberating to you and it gives you a feeling of freedom that you can take the courses and major(s) that you want and still choose from a wide variety of job possibilities when you graduate. Liberal arts graduates spread themselves across the entire landscape of the world of work.

It's fine to seek a major that relates to your career interests. You may well develop a strong connection between your major field and your future work. However, the key is not to allow your major to create artificial boundaries around your career aspirations. Your job and career opportunities are many times broader than anything your major may seem to suggest—let yourself roam wherever you please.

What about all these liberal arts graduates who are rushing off to complete MBA programs? Is the MBA required for entry into the business world? Definitely not. Many businesses prefer to train you themselves. Entrepreneurial opportunities also do not require an MBA, as many dot.com adventurers and more conventional business owners are demonstrating.

The more enthusiasm you have about your major, the more you'll learn and the more skills you'll acquire from it. Why would anyone take a major and not be enthusiastic about it? Sometimes students enroll in a major because they believe it will help them in their careers, even though they are not thrilled about the subject matter. For example, a student who aspires to the business world may choose economics as a major, even though he doesn't especially resonate to it. Better to study what he does like, and approach the business world later on. As subsequent chapters note, employers are looking for a variety of skills that you can acquire across the entire liberal arts program.

AN CHOOSING A MAJOR BE CHOOSING A PHILOSOPHY?

Each major field represents a different set of lenses with which to view the world. A biologist sees life forms, how they evolved, how they will continue to change. A biologist's philosophy is that organisms tell us the nature of life. A sociologist views life as the interaction of human life forms. A political scientist proposes the philosophy that living things must form an organized society, lest they degenerate into barbarians. An art historian feels that the values of a culture are revealed through its art. Each academic discipline offers a viewpoint about what is important to observe, a philosophy of meaning. When choosing a major, you have an opportunity to make a beginning statement about your personal philosophy, about where you think some of the meaning is in life.

> Whether you succeed or not is irrelevant—there is no such thing. Making your unknown known is the important thing—and keeping the unknown always beyond you.
>
> GEORGIA O'KEEFE, *LETTER TO SHERWOOD ANDERSON, 1923*

Your choice of a major offers much more than the development of skills for your career. Aim for something much higher in your choice of major. The major is an opportunity to study a field in depth, a chance for you to immerse yourself in a philosophy of learning and see where it takes you. You can sit side-by-side with leading thinkers and decide where you place your beliefs about what is "true" in that discipline. Your major gives you a chance to be at the leading edge of what people are saying in that field, and to think about how you might carry it a step farther.

In his book, *Plato, Not Prozac!*, Lou Marinoff discusses the application of philosophy to everyday life.[2]

. . . at its heart, philosophy examines the questions we all ask: What is a good life? What is good? What is life about? Why am I here? Why should I do the right thing? What is the right thing? (p. 5)

*   *   *

The great thing about having thousands of years of thinking to draw on is that many of history's wisest minds have weighed in on these subjects and have left insights and guidelines for us to use. But philosophy is also personal—you are your own philosopher too. Take what you can learn from other sources, but to arrive at a way of approaching the world that works for you, you'll have to do the thoughtful work yourself. The good news is that, with proper encouragement, you can think effectively for yourself. (pp. 5–6)

WHAT ARE THE VIRTUES OF BEING "UNDECIDED"?

"Undecided" students win the Courage Award. In the face of parents and peers who say, "What are you going to major in? You don't know? Well, when are you going to decide?", it takes courage to say, "I don't know yet."

Maybe you think you'll never know. It will come; however, it's not fun answering the barrage of questions about being "undecided."

Liberal arts students are often decidedly undecided and that's not a bad thing! They're undecided about their majors, their career goals, and even about the courses they'll take next semester. Well, why not? It takes time to reflect on what you want.

Don't let people call you wishy-washy. Undecidedness is part of the normal human condition. For any decision, you need a period of "incubation" while your unconscious sifts and sorts all of the information and possibilities. You also need to gather "experience" that will help you decide. In the case of a major, you should sample courses, talk to students who have taken specific courses, and experience more of yourself as a student—what you resonate to.

Life is an ongoing parade of undecidedness. Careers are especially fluid. Don't rush the process. Premature decisions are usually made to satisfy somebody else. Be comfortable with your undecidedness. It's a sign of your maturity that you're not picking the first major that smiles at you.

A decision about a major may wait until you have had summer jobs, internships, or informal exposure to people in the world of work. Or simply until your unconscious has had time to sort through how you feel

REAL WORLD PERSPECTIVE

Karen Bamberger, *Loyola Marymount University, 1995, Majors:*
Humanities and Philosophy

"What do you do with a humanities major? You're already
human!" That was what my father said to me when I
announced that I had changed my major from business to
humanities. He wasn't joking. Then, for good measure, I added
philosophy to my humanities major. My parents were somewhat appalled.
My brothers and sisters hadn't finished college, so they said, "Well, as long
as you finish," but they had no idea what I was going to do. My parents
could never get my majors right. People would ask, "What's she majoring
in?" and they'd say, "We don't know."

I pretty much assumed that I would get a job because I was going to
have a degree. But I had no idea where my degree was going to take me. I
figured out early on that my learning skills would be the key to my future
employment. And I decided those learning skills could be acquired, perhaps
even maximized, in the liberal arts.

I first majored in business but everyone I talked to told me, "Major in
something that you love because it doesn't matter what you major in as far
as getting a job. A business will teach you how to do what they need done."

My first job after LMU was with an infomercial company. I quickly
became turned off because of ethical considerations. In the infomercial
world, I was asking myself, "Why are people stealing from each other? And
why should I be a part of this?"

Then, I got a job as assistant director of employer relations at Loyola
Marymount University. This was a management position in which I coordi-
nated on-campus recruitment and "sold" employers on the merits of LMU
graduates.

My present job is working as a recruiter for one of the "Big Five"
accounting firms. I'm on the opposite side of the fence. I recruit college
graduates instead of preparing them to meet with recruiters. *(continued)*

Philosophy has helped me make order out of chaos when I am given a project. There are many ideas when you start a project, and philosophy helped me figure out what to do: Where to go to find the answer, or where to go to begin the search. When it's open-ended, a liberal arts background helps.

It's inherent in a liberal arts major to know where to find answers, or where to look, or where to start . . . knowing how to use references in books, and find where the information is.

In liberal arts, you have to be creative. Non-liberal arts majors may have "functional fixedness"—looking at a problem and only seeing one thing. They may look at a pencil and only see that it can be used as a pencil.

A liberal arts major is going to be able to talk to interviewers about life and culture, not just about business. Liberal arts graduates can sell themselves to many different employers based on the skills they bring—organizing oneself, thinking, communicating, researching, interacting with people one-on-one, and so on.

Taking a logic course taught me how to think critically, evaluate arguments, and formulate logical, coherent ideas. A previous boss always said I had the ability to organize chaos. She would often call on me and say "Karen, with your logical mind, what do you think about . . . ?"

I try to tell students that there can be many answers to one question and that it's okay if they do not have a specific career goal for the future. I think it is scary for students to not know what they are going to do after college—so much of their lives up to this point has been predetermined by their parents. Now they have to choose for themselves.

I always think of Plato's Cave and how the prisoners reacted when they were able to escape from the cave and learn so much about the world around them. Hopefully, students will impart their knowledge to those who have not yet "escaped."

(continued)

I also take an existential stance. I believe that our choices are our own and that we need to take responsibility for our actions.

Many feel like they need to have a career plan or specific profession after they graduate (i.e., must be a doctor, lawyer, or accountant). And they feel inadequate if these decisions aren't made before graduation. One aspect of my previous job was letting them know it's okay not to have it all planned out. I told them not to compare themselves to those who have "set careers," because many times those with set careers have made their decisions in error and may not be happy in the careers they have chosen.

I emphasize networking. As scary as it may be for some students, I stress how important it is develop rapport with as many people as possible. Most jobs people obtain are the ones where a "friend of a friend" referred a job opportunity.

My dream job is to be a travel writer. I believe I have all of the thinking and interpersonal tools to do it. I just have to decide when.

WHAT DO YOU DO WITH A HUMANITIES MAJOR? YOU'RE ALREADY HUMAN!

My husband works in the entertainment industry. He is currently developing a project directly related to traveling and is interviewing people around the country. If this takes off, who knows, I may write for the show. We are trying to think of creative ways we can be self-employed and be able to work together on something we both love.

We both majored in philosophy during college. Two philosophy majors who are married. Sometimes we think so hard when we have discussions that we get headaches.

I think my parents are pleased about my career path. Originally, they were a bit skeptical that I would be qualified to do much after I graduated. I think I've surprised them.

about various options. The unconscious, intuitive side of you—the part that makes the important decisions—needs time to function.

What happens when you rush decisions? What happens when you make a premature choice to satisfy those who've been asking? You choose a major that "sounds good" and has little to do with how you feel. Having made that hurried choice, you feel a little sick because you know that you'll change your mind later and have to "justify" that. A premature choice is usually one that you'll regret.

What to Tell Your Family

Your family is waiting for some sign about how it's going at college and what your major will be. Families can get a little edgy, so it's useful to have something to tell them.

The following are suggestions on how to explain your "undecidedness" to your family.

1. You're taking courses in several different departments in your ongoing search for meaning. Family members may not know exactly what you're talking about, but they will respect you.

2. You're investigating several major fields, but you don't want to make any sort of commitment until you've completed your research. Provide them with two or more career possibilities that you've been researching.

3. Explain that the skills you're developing will enable you to get a wide variety of jobs.

HOW DO YOU CREATE YOUR OWN MAJOR?

Suppose you don't like *any* of the majors that are offered? At many colleges, it is possible to create your own major. This might be a good way to express your personal philosophy.

Typically, the college has a procedure to follow to develop a major:

1. Decide on a theme or an area of interest. Write a statement regarding the nature of the theme, and why you believe it's important to study.

2. Identify an array of courses in the college catalog that you believe are most suitable for studying this theme.

3. Add subject areas not specified as courses for "independent study" with particular professors.

4. Write a summary statement about what you expect to learn from this self-created major.

Of course, there will be faculty to help you develop this unique major. They may suggest a change of emphasis, or perhaps even redirect your thinking if your theme seems overly large or difficult to investigate. The final curriculum for your self-created major will be a product of your work and the advice of one or more faculty.

Creating your own major allows you to pour your energy into a subject area that you find compelling. It encourages you to be creative, self-disciplined, and resourceful. You may not immediately find all of the courses or subject areas that you need, but the hunt is half the fun.

A self-created major also allows you to combine existing disciplines and examine the connections between them, such as music and mathematics, religion and sociology, political science and philosophy, or economics and psychology. For example, you might study why people make psychologically irrational decisions about money.[3]

Helen changed her major six times, each change in response to a new course that she liked. Everyone kept asking, "Are you sampling everything and you'll stay here 10 years? What's your flavor of the month today?" Does it matter that people questioned her? No. Helen was shopping the merchandise, experimenting. She eventually created her own major—science in pre-scientific history—and, after graduation, began her own successful eclectic antique store.

HOW DO YOU EXPLAIN YOUR LIBERAL ARTS CHOICE?

The poem on pages 6 and 7 by Carol Jin Evans ("I Tell Them I'm a Liberal Arts Major") provides an excellent answer to this question. Here are a few more suggestions:

1. You feel very satisfied with the critical thinking, communication, and research skills you are developing, and you plan to apply these to whatever work you choose.

2. Because liberal arts has introduced you to the many key issues, problems, perspectives, and joys of humanity, you are satisfied that your life will be productive.

3. You're going to use liberal arts to continue as a lifelong learner.

4. You're going to create a career unique to your abilities because your liberal education gives you the freedom to build your career across many different jobs, industries, and enterprises.

HOULD YOU PURSUE A DOUBLE MAJOR?

Many liberal arts students take two majors in the hope that the combination will have a greater career potential. Before pursuing this strategy, here are some of the possible negatives.

Completing a second major forces you to reduce the range of "electives" that you can take from other departments. Ask yourself whether your double major choice is a way to avoid courses you don't like. If so, rethink your choice because it will reduce the breadth of your curriculum and your exposure to courses that are new and unfamiliar.

A double major may comprise 60 percent or more of your entire college curriculum. Consider whether it is best to devote 60 percent of your courses to two areas.

Nevertheless, you may still like the idea of a second major. Sometimes the second major is outside liberal arts, perhaps in the business school. You may feel you need something "practical" to balance your liberal arts major. The advantages might be illusory. You might sacrifice courses that build your communication or analytical thinking skills, or courses that enlarge your world perspective, in exchange for so-called "practical" courses. At least one study has refuted the idea that a second major in business is a good thing to do: "Our findings cast doubt on the belief that liberal arts graduates will gain a competitive edge by taking a second major in business."[4]

There are, however, reasons that support choosing a double major. When you choose two liberal arts majors that represent an interesting combination of perspectives, and these perspectives help you to examine life problems or issues that you find exciting, then two majors can be enriching. The interactions between geology and religion, for example, would lead to some interesting views.

Try to estimate what may be lost when you give up numerous elective courses in exchange for a second major. Breadth of curriculum and intellectual experimentation give you the confidence to delve into many different areas of knowledge. If you complete two majors, you will sacrifice some of this intellectual versatility. Ask yourself, "Is having two majors worth this loss?"

HOULD YOU EVER CHANGE YOUR MAJOR?

Why not? There are many reasons to change your major, and most of them are good ones. If you're unhappy in your present major, look for one that suits you better.

College students change their majors quite frequently. In most colleges, 50 percent or more change majors at least once, some as many as three or four times. Change as frequently as you need to. You often don't really know what a subject area is like until you experience it.

Some students change their majors because they declare the initial major too early. They're in a hurry to have a "major identity." Do not hang onto an initial major just because that's what you said when you had less exposure to the curriculum. You have a right to change based on your new experiences and the courses you've been taking.

Before officially changing your major, you should "sit in" on classes in other departments (without actually being enrolled) to see what the courses, the students, and the professors are like. You can usually ask the professors' permission to do this; it's the best way to sample a potential new major without committing to it.

It may be better to be "undecided" for a while, instead of changing to a new major field. As noted earlier, undecidedness is a virtue; it's a sign of your patience and judgment in considering several possibilities before declaring a new major.

Connie wanted to change from sociology to physics/astronomy, but it would add two full semesters to her degree plan. More money, more time, more postponing income. Would it be worth it? She took more time to repay her loans than she had wanted, but she eventually became a noted astronomer and looks back happily on her change of major.

I S YOUR MAJOR A KEY TO SUCCESS?

Is your major a union card that will get you into certain jobs or careers, a badge of entry? That's what many students would like it to be, but it is not. A major is a sign of your interest and that you possess certain knowledge. More importantly, it reveals many of the values in your personal philosophy. Nonetheless, graduates from other majors can apply for many of the same jobs you can.

Even computer jobs, though they are technical, are wide open to a variety of majors. Having a computer science degree is no guarantee of a job, and not having a computer science degree is not a barrier to entry.

Your liberal arts degree gives you the versatility that graduates with "vocational" majors wish they had. For example, if you're an English major, you can apply for jobs in writing-related fields, management consulting, computer firms, government agencies, businesses, arts organizations, banks, and social service agencies, to name just a few.

Your keys to success are in this book, and in the study skills, learning skills, speaking and writing skills, time management ability, and attitudes that you learn during your liberal arts experience.

J OURNAL ENTRY

To record your thoughts, use a separate sheet or journal.

Did you start thinking about your major long before you even enrolled in college, or are you still undecided about it? Either way is okay. What factors are going to guide your choice of a major? Your major may have a career-relevant component, or you may choose it largely because of an interest in the subject matter. Are you considering more than one major? If so, for what reasons? Do you see good reasons to stay undecided about your major for a while? How will you explore the possibilities?

Self-Awareness

KNOWING WHO YOU ARE AND HOW YOU LEARN

This chapter extends the material you explored in Chapter 2, Liberal Arts Courses. You probably will want to take courses based on your preferred learning styles; however, you should also take some courses that challenge you to strengthen other learning styles.

The ability to learn is much more than a college skill. Being a learner for life means that you will be able to keep pace with rapidly changing workplace technology, stay aware of world developments and how they affect you, and continue to grow as a person. To learn effectively, you need to understand *how* you learn. This chapter will help by introducing you to two different personal assessments—one focusing on how you take in information, and one that helps you determine how you interact with others. You will then explore other important elements of self: your self-perception, interests, and habits. The more you know about your learning style, interests, and abilities, the better prepared you will be to choose a career that makes the most of who you are and what you can do.

In this chapter, you will explore answers to the following questions:

- Is there one best way to learn?
- What are the benefits of knowing your learning style?
- How can you discover your learning style?
- How do you explore who you are?

IS THERE ONE BEST WAY TO LEARN?

Your mind is the most powerful tool you will ever possess. You are accomplished at many skills and can process all kinds of information. However, when you have trouble accomplishing a particular task, you may become convinced that you can't learn how to do anything new. Not only is this perception incorrect, it can also damage your belief in yourself.

Every individual is highly developed in some abilities and underdeveloped in others. Many famously successful people were brilliant in one area but functioned poorly in other areas. Winston Churchill failed the sixth grade. Abraham Lincoln was demoted to a private in the Black Hawk war. Louis Pasteur was a poor student in chemistry. Walt Disney was fired from a job and told he had no good ideas. What some might interpret as a deficiency or disability may be simply a different method of learning. People have their own individual gifts—the key is to identify them.

There is no one "best" way to learn. Instead, there are many different learning styles, each suited to different situations. Each person's *learning style* is unique. Knowing how you learn is one of the first steps in discovering who you are. Before you explore your learning style, consider how the knowledge you will gain can help you.

WHAT ARE THE BENEFITS OF KNOWING YOUR LEARNING STYLE?

Although it takes some work and exploration, understanding your learning style can benefit you in many ways—in your studies, the classroom, and the workplace.

Study Benefits

Most students aim to maximize learning while minimizing frustration and time spent studying. If you know your strengths and limitations, you can use techniques that take advantage of your highly developed areas while helping you through your less developed ones. For example, say you perform better in smaller, discussion-based classes. When you have the opportunity, you might choose a course section that is smaller or that is taught by an instructor who prefers group discussion. You might also apply specific strategies to improve your retention in a large-group lecture situation.

Following each of this chapter's two assessments, you will see information about study techniques that tend to complement the strengths and shortcomings of each intelligence or spectrum. Remember that you have abilities in all areas, even though some are dominant. Therefore, you may encounter useful suggestions under any of the headings. What's important is that you use what works. During this course, try a large number of new study techniques, eventually keeping those you find to be useful.

Classroom Benefits

Knowing your learning style can help you make the most of the teaching styles of your instructors. Your particular learning style may work well with the way some instructors teach and be a mismatch with other instructors. Remember that an instructor's teaching style often reflects his or her learning style. After perhaps two class meetings, you should be able to make a pretty good assessment of teaching styles (instructors may exhibit more than one). Once you understand the various teaching styles you encounter, plan to make adjustments that maximize your learning. See Table 4.1 for some common teaching styles.

Assess how well your own styles match up with the various teaching styles. If your styles mesh well with an instructor's teaching styles, you're in luck. If not, you have a number of options.

Bring extra focus to your weaker areas. Although it's not easy, working on your weaker points will help you break new ground in your learning. For

TABLE 4.1	Teaching styles.
Lecture	Instructor speaks to the class for the entire period, little to no class interaction.
Group discussion	Instructor presents material but encourages discussion throughout.
Small groups	Instructor presents material and then breaks class into small groups for discussion or project work.
Visual focus	Instructor uses visual elements such as diagrams, photographs, drawings, transparencies.
Verbal focus	Instructor relies primarily on words, either spoken or written on the board or overhead projector.
Logical presentation	Instructor organizes material in a logical sequence, such as by time or importance.
Random presentation	Instructor tackles topics in no particular order, jumps around a lot, or digresses.

example, if you're a verbal person in a math- and logic-oriented class, increase your focus and concentration during class so that you get as much as you can from the presentation. Then spend extra study time on the material, make a point to ask others from your class to help you, and search for additional supplemental materials and exercises to reinforce your knowledge.

Ask your instructor for additional help. For example, a visual person might ask an instructor to recommend visuals that would help to illustrate the points made in class. If the class breaks into smaller groups, you might ask the instructor to divide those groups roughly according to learning style, so that students with similar strengths can help each other.

"Convert" class material during study time. For example, an interpersonal learner takes a class with an instructor who presents big-picture information in lecture format. This student might organize study groups and, in those groups, focus on filling in the factual gaps using reading materials assigned for that class. Likewise, a visual student might rewrite notes in different colors to add a visual element—for example, assigning a different color to each main point or topic, or using one color for central ideas, another for supporting examples.

Instructors are as individual as students. Taking time to focus on their teaching styles, and on how to adjust, will help you learn more effectively and avoid frustration. Don't forget to take advantage of your instructor's office hours when you have a learning style issue that is causing you difficulty.

Career Benefits

Because different careers require differing abilities, there is no one "best" learning style. Develop self-knowledge through honest analysis and then accurately match what you do best with a career that makes the most of your strengths. Specifically, how can knowing your learning style help you in your career?

You will perform more successfully. Your learning style is essentially your working style. If you know how you learn, you will be able to look for an environment that suits you best. You will perform at the top of your ability if you work at a job in which you feel competent and happy. Even when you are working at a job that isn't your ideal, knowing yourself can lead you to on-the-job choices that make your situation as agreeable as possible.

You will be able to function well in teams. Teamwork is a primary feature of the modern workplace. The better your awareness of your abilities, the better you will be able to identify what tasks you will best be able to perform in a team situation. The better your awareness of personality traits—your own as well as those of others—the more skillful you will be at communicating with and relating to your coworkers.

You will be more able to target areas that need improvement. Awareness of your learning styles will help you pinpoint the areas that are more difficult for you. That has two advantages: One, you can begin to work on difficult areas, step by step. Two, when a task requires a skill that is tough for you, you can either take special care with it or suggest someone else whose style may be better suited to it.

Now that you know you have something to gain, look at some ways you can explore your particular learning style.

OW CAN YOU DISCOVER YOUR LEARNING STYLE?

Many different types of assessments are available to promote self-discovery. Each type provides a different means of exploring strengths and weaknesses, abilities and limitations. This chapter contains one each of two particular types—learning style assessments and personality assessments.

Learning style assessments focus on the process by which you take in, retain, and use information. Students may use learning style assessment results to maximize study efficiency and to choose courses that suit their styles. *Personality assessments* indicate how you respond to both internal and external situations—in other words, how you react to thoughts and feelings as well as to people and events. Employers may give such assessments to employees and use the results to set up and evaluate teams.

The learning styles assessment in this chapter is called *Pathways to Learning* and is based on the Multiple Intelligences Theory, discussed below. It can help you determine how you best take in information as well as how you can improve areas in which you have more trouble learning. The second assessment tool, the *Personality Spectrum*, is a personality assessment that helps you evaluate how you react to people and situations in your life. *Pathways to Learning* and the *Personality Spectrum* provide two different perspectives that together will give you a more complete picture of how you interact with everything you encounter—information, people, and your own inner thoughts.

Multiple Intelligences Theory

There is a saying, "It is not how smart you are, but how you are smart." In 1983, Howard Gardner, a Harvard University professor, changed the way people perceive *intelligence* and learning with his theory of *Multiple Intelligences*. Gardner believes there are at least eight distinct intelligences possessed by all people, and that every person has developed some intelligences more fully than others. Most people have at one time learned something quickly and comfortably. Most have also had the opposite experience: no matter how hard they try, something they want to learn just won't sink in. According to the Multiple Intelligences Theory, when you find a task or subject easy, you are probably using a more fully developed intelligence; when you have more trouble, you may be using a less developed intelligence.[1]

Table 4.2 offers brief descriptions of the focus of each of the intelligences. You will find information on related skills and study techniques on pages 78 and 79. The *Pathways to Learning* assessment will help you determine the levels to which your intelligences are developed.

Multiple intelligences.

INTELLIGENCE	DESCRIPTION
Verbal–Linguistic	Ability to communicate through language (listening, reading, writing, speaking)
Logical–Mathematical	Ability to understand logical reasoning and problem solving (math, science, patterns, sequences)
Bodily–Kinesthetic	Ability to use the physical body skillfully and to take in knowledge through bodily sensation (coordination, working with hands)
Visual–Spatial	Ability to understand spatial relation and to perceive and create images (visual art, graphic design, charts and maps)
Interpersonal	Ability to relate to others, noticing their moods, motivations, and feelings (social activity, cooperative learning, teamwork)
Intrapersonal	Ability to understand one's own behavior and feelings (self-awareness, independence, time spent alone)
Musical	Ability to comprehend and create meaningful sound (music, sensitivity to sound, understanding patterns)
Naturalistic	Ability to understand features of the environment (interest in nature, environmental balance, ecosystem, stress relief brought by natural environments)

Personality Spectrum

One of the first instruments to measure psychological types, the Myers-Briggs Type Inventory® (MBTI), was designed by Katharine Briggs and her daughter, Isabel Briggs Myers. Later, David Keirsey and Marilyn Bates combined the 16 Myers-Briggs types into 4 temperaments and developed an assessment based on those temperaments, called the Keirsey Sorter. These assessments are two of the most widely used personality tests, both in psychology and in the business world.

The *Personality Spectrum* assessment in this chapter can help you better understand yourself and those around you. Based on the Myers-Briggs and Keirsey theories, it adapts and simplifies their material into four personality types—Thinker, Organizer, Giver, and Adventurer—and was developed by Joyce Bishop (1997).[2] The *Personality Spectrum* will give you a personality perspective on how you can maximize your functioning at school and at work. Each personality type has its own abilities that improve work and school performance, suitable learning techniques, and ways of relating in interpersonal relationships. Pages 82 and 83 will give you more details about each type.

Using the Assessments

The two assessments follow this section of text. After each assessment you will find details of the traits of each dimension and strategies to help you make the most of that dimension's tendencies.

Complete both assessments, trying to answer the questions objectively—in other words, mark the answers that best indicate who you are, not who you want to be. The more closely you can see yourself today, the more effectively you can set goals for where you want to go from here. Then, enter your scores on page 84, where you will see a brain diagram on which to plot *Personality Spectrum* scores and boxes in which to enter your *Pathways to Learning* scores. This page is organized so that you can see your scores for both assessments at a glance, giving you an opportunity to examine how they relate to one another. Don't be concerned if some of your scores are low—that is true for most everyone. For *Pathways to Learning,* 21–24 indicates a high level of development in that particular type of intelligence, 15–20 a moderate level, and below 15 an underdeveloped intelligence. For the *Personality Spectrum,* 26–36 indicates a strong tendency in that dimension, 14–25 a moderate tendency, and below 14 a minimal tendency.

Knowing how you learn will help you improve your understanding of yourself—how you may function at school, in the workplace, and in your personal life. Keep in mind that these or any other assessments are intended not to label you but to be *indicators* of who you are. Your thinking skills—your ability to evaluate sources of information—will best enable you to see yourself as a whole, including both gifts and areas for growth. Your job is to verify and sift each piece of information and arrive at the most accurate portrait of yourself at this point in time.

Perspective on Learning Style

Both of the assessments in the chapter provide you with self-knowledge that can help you manage yourself in school, at work, and at home in the most effective way possible. However, no one assessment can give you the final word on who you are and what you can and cannot do. It's human to want an easy answer—a one-page printout of the secret to your identity—but this kind of quick fix does not exist. You are a complex person who cannot be summed up by a test or evaluation.

> To be what we are, and to become what we are capable of becoming, is the only end of life.
>
> ROBERT LOUIS STEVENSON

Use Assessments for Reference

The most reasonable way to approach any assessment is as a reference point rather than as a label. There are no "right" answers, no "best" set of scores. Instead of boxing yourself into one or more categories, which limits you, approach any assessment as a tool with which you can expand your idea of yourself. Think of it as a new set of eyeglasses for a person with somewhat blurred vision. The glasses will not create new paths and possibilities for you, but they will help you see more clearly the paths and possibilities that already exist. They give you the power to explore, choose, and act with confidence.

You will continually learn, change, and grow throughout your life. Any evaluation is simply a snapshot, a look at who you are in a given moment. The answers can, and will, change as you change and as circumstances change. They provide an opportunity for you to identify a moment and learn from it by asking questions: Who am I right now? How does this compare to who I want to be?

Use Assessments for Understanding

Understanding your tendencies will help you understand yourself. Avoid labeling yourself narrowly by using one intelligence or personality type, such as if you were to say, "I'm no good in math" or "I'm never a thinker." Anyone can learn math; however, some people learn math more efficiently through intelligences other than logical–mathematical. For example, a visual–spatial learner may want to draw diagrams of as much of a math problem as possible. Everyone is a thinker; however, some people tend to approach life situations more analytically than others.

People are a blend of all the intelligences and personality types, in proportions unique to them. Most often one or two intelligences or types are dominant. When material is very difficult or when you are feeling insecure about learning something new, use your most dominant areas. When something is easy for you, however, this is an opportunity for you to improve your less developed areas. All of your abilities will continue to develop throughout your lifetime.

In addition, you may change which abilities you emphasize, depending on the situation. For example, an organizer-dominant student might find it easy to take notes in outline style when the instructor lectures in an organized way. However, if another instructor jumps from topic to topic, the same student might choose to use a think link. The more you know yourself, the more you will be able to assess any situation and set appropriate goals.

Elsewhere in the text you will see how your personality types and intelligences influence other skills and life areas. As you read, try to examine how your tendencies affect you in different areas—study techniques, time management, personal wellness, communication, and so on. Knowing your style can help you improve how you function in every area of your life.

REAL WORLD PERSPECTIVE

Robert Knowles, *Whittier College, 1997, Majors: Chemistry and Spanish*

I am a 1997 graduate of Whittier College with majors in chemistry and Spanish. I originally wanted to be an architect. Then, I became a pre-medical student, but didn't get into medical school.

After graduation, I landed a job at Beckman Corporation—a manufacturer of medical diagnostic instruments. I learned how to do this job through on-the-job training and training courses provided by the employer.

My job involves working on electronics and prototype designs of diagnostic medical analyzer subsystems. I also represent my department and field engineers on developmental task forces. I provide technical assistance to field engineers and conduct training classes on our instruments and tools. The training component allows me to be a teacher, which I enjoy. I ran a tutorial business during college.

(continued)

I will complete an MBA degree at California State University–Fullerton in 2002. Liberal arts was great preparation for the MBA program because in business you need to know more than just the numbers. In marketing and finance one learns to examine a potential market or company from outside the box, looking at the corporate culture as well as the people who make up that environment. Liberal arts has given me an appreciation for an open mind.

What I liked about liberal education was that when the classes are small, the teachers can push you to the next level because they can demand more from you. In small classes, there's no hiding.

Working in a lab, you can just work by yourself if you want.

If you want to get ahead in life, I recommend liberal arts, because of the exposure you get to politics, religion, everything.

IF YOU WANT TO GET AHEAD IN LIFE, I RECOMMEND LIBERAL ARTS.

Whittier helped me to be more open to diverse kinds of people, and there's a lot of diversity in the workplace. You get a lot more accomplished when you can sit down with a person and chat with them about subjects completely unrelated to the office. That's where my liberal education helps. It helps me to stay open-minded.

Liberal arts taught me to see the world without blinders on. In the past, because my preference is with the sciences, I tended to look at the world as a cut and dried place based on facts and numbers. I wouldn't deviate much from my perception of how things should be. Liberal arts, however, gave me a worldly view of my surroundings. For example, the classes I took on religion, Spanish culture, and politics allowed me to see on what others base their norms and values of daily life.

It seems in the workplace today, they don't want somebody who can just do one thing. They want somebody who has a broad background.

PATHWAYS TO LEARNING*

Name   Date

Directions: Rate each statement as follows: 1 = rarely, 2 = sometimes, 3 = usually, 4 = always. Write the number of your response (1–4) on the line next to the statement and total each set of six questions.

1. _____ I enjoy physical activities.
2. _____ I am uncomfortable sitting still.
3. _____ I prefer to learn through doing.
4. _____ When sitting I move my legs or hands.
5. _____ I enjoy working with my hands.
6. _____ I like to pace when I'm thinking or studying.
   _____ TOTAL for Bodily–Kinesthetic

7. _____ I enjoy telling stories.
8. _____ I like to write.
9. _____ I like to read.
10. _____ I express myself clearly.
11. _____ I am good at negotiating.
12. _____ I like to discuss topics that interest me.
    _____ TOTAL for Verbal–Linguistic

13. _____ I use maps easily.
14. _____ I draw pictures/diagrams when explaining ideas.
15. _____ I can assemble items easily from diagrams.
16. _____ I enjoy drawing or photography.
17. _____ I do not like to read long paragraphs.
18. _____ I prefer a drawn map over written directions.
    _____ TOTAL for Visual–Spatial

19. _____ I like math in school.
20. _____ I like science.
21. _____ I problem solve well.
22. _____ I question how things work.
23. _____ I enjoy planning or designing something new.
24. _____ I am able to fix things.
    _____ TOTAL for Logical–Mathematical

*Developed by Joyce Bishop, Ph.D., and based upon Howard Gardner's *Frames of Mind: The Theory of Multiple Intelligences*.

PATHWAYS TO LEARNING, Continued

25. _____ I listen to music.
26. _____ I move my fingers or feet when I hear music.
27. _____ I have good rhythm.
28. _____ I like to sing along with music.
29. _____ People have said I have musical talent.
30. _____ I like to express my ideas through music.
_____ TOTAL for Musical

31. _____ I need quiet time to think.
32. _____ I think about issues before I want to talk.
33. _____ I am interested in self-improvement.
34. _____ I understand my thoughts and feelings.
35. _____ I know what I want out of life.
36. _____ I prefer to work on projects alone.
_____ TOTAL for Intrapersonal

37. _____ I like doing a project with other people.
38. _____ People come to me to help settle conflicts.
39. _____ I like to spend time with friends.
40. _____ I am good at understanding people.
41. _____ I am good at making people feel comfortable.
42. _____ I enjoy helping others.
_____ TOTAL for Interpersonal

43. _____ I enjoy nature whenever possible.
44. _____ I think about having a career involving nature.
45. _____ I enjoy studying plants, animals, or oceans.
46. _____ I avoid being indoors except when I sleep.
47. _____ As a child I played with bugs and leaves.
48. _____ When I feel stressed I want to be out in nature.
_____ TOTAL for Naturalistic

PATHWAYS TO LEARNING: MULTIPLE INTELLIGENCES APPLIED*

	SKILLS
Verbal–Linguistic	Analyzing own use of language Remembering terms easily Explaining, teaching, learning, using humor Understanding syntax and meaning of words Convincing someone to do something
Musical–Rhythmic	Sensing tonal qualities Creating or enjoying melodies and rhythms Being sensitive to sounds and rhythms Using "schemas" to hear music Understanding the structure of music
Logical–Mathematical	Recognizing abstract patterns Reasoning inductively and deductively Discerning relationships and connections Performing complex calculations Reasoning scientifically
Visual–Spatial	Perceiving and forming objects accurately Recognizing relationships between objects Representing something graphically Manipulating images Finding one's way in space
Bodily–Kinesthetic	Connecting mind and body Controlling movement Improving body functions Expanding body awareness to all senses Coordinating body movement
Intrapersonal	Evaluating own thinking Being aware of and expressing feelings Understanding self in relationship to others Thinking and reasoning on higher levels
Interpersonal	Seeing things from others' perspectives Cooperating within a group Communicating verbally and nonverbally Creating and maintaining relationships
Naturalist	Deep understanding of nature Appreciation of the delicate balance in nature

*Adapted by Joyce Bishop, Ph.D., from *Seven Pathways of Learning,* David Lazear, © 1994.

PATHWAYS TO LEARNING: MULTIPLE INTELLIGENCES APPLIED

	STUDY TECHNIQUES
Verbal–Linguistic	Read text and highlight no more than 10% Rewrite notes Outline chapters Teach someone else Recite information or write scripts/debates
Musical–Rhythmic	Create rhythms out of words Beat out rhythms with hand or stick Play instrumental music/write raps Put new material to songs you already know Take music breaks
Logical–Mathematical	Organize material logically Explain material sequentially to someone Develop systems and find patterns Write outlines and develop charts and graphs Analyze information
Visual–Spatial	Develop graphic organizers for new material Draw mind maps Develop charts and graphs Use color in notes to organize Visualize material (method of loci)
Bodily–Kinesthetic	Move or rap while you learn; pace and recite Use "method of loci" or manipulatives Move fingers under words while reading Create "living sculptures" Act out scripts of material, design games
Intrapersonal	Reflect on personal meaning of information Visualize information/keep a journal Study in quiet settings Imagine experiments
Interpersonal	Study in a group Discuss information Use flash cards with others Teach someone else
Naturalist	Connect with nature whenever possible Form study groups of people with like interests

PERSONALITY SPECTRUM I

Name   Date

STEP 1: Rank order all four responses to each question from most like you (4) to least like you (1). Place a 1, 2, 3, or 4 in each box next to the responses.

1. I like instructors who
    a. ☐ tell me exactly what is expected of me.
    b. ☐ make learning active and exciting.
    c. ☐ maintain a safe and supportive classroom.
    d. ☐ challenge me to think at higher levels.

2. I learn best when the material is
    a. ☐ well organized.
    b. ☐ something I can do hands-on.
    c. ☐ about understanding and improving the human condition.
    d. ☐ intellectually challenging.

3. A high priority in my life is to
    a. ☐ keep my commitments.
    b. ☐ experience as much of life as possible.
    c. ☐ make a difference in the lives of others.
    d. ☐ understand how things work.

4. Other people think of me as
    a. ☐ dependable and loyal.
    b. ☐ dynamic and creative.
    c. ☐ caring and honest.
    d. ☐ intelligent and inventive.

5. When I experience stress I would most likely
    a. ☐ do something to help me feel more in control of my life.
    b. ☐ do something physical and daring.
    c. ☐ talk with a friend.
    d. ☐ go off by myself and think about my situation.

PERSONALITY SPECTRUM I

6. I would probably not be close friends with someone who is
   a. ☐ irresponsible.
   b. ☐ unwilling to try new things.
   c. ☐ selfish and unkind to others.
   d. ☐ an illogical thinker.

7. My vacations could be described as
   a. ☐ traditional.
   b. ☐ adventuresome.
   c. ☐ pleasing to others.
   d. ☐ a new learning experience.

8. One word that best describes me is
   a. ☐ sensible.
   b. ☐ spontaneous.
   c. ☐ giving.
   d. ☐ analytical.

STEP 2: Add up the total points for each letter.

TOTAL for a. ☐ Organizer

TOTAL for b. ☐ Adventurer

TOTAL for c. ☐ Giver

TOTAL for d. ☐ Thinker

STEP 3: Plot these numbers on the brain diagram on page 84.

PERSONALITY SPECTRUM: DESCRIPTION OF TYPES

Thinker

Personal strengths—You enjoy solving problems and love to develop models and systems. You have an abstract and analytical way of thinking. You love to explore ideas. You dislike unfairness and wastefulness. You are global by nature, always seeking universal truth.

Work/school—You work best when assigned projects that require analytical thinking and problem solving. You are inspired by futuristic ideas and potentials. You need the freedom to go beyond the established rules. You feel appreciated when praised for your ingenuity. You dislike repetitive tasks.

Relationships—You thrive in relationships that recognize your need for independence and private time to think and read. Stress can come from the fear of appearing foolish. You want others to accept that you feel deeply even though you may not often express it.

Learning—You like quiet time to reflect on new information. Learning through problem solving and designing new ways of approaching issues is most interesting to you. You may find it effective to convert material you need to learn into logical charts and graphs.

Organizer

Personal strengths—You value the traditions of family and support social structures. You never take responsibility lightly. You have a strong sense of history, culture, and dignity. You value order and predictability. You dislike disobedience or nonconformity. You value loyalty and obligation.

Work/school—You enjoy work that requires detailed planning and follow-through. You prefer to have tasks defined in clear and concrete terms. You need a well-structured, stable environment, free from abrupt changes. You feel appreciated when you are praised for neatness, organization, and efficiency. You like frequent feedback so you know you are on the right track.

Relationships—You do best in relationships that provide for your need of security, stability, and structure. You appreciate it when dates that are important to you are remembered by others.

Learning—You must have organization to the material and know the overall plan and what will be required of you. Depending on your most developed Multiple Intelligences, organizing the material could include any of the following: highlighting key terms in text, rewriting and organizing notes from class or text, making flash cards.

PERSONALITY SPECTRUM: DESCRIPTION OF TYPES

Giver

Personal strengths—You value honesty and authenticity above all else. You enjoy close relationships with those you love and there is a strong spirituality in your nature. Making a difference in the world is important to you, and you enjoy cultivating potential in yourself and others. You are a person of peace. You are a natural romantic. You dislike hypocrisy and deception.

Work/school—You function best in a warm, harmonious working environment with the possibility of interacting with openness and honesty. You prefer to avoid conflict and hostility. You thrive when your creative approach to your work is appreciated and praised.

Relationships—You thrive in relationships that include warm, intimate talks. You feel closer to people when they express their feelings and are open and responsive. You think romance, touch, and appreciation are necessary for survival. You blossom when others express a loving commitment to you and you are able to contribute to the relationship.

Learning—You enjoy studying with others and also helping them learn. Study groups are very effective for you to remember difficult information.

Adventurer

Personal strengths—Your strength is skillfulness. You take pride in being highly skilled in a variety of fields. Adventure is your middle name. A hands-on approach to problem solving is important to you. You need variety, and waiting is like "emotional death." You live in the here and now. It is your impulsiveness that drives everything you do. You dislike rigidity and authority.

Work/school—You function best in a work environment that is action-packed with a hands-on approach. You appreciate the opportunity to be skillful and adventurous, and to use your natural ability as a negotiator. You like freedom on the job so you can perform in nontraditional ways and in your own style. Keeping a good sense of humor and avoiding boredom on the job are important to you. You feel appreciated when your performance and skills are acknowledged.

Relationships—You function best in relationships that recognize your need for freedom. You thrive on spontaneous playfulness and excitement.

Learning—You learn exciting and stimulating information easiest, so pick classes and instructors carefully. Study with fun people in a variety of ways and places. Keep on the move. Develop games and puzzles to help memorize terminology.

PERSONALITY SPECTRUM II

THINKER
Technical
Scientific
Mathematical
Dispassionate
Rational
Analytical
Logical
Problem Solving
Theoretical
Intellectual
Objective
Quantitative
Explicit
Realistic
Literal
Precise
Formal

ORGANIZER
Tactical
Planning
Detailed
Practical
Confident
Predictable
Controlled
Dependable
Systematic
Sequential
Structured
Administrative
Procedural
Organized
Conservative
Safekeeping
Disciplined

Directions: Place a dot on the appropriate number line for each of your four scores, connect the dots, and color the polygon. Write your scores in the four shaded boxes.

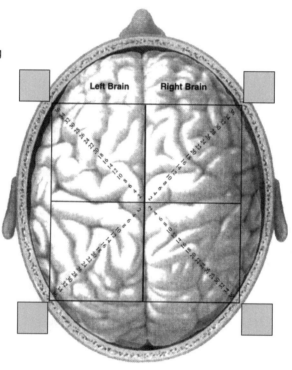

Left Brain   Right Brain

Source: *Understanding Psychology,* 3/e, by Morris, © 1996. Adapted by permission of Prentice-Hall, Inc., Upper Saddle River, NJ.

PATHWAYS TO LEARNING

From pages 76 and 77, write your eight intelligences in the boxes, according to your total scores.

GIVER
Interpersonal
Emotional
Caring
Sociable
Giving
Spiritual
Musical
Romantic
Feeling
Peacemaker
Trusting
Adaptable
Passionate
Harmonious
Idealistic
Talkative
Honest

ADVENTURER
Active
Visual
Risking
Original
Artistic
Spatial
Skillful
Impulsive
Metaphoric
Experimental
Divergent
Fast-paced
Spontaneous
Competitive
Imaginative
Open-minded
Adventuresome

21–24 = highly developed	15–20 = moderately developed	below 15 = underdeveloped

Avoid Overreacting to Challenges

The assessments you complete reveal areas of challenge as well as ability. If you assume that your limitations are set in stone or let them dominate your self-image, you may deny yourself growth. Rather than dwelling on limitations (which often results in a negative self-image) or ignoring them (which often leads to unproductive choices), use what you know from the assessments to face your limitations and work to improve them.

In any area of challenge, look at where you are and set goals that will help you reach where you want to be. If a class is difficult, examine what improvements you need to make in order to succeed. If a work situation requires you to perform in an area that causes trouble for you, face your limitations head-on and ask for help. Exploring what you will gain from working on a limitation will help you gain the motivation you need to move ahead.

If you are interested in an additional method of self-discovery you might also find additional assessments and information through your school's career counselors.

Your learning style is one important part of self-knowledge. Following the assessments, you will explore other important factors that help to define you.

OW DO YOU EXPLORE WHO YOU ARE?

You are an absolutely unique individual. Although you may share individual characteristics with others, your combination of traits is one-of-a-kind. It could take a lifetime to learn everything there is to know about yourself because you are constantly changing. However, you can start by exploring these facets of yourself: self-perception, interests, and habits.

Self-Perception

Having an accurate *self-perception* isn't easy. It's important to see yourself in a broad capacity, not limited by the ideas that you or others may have of you. How you react to your assessment scores is an indicator of your self-perception. As mentioned earlier in the chapter, the most productive reaction involves seeing the scores as informational indicators, not as defining and undeniable labels.

Feeling inadequate from time to time is normal, but a constantly negative self-perception is likely to have destructive effects. Negative self-perception can be a self-fulfilling prophecy: First you believe that you are incapable of being or doing something, then you neglect to try, and finally you probably don't do or become what you had already decided was impossible. For example, say you think you can't pass a certain course.

Because you feel you don't have a chance, you don't put as much effort into the work. Sure enough, at the end of the semester, you don't pass. Unfortunately, you may see your failure as proof of your incapability, instead of realizing that you didn't allow yourself to try. When this chain of events occurs in the workplace, people lose jobs. When it happens in personal life, people lose relationships.

Negative self-images may come from one or more different sources, some of which are shown in Figure 4.1. The following strategies might help you refine your self-image so that it reflects more of your true self.

- Believe in yourself. If you don't believe in yourself, others may have a harder time believing in you. Work to eliminate negative self-talk. Have faith in your areas of strength. When you set your goals, stick to them. Know that your mind and will are very powerful.
- Talk to other people whom you trust. People who know you well often have a more realistic perception of you than you do of yourself.
- Take personal time. Stress makes having perspective on your life more difficult. Take time out to clear your mind and think realistically about who you are and who you want to be.
- Look at all of the evidence. Mistakes and limitations can loom large in your mind. Consider what you do well and what you have accomplished as carefully as you consider your stumbles.

The greatest discovery of any generation is that human beings can alter their lives by altering their attitudes of mind.

ALBERT SCHWEITZER

Building a positive self-perception is a lifelong challenge. If you maintain a bright but realistic vision of yourself, it will take you far along the road toward achieving your goals.

Interests

Taking time now to explore your interests will help you later when you select a major and a career. Looking at your dominant intelligences and personality traits may give you clues about your interests. For example, a giver may be interested in service professions, an interpersonal learner may want to work with people, or a naturalistic learner might have nature as a primary interest.

Other ideas about your interests may come from asking yourself questions such as these:

- What areas of study do I like?
- What activities make me happy?

FIGURE 4.1

Self-Image sources.

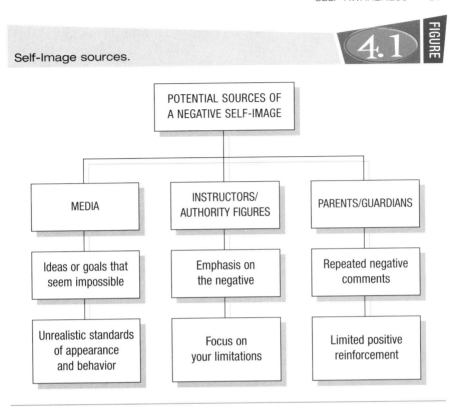

POTENTIAL SOURCES OF
A NEGATIVE SELF-IMAGE

MEDIA

INSTRUCTORS/
AUTHORITY FIGURES

PARENTS/GUARDIANS

Ideas or goals that
seem impossible

Emphasis on
the negative

Repeated negative
comments

Unrealistic standards
of appearance
and behavior

Focus on
your limitations

Limited positive
reinforcement

- What careers seem interesting to me?
- What kind of daily schedule do I like to keep (early riser or night owl)?
- What type of home and work environment do I prefer?

Interests play an important role in the workplace. Many people, however, do not take their interests seriously when choosing a career. Some make salary or stability their first priority. Some take the first job that comes along. Some may not realize they can do better. Not considering what you are interested in may lead to an area of study or a job that leaves you unhappy, bored, or unfulfilled.

Choosing to consider your interests and happiness takes courage but brings benefits. Think about your life. You spend hours attending classes and studying outside of class. You will probably spend at least 8 hours a day, 5 or more days a week, up to 50 or more weeks a year as a working contributor to the world. Although your studies and work won't always make you deliriously happy, it is possible to spend your school and work time in a manner that suits you.

Here are three positive effects of focusing on your interests:

You will have more energy. When you're doing something you like, time seems to pass quickly. Contrast this with how you feel about disagreeable activities. The difference in your energy level is immense. You will be able to get much more done in a subject or career area that you enjoy.

You will perform better. When you were in high school, you probably got your best grades in your favorite classes. That doesn't change as you get older. The more you like something, the harder you work at it—and the harder you work, the more you will improve.

You will have a positive attitude. A positive *attitude* creates a positive environment and might even make up for areas in which you lack ability or experience. This is especially important when working in a team. Because businesses currently emphasize teamwork to such a great extent, your ability to maintain a positive attitude might mean the difference between success and failure.

Habits

A preference for a particular action that you do a certain way, and often on a regular basis or at certain times, is a *habit*. You might have a habit of showering in the morning, channel surfing with the TV remote control, talking for hours on the phone, or studying late at night. Habits can be linked to personality types and intelligences. A verbal learner might have a habit of reading the paper every morning, while a visual learner may prefer to get the news from TV. An adventurer may habitually go out of town on the weekend, while an organizer may spend weekends getting things in order at home. Your habits reveal a lot about you. Some habits you consider to be good habits, and some may be bad habits.

Bad habits earn that title because they can prevent you from reaching important goals. Some bad habits, such as chronic lateness, cause obvious problems. Other habits, such as renting movies three times a week, may not seem bad until you realize that you needed to spend those hours studying. People maintain bad habits because they offer immediate, enjoyable rewards, even if later effects are negative. For example, going out to eat frequently may drain your budget, but at first it seems easier than shopping for food, cooking, and washing dishes.

Good habits are those that have positive effects on your life. You often have to wait longer and work harder to see a reward for good habits, which makes them harder to maintain. If you cut out fattening foods, you won't lose weight in two days. If you reduce your nights out to gain study time, your grades won't improve in a week. When you strive to maintain good habits, trust that the rewards are somewhere down the road. Changing a habit can be a long process.

Take time to evaluate your habits. Look at the positive and negative effects of each, and decide which are helpful and which harmful to you. Here are steps you can take to evaluate a habit and, if necessary, make a change (if the habit has more negative effects than positive ones). Be careful to change only one habit at a time—trying to reach perfection in everything all at once can overwhelm you.

> To fall into a habit is to begin to cease to be.
>
> **MIGUEL UNAMUNO**

1. *Honestly admit your habit.* Admitting negative or destructive habits can be hard to do. You can't change a habit until you admit that it is a habit.

2. *Evaluate your habit.* What are the negative and positive effects? Are there more negatives than positives, or vice versa? Look at effects carefully, because at times the trouble may not seem to come directly from the habit. For example, spending every weekend working on the house may seem important, but you may be overdoing it and ignoring friends and family members.

3. *If necessary, decide to change.* You might realize what your bad habits are but not yet care about their effects on your life. Until you are convinced that you will receive a benefit, efforts to change will not get you far.

4. *Start today.* Don't put it off until after this week, after the family reunion, or after the semester. Each day lost is a day you haven't had the chance to benefit from a new lifestyle.

5. *Reward yourself appropriately for positive steps taken.* If you earn a good grade, avoid slacking off on your studies the following week. If you've lost weight, avoid celebrating in an ice-cream parlor. Choose a reward that will not encourage you to stray from your target.

6. *Keep it up.* To have the best chance at changing a habit, be consistent for at least three weeks. Your brain needs time to become accustomed to the new habit. If you go back to the old habit during that time, you may feel like you're starting all over again.

Finally, don't get too discouraged if the process seems difficult. Rarely does someone make the decision to change and do so without a setback or two. Being too hard on yourself might cause frustration that tempts you to give up and go back to the habit. Take it one step at a time.

All of the self knowledge you are building will be very important for your educational decisions. Take what you know into account when thinking about your choice of major, which we discussed earlier, in Chapter 3.

J OURNAL ENTRY

To record your thoughts, use a separate sheet or journal.

Discuss the insights you have gained through exploring your multiple intelligences. What strengths have come to your attention? What challenges have been clarified? Talk about your game plan for using your strengths and addressing your challenges both at school and in the real world.

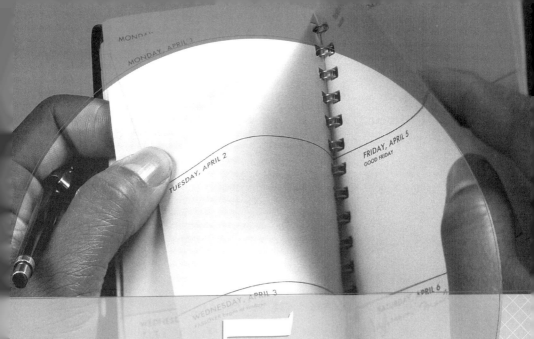

Goal Setting and Time Management

MAPPING YOUR COURSE

People dream of what they want out of life, but dreams often seem too difficult or completely out of your reach. When you set goals, prioritize, and manage your time effectively, you can develop the kind of "big picture" vision that will help you achieve what you dream. This chapter explains how taking specific steps toward goals can help you turn your dreams into reality. The section on time management will discuss how to translate your goals into daily, weekly, monthly, and yearly steps. Finally, you will explore how procrastination can derail your dreams and how to avoid it.

In this chapter, you will explore answers to the following questions:

- What defines your values?
- How do you set and achieve goals?
- What are your priorities?
- How can you manage your time?
- Why is procrastination a problem?

WHAT DEFINES YOUR VALUES?

Your personal *values,* for example, family togetherness, a good education, caring for others, and worthwhile employment, are the beliefs that guide your choices. The total of all your values is your *value system.* You demonstrate your particular value system in the priorities you set, how you communicate with others, your family life, your educational and career choices, and even the material things with which you surround yourself.

Choosing and Evaluating Values

Examining the sources of your values—family, friends, religion, media, school, and/or work—can help you define those values, trace their origin, and question the reasons why you have adopted them. Value sources, however, aren't as important as the process of considering each value carefully to see if it makes sense to you. Your individual value system is unique. Your responsibility is to make value choices based on what feels right for you, for your life, and for those involved in your life.

You can be more sure of making choices that are right for you if you try to periodically question and evaluate your values. Ask yourself: Does this value feel right? What effects does it, or might it, have on my life? Am I choosing it to please someone else, or is it truly my choice? Values are a design for life, and you are the one who has to live the life you design.

Life change and new experiences may bring a change in values. From time to time, try to evaluate the effects that each value has on your life and see if a shift in values might suit your changing circumstances. For example, after growing up in a homogeneous town, a student who meets other students from unfamiliar backgrounds may come to value living in a diverse community. Your values will grow and develop as you do if you continue to think them through.

How Values Relate to Goals

Understanding your values will help you set goals because any goal can help you achieve what you value. If you value spending time with your family, a related goal may be living near your parents. A value of financial independence may generate goals, such as working part-time and keeping credit card debt low, that reflect this value. If you value helping others, you might make time for volunteer work.

Goals enable you to put values into practice. When you set and pursue goals that are based on values, you demonstrate and reinforce values by taking action. The strength of those values, in turn, reinforces your goals. You will experience a stronger drive to achieve if you build goals around what is most important to you.

HOW DO YOU SET AND ACHIEVE GOALS?

A goal can be something as concrete as buying a health insurance plan or as abstract as working to control your temper. When you set goals and work to achieve them, you engage your intelligence, abilities, time, and energy in order to move ahead. From major life decisions to the tiniest day-to-day activities, setting goals will help you define how you want to live and what you want to achieve.

Paul Timm, an expert in self-management, believes that focus is a key ingredient in setting and achieving goals: "Focus adds power to our actions. If somebody threw a bucket of water on you, you'd get wet. . . . But if water was shot at you through a high-pressure nozzle, you might get injured. The only difference is focus."[1] Focus your goal-setting energy by defining a personal mission, placing your goals in long-term and short-term time frames, evaluating goals in terms of your values, and exploring different types of goals.

> Obstacles are what people see when they take their eyes off the goal.
>
> **NEW YORK SUBWAY BULLETIN BOARD**

Identifying Your Personal Mission

If you choose not to set goals or explore what you want out of life, you may look back on your past with a sense of emptiness. You may not know what you've done or why you did it. However, you can avoid that emptiness by periodically thinking about where you've been and where you want to be.

One helpful way to determine your general direction is to write a personal mission statement. Dr. Stephen Covey, author of *The Seven Habits of Highly Effective People,* defines a mission statement as a philosophy outlining what you want to be (character), what you want to do (contributions and achievements), and the principles by which you live. Dr. Covey compares the personal mission statement to the Constitution of the United States, a statement of principles that gives this country guidance and standards in the face of constant change.[2]

Your personal mission isn't written in stone. It should change as you move from one phase of life to the next—from single person to spouse, from student to working citizen. Stay flexible and reevaluate your personal mission from time to time.

The following personal mission statement was written by Carol Carter, one of the authors of this text.

> My mission is to use my talents and abilities to help people of all ages, stages, backgrounds, and economic levels achieve their human potential through fully developing their minds and their talents. I also aim to balance work with people in my life, understanding that my family and friends are a priority above all else.

A company, like a person, needs to establish standards and principles that guide its many activities. Companies often have mission statements so that each member of the organization clearly understands what to strive for. If a company fails to identify its mission, thousands of well-intentioned employees might focus their energies in just as many different directions, creating chaos and low productivity.

Here is a mission statement from the company that publishes this text:

> To provide the most innovative resources—books, technology, programs—to help students of all ages and stages achieve their academic and professional goals inside the classroom and out.

You will have an opportunity to write your own personal mission statement at the end of this chapter. Thinking through your personal mission can help you begin to take charge of your life. It can put you in control instead of allowing circumstances and events to control you. If you frame your mission statement carefully so that it truly reflects your goals, it can be your guide in everything you do.

Placing Goals in Time

Everyone has the same 24 hours in a day, but it often doesn't feel like enough. Your commitments can overwhelm you unless you decide how to use time to plan your steps toward goal achievement.

If developing a personal mission statement establishes the big picture, placing your goals within particular time frames allows you to bring individual areas of that picture into the foreground. Planning your progress step-by-step will help you maintain your efforts over the extended time period often needed to accomplish a goal. There are two categories: long-term goals and short-term goals.

Setting Long-Term Goals

Establish first the goals that have the largest scope, the long-term goals that you aim to attain over a lengthy period of time, up to a few years or more. As a student, you know what long-term goals are all about. You have set yourself a goal to attend school and earn a degree or certificate. Becoming educated is an admirable goal that often takes years to reach.

Some long-term goals are lifelong, such as a goal to continually learn more about yourself and the world around you. Others have a more definite end, such as a goal to complete a course successfully. To determine your long-term goals, think about what you want out of your professional, educational, and personal life. Here is Carol Carter's long-term goal statement:

> To accomplish my mission through writing books, giving seminars, and developing programs that create opportunities for students to learn and develop. To create a personal, professional, and family environment that allows me to manifest my abilities and duly tend to each of my responsibilities.

For example, you may establish long-term goals such as these:

- I will graduate from school and know that I have learned all that I could, whether my grade point average reflects this or not.
- I will use my current and future school experience to develop practical skills that will help me get a satisfying, well-paying job.

Long-term goals don't have to be lifelong goals. Considering what you want to accomplish in a year's time will give you clarity, focus, and a sense of what needs to take place right away. When Carol thought about her long-term goals for the coming year, she came up with the following:

1. Develop programs to provide internships, scholarships, and other quality initiatives for students.
2. Allow time in my personal life to eat well, run five days a week, and spend quality time with family and friends. Allow time daily for quiet reflection and spiritual devotion.

In the same way that Carol's goals are tailored to her personality and interests, your goals should reflect who you are. Personal missions and goals are as unique as each individual. Continuing the example above, you might adopt these goals for the coming year:

- I will look for a part-time job with a local newspaper or newsroom.
- I will learn to navigate the Internet and research topics on-line.

Setting Short-Term Goals

When you divide your long-term goals into smaller, manageable goals that you hope to accomplish within a relatively short time, you are setting short-term goals. Short-term goals narrow your focus, helping you to maintain your progress toward your long-term goals. Say you have set the long-term goals you just read in the previous section. To stay on track toward those goals, you may want to accomplish these short-term goals in the next six months:

- I will make an effort to ask my coworkers for advice on how to get into the news business.
- I will write an assigned paper using information found on the Internet.

These same goals can be broken down into even smaller parts, such as the following one-month goals:

- I will have lunch with my office mate at work so that I can talk with him about his work experience.
- I will learn to conduct Internet research using search directories.

In addition to monthly goals, you may have short-term goals that extend for a week, a day, or even a couple of hours in a given day. Take as an example the Internet research goal. Such short-term goals may include the following:

- Three weeks from now: Research my topic using the two search directories that have the most helpful information.
- Two weeks from now: Experiment with search directories to see which ones will be most useful to me.
- One week from now: Read an Internet guide book to learn how to use search directories effectively.
- By the end of today: Find out what the major search directories are.

As you consider your long- and short-term goals, notice how all of your goals are linked to one another. As Figure 5.1 shows, your long-term goals establish a context for the short-term goals. In turn, your short-term goals make the long-term goals seem clearer and more reachable.

Linking Goals with Values

If you are not sure how to start formulating your mission statement, look to your values to guide you. Define your mission and goals based on what is important to you. For example, if you value physical fitness, your mission

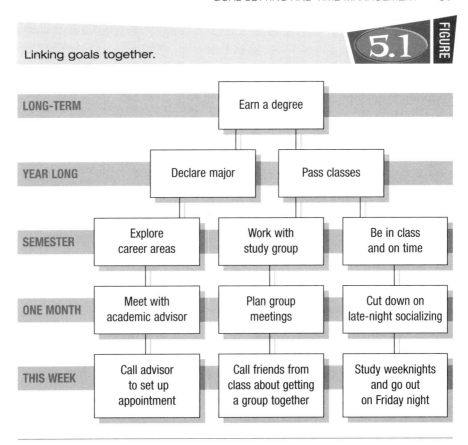

Linking goals together.

FIGURE 5.1

LONG-TERM	Earn a degree
YEAR LONG	Declare major / Pass classes
SEMESTER	Explore career areas / Work with study group / Be in class and on time
ONE MONTH	Meet with academic advisor / Plan group meetings / Cut down on late-night socializing
THIS WEEK	Call advisor to set up appointment / Call friends from class about getting a group together / Study weeknights and go out on Friday night

statement might emphasize your commitment to staying in shape through-out your life. Your long-term goal might be to run a marathon, while your short-term goals might involve your weekly exercise and eating plans.

When you use your values as a compass for your goals, make sure the compass is pointed in the direction of your real feelings. Watch out for the following two pitfalls:

Setting goals according to other people's values. Friends or family may encourage you to strive for what they think you should value. You may, of course, share their values. If you follow advice that you don't believe in, however, you may have a harder time sticking to your path. Staying in tune with your own values will help you make decisions that are right for you.

Setting goals that reflect values you held in the past. Life changes can alter your values. For example, a person who has been through a near-fatal car accident may experience a dramatic increase in how he values time with friends and family and a decrease in how he values material possessions. Keep in touch with your life's changes so your goals can reflect who you are today.

Different Kinds of Goals

People have many different goals, involving different parts of life and different values. Because school is currently a focus in your life, examine your educational goals.

Identifying Educational Goals

People have many reasons for attending college. You may identify with one or more of the following:

- I want to earn a higher salary.
- I want to build marketable skills in a particular career area.
- My supervisor at work says that a degree will help me move ahead in my career.
- Most of my friends were going.
- I want to learn.
- I am recently divorced and need to find a way to earn money.
- Everybody in my family goes to college; it's expected.
- I don't feel ready to jump into the working world yet.
- My friend loves her job and encouraged me to take courses in the field.
- My parent (or a spouse or partner) pushed me to go to college.
- I need to increase my skills so I can provide for my kids.
- I don't really know.

All of these answers are legitimate, even the last one. Whatever your reasons for being here, thinking about your educational goals—what you want out of being here—will help you make the most of your time. Consider what is available to you, for example, classes, instructors, class schedule, and available degrees or certificates. If you have an idea of the career you want to pursue, consider the degree(s), certificate(s), or test(s) that may be required. Don't forget to ponder what you want in terms of learning, relationships, and personal growth.

Goals in Your Career and Personal Life

Establish your long- and short-term goals for your other two paths— career and personal life—as well as for your educational path. Remember that all your goals are interconnected. A school goal is often a step toward a career goal and can affect a personal goal.

Career. Think of your career goals in terms of both job and financial goals.

- First, consider the job you want after you graduate—requirements, duties, hours, coworkers, salary, transportation, and company size, style, and location.

- Then, consider financial goals. How much money do you need to pay your bills, live comfortably, and save for the future? Compare your current financial picture to how you want to live, and set goals that will help you bridge the gap.

Personal Life. Consider personal goals in terms of self, family, and lifestyle.

- First, look at yourself—character, personality, health/fitness, and conduct. Examine the difference between who you are and who you want to be.

- Then, consider your family goals. Do you want to stay single, be married, be a parent, or increase a family you've already started? Do you want to improve relations with a spouse or other family members?

- Finally, consider your ideal lifestyle—where you want to live, in what kind of space, and with whom. Consider goals that allow you to live the way you want to live.

Like learning a new physical task, setting and working toward goals takes a lot of practice and repeated efforts. As long as you do all that you can to achieve a goal, you haven't failed, even if you don't achieve it completely or in the time frame you had planned.

Achieving goals becomes easier when you are realistic about what is possible. Setting priorities will help you make that distinction.

WHAT ARE YOUR PRIORITIES?

When you set a *priority*, you identify what's important at any given moment. Prioritizing helps you focus on your most important goals, especially when the important ones are the most difficult. Human nature often leads people to tackle easy goals first and leave the tough ones for later. The risk is that you might never reach for goals that are crucial to your success.

To explore your priorities, think about your personal mission and look at your school, career, and personal goals. Do one or two of these paths take priority for you right now? In any path, which goals take priority? Which goals take priority over all others?

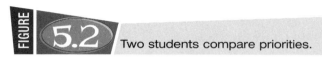

FIGURE 5.2 Two students compare priorities.

K. COLE
returning adult student

M. CONNELL
traditional-aged freshman

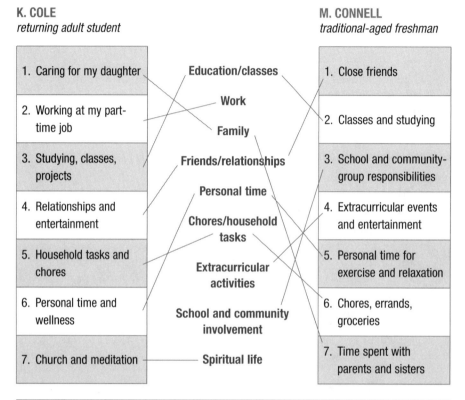

You are a unique individual, and your priorities are yours alone. What may be top priority to someone else may not mean that much to you, and vice versa. You can see this in Figure 5.2, which compares the priorities of two very different students. Each student's priorities are listed in order, with the first priority at the top and the lowest priority at the bottom.

First and foremost, your priorities should reflect your goals. In addition, they should reflect your relationships with others. For example, if you are a parent, your children's needs will probably be high on the priority list. You may be in school so you can get a better job than you have now and give them a better life. If you are in a committed relationship, you may schedule your classes so that you and your partner are home together as often as possible. Even as you consider the needs of others, though, be true to your own goals and priorities so that you can make the most of who you are.

REAL WORLD PERSPECTIVE

Gerard Tamparong, *Loyola Marymount University, 1998, Major: Biology, Minor: Art History*

I graduated from Loyola Marymount University in 1998 with a major in biology and an art history minor. I initially wanted to become a medical doctor, but gradually that gave way to my strong interest in a wide variety of community service. That direction was fueled by my leadership of the Special Games program at LMU.

I was Director of the Games for two years; this program brought hundreds of special education athletes to the LMU campus for competition. Special Games was one of the most successful community service events ever held at LMU.

Special Games taught me how to get along with other people. You will not always get your way.

I doubt that this program would have been supported at a non-liberal arts school. A liberal arts institution invokes a higher standard of educating the spirit than would a technical school. It challenges the individual to become more than just a student of scholastics. We were expected to become students of life. This environment fosters enriching programs such as Special Games.

The experience with Special Games—which involved directing large numbers of people—helped me get my first job after college, an operations position with Franklin Templeton.

I was far from a perfectly qualified person for Franklin Templeton. I was a biology major. However, I got this job by telling them that I had managed 400 people—I can hire, fire, train, and motivate. I beat out finance, marketing, and other business majors for the job.

I knew nothing about the job, and I knew *even less* once I started. I didn't even know what a mutual fund was.

My present job is with Wells Fargo Bank. I am the Coordinator of Community Services. This involves directing the Blood Drive, the Toys Drive, and many other community service projects that help people and deepen Wells Fargo's involvement in the local community. I was hired by Wells Fargo to sell financial products, but I decided that I was more energized by the community service work, so I sold the concept to my supervisor, and the job was created for me. *(continued)*

I wanted to do that job and I believed it would bring great value to the bank. My ultimate goal is to get to the Wells Fargo Foundation and broaden my involvement by helping the bank to generate local, regional, and national community service projects.

In order to reach this goal, aside from knocking on the proverbial door to opportunity with every chance I get, I must exhibit an extreme amount of patience. In the past eight years, there have been only two opportunities for regular employment with the Foundation. I have in essence created my own Wells Fargo Foundation in my area by making sure my name was attached to anything that was remotely associated with community development or outreach. From constructing administrative reports to leading volunteers in a fund-raising drive, I have made it a prime directive to be nothing less than the first point of contact on behalf of the bank.

I BEAT OUT FINANCE, MARKETING, AND OTHER BUSINESS MAJORS FOR THE JOB. . . . I DIDN'T EVEN KNOW WHAT A MUTUAL FUND WAS.

The value of a liberal education is evident in my career. First of all, liberal arts is pre-everything! In liberal arts, you have time to figure out where you want to go. The variety of courses helps you figure out where your talents lie. It helps you find out what you're made of.

As a liberal arts major, more doors open to you, instead of just one track. By exposing you to many areas of knowledge, a liberal education helps you to make a more informed career choice.

Philosophy made me think for myself. My ethics course made me think about the costs (consequences) and benefits of any action.

I like doing social service work within a business environment. Simply put, I have been given the best of both worlds: the job security and benefits associated with a corporate environment *and* the opportunities to make a substantial difference to our local communities.

Nonprofit work brings visibility to a company and visibility is a precursor to more business avenues. This, in turn, allows for more nonprofit interaction due to a larger pool of deposit growth on hand. It's a total "win–win" situation.

Setting priorities moves you closer to accomplishing specific goals. It also helps you begin planning to achieve your goals within specific time frames. Being able to achieve your goals is directly linked to effective time management.

H OW CAN YOU MANAGE YOUR TIME?

Everyone has the same 24 hours in a day, every day; your responsibility and potential for success lie in how you use yours. You cannot change how time passes, but you can spend it wisely. Efficient time management helps you achieve your goals in a steady, step-by-step process.

People have a variety of approaches to time management. Your learning style (see Chapter 4) can help you understand how you use time. For example, students with strong logical–mathematical intelligence and Thinker types tend to organize activities within a framework of time. Because they stay aware of how long it takes them to do something or travel somewhere, they are usually prompt. By contrast, Adventurer types and less logical learners with perhaps stronger visual or interpersonal intelligences may neglect details such as how much time they have to complete a task. They can often be late without meaning to be.

Time management, like physical fitness, is a lifelong pursuit. Throughout your life, your ability to manage your time will vary with your stress level, how busy you are, and other factors. Don't expect perfection—just do your best and keep working at it. Time management involves building a schedule, taking responsibility for how you spend your time, and being flexible.

Building a Schedule

Just as a road map helps you travel from place to place, a schedule is a time-and-activity map that helps you get from the beginning of the day (or week, or month) to the end as smoothly as possible. Schedules help you gain control of your life in two ways: They allocate segments of time for the fulfillment of your daily, weekly, monthly, and longer-term goals, and they serve as a concrete reminder of tasks, events, due dates, responsibilities, and deadlines.

Keep a Date Book

Gather the tools of the trade: a pen or pencil and a date book (sometimes called a planner). A date book is indispensable for keeping track of your time. Some of you have date books and may have used them for years.

Others may have had no luck with them or have never tried. Even if you don't feel you would benefit from one, give it a try. Paul Timm says, "Most time management experts agree that rule number one in a thoughtful planning process is: Use some form of a planner where you can write things down."[3]

There are two major types of date books. The day-at-a-glance version devotes a page to each day. Although it gives you ample space to write the day's activities, it's harder to see what's ahead. The week-at-a-glance book gives you a view of the week's plans but has less room to write per day. If you write detailed daily plans, you might like the day-at-a-glance version. If you prefer to remind yourself of plans ahead of time, try the book that shows a week's schedule all at once. Some date books contain sections for monthly and yearly goals.

Another option is an electronic planner—a compact minicomputer that can hold a large amount of information. You can use it to schedule your days and weeks, make to-do lists, and create and store an address book. Electronic planners are powerful, convenient, and often fun. However, they certainly cost more than the paper version, and you can lose a lot of important data if something goes wrong with the computer inside. Evaluate your options and decide what works best for you.

Set Weekly and Daily Goals

The most ideal time management starts with the smallest tasks and builds to bigger ones. Setting short-term goals that tie in to your long-term goals lends the following benefits:

- increased meaning for your daily activities
- shaping your path toward the achievement of your long-term goals
- a sense of order and progress

For college students as well as working people, the week is often the easiest unit of time to consider at one shot. Weekly goal setting and planning allows you to keep track of day-to-day activities while giving you the larger perspective of what is coming up during the week. Take some time before each week starts to remind yourself of your long-term goals. Keeping long-term goals in mind will help you determine related short-term goals you can accomplish during the week to come.

Figure 5.3 shows parts of a daily schedule and a weekly schedule.

Link Daily and Weekly Goals with Long-Term Goals

After you evaluate what you need to accomplish in the coming year, semester, month, week, and day to reach your long-term goals, use your schedule to record those steps. Write down the short-term goals that will

Daily and weekly schedule.

FIGURE 5.3

Monday, March 20

Time	Tasks	Priority
7:00 AM		
8:00	Up at 8am — finish homework	*
9:00	Class	
10:00		
11:00	Class	
12:00 PM	Renew driver's license @ DMV	*
1:00	Lunch	
2:00	Writing Seminar (peer editing today)	*
3:00	↓	
4:00	check on Ms. Schwartz's office hrs.	
5:00	5:30 work out	
6:00	└→6:30	
7:00	Dinner	
8:00	Read two chapters for Chemistry	
9:00		
10:00		
11:00		

Monday, March 20

8		Call: Mike Blair	1
9	BIO 212	Financial Aid Office	2
10		EMS 262 *Paramedic	3
11	CHEM 203	role-play*	4
12			5
Evening	6pm yoga class		

Tuesday, March 21

8	Finish reading assignment!	Work @ library	1
9			2
10	ENG 112	(study for quiz)	3
11	↓		4
12			5
Evening		↓ until 7pm	

Wednesday, March 22

8		Meet w/advisor	1
9	BIO 212		2
10		EMS 262	3
11	CHEM 203 *Quiz		4
12		Pick up photos	5
Evening	6pm Aerobics		

enable you to stay on track. Here is how a student might map out two different goals over a year's time:

This year: Complete enough courses to graduate.
              Improve my physical fitness.

This semester: Complete my accounting class with a B average or higher.
                Lose 10 pounds and exercise regularly.

This month: Set up study group schedule to coincide with quizzes.
              Begin walking and weight lifting.

This week: Meet with study group; go over material for Friday's quiz.
              Go for a fitness walk three times; go to weight room twice.

Today: Go over Chapter 3 in accounting text.
              Walk for 40 minutes.

Even if you're on the right track, you'll get run over if you just sit there.

WILL ROGERS

Prioritize Goals

Prioritizing enables you to use your date book with maximum efficiency. On any given day, your goals will have varying degrees of importance. Record your goals first, and then label them according to their level of importance, using these categories: Priority 1, Priority 2, and Priority 3. Identify these categories by using any code that makes sense to you. Some people use numbers, as above. Some use letters (A, B, C). Some write activities in different colors according to priority level. Some use symbols (*, +, −).

Priority 1 activities are the most important things in your life. They may include attending class, picking up a child from day care, and paying bills.

Priority 2 activities are part of your routine. Examples include grocery shopping, working out, participating in a school organization, or cleaning. Priority 2 tasks are important but more flexible than Priority 1 tasks.

Priority 3 activities are those you would like to do but can reschedule without much sacrifice. Examples might be a trip to the mall, a visit to a friend, a social phone call, or a sports event. Many people don't enter Priority 3 tasks in their date books until they are sure they have time to get them done.

Prioritizing your activities is essential for two reasons. First, some activities are more important than others, and effective time management requires that you focus most of your energy on Priority 1 items. Second, looking at all your priorities helps you plan when you can get things done. Often, it's not possible to get all your Priority 1 activities done early in the day, especially if they involve scheduled classes or meetings. Prioritizing helps you set Priority 1 items and then schedule Priority 2 and 3 items around them as they fit.

Keep Track of Events

Your date book also enables you to schedule events. Think of events in terms of how they tie in with your long-term goals, just as you would your other tasks. For example, being aware of quiz dates, due dates for assignments, and meeting dates will aid your goals to achieve in school and become involved.

Note events in your date book so that you can stay aware of them ahead of time. Write them in daily, weekly, monthly, or even yearly sections, where a quick look will remind you that they are approaching. Writing them down will also help you see where they fit in the context of all your other activities. For example, if you have three big tests and a presentation all in one week, you'll want to take time in the weeks before to prepare for them.

Following are some kinds of events worth noting in your date book:

- due dates for papers, projects, presentations, and tests
- important meetings, medical appointments, or due dates for bill payments
- birthdays, anniversaries, social events, holidays, and other special occasions
- benchmarks for steps toward a goal, such as due dates for sections of a project or a deadline for losing 5 pounds on your way to 20

Taking Responsibility for How You Spend Your Time

When you plan your activities with an eye toward achieving your most important goals, you are taking responsibility for how you live. The following strategies will help you stay in charge of your choices:

Plan your schedule each week. Before each week starts, note events, goals, and priorities. Decide where to fit activities like studying and Priority 3 items. For example, if you have a test on Thursday, you can plan study sessions on the preceding days. If you have more free time on Tuesday and

5.4   A sample monthly calendar.

SUNDAY	MONDAY	TUESDAY	WEDNESDAY	THURSDAY	FRIDAY	SATURDAY
1	2 WORK	3 Turn in English paper topic	4	5 Chem test	6 Yoga 6 pm	7
8 Frank's Birthday	9 9 am Psych test WORK	10 6:30 pm mtg @ student ctr.	11	12 History study group	13 WORK	14 WORK
15	16 English paper due WORK	17	18 WORK	19 Dentist 2 pm	20 Yoga 6 pm	21 Dinner @ Ann's
22	23 WORK	24 Statistics test	25	26 History study group	27 WORK	28 WORK
29	30 WORK	31				

Friday than on other days, you can plan workouts or Priority 3 activities at those times. Looking at the whole week will help you avoid being surprised by something you had forgotten was coming up.

Make and use to-do lists. Use a to-do list to record the things you want to accomplish. If you generate a daily or weekly to-do list on a separate piece of paper, you can look at all tasks and goals at once. This will help you consider time frames and priorities. Some people create daily to-do lists right on their date book pages. You can tailor a to-do list to an important event, such as exam week, or an especially busy day. This kind of specific to-do list can help you prioritize and accomplish an unusually large task load.

Post monthly and yearly calendars at home. Keeping a calendar on the wall will help you stay aware of important events. Use a yearly or a monthly version (Figure 5.4 shows part of a monthly calendar), and keep it where you can refer to it often. If you live with family or friends, make the calendar a group project so that you stay aware of each other's plans. Knowing each other's schedules can also help you avoid problems such as two people needing the car at the same time.

Schedule downtime. When you're wiped out from too much activity, you don't have the energy to accomplish as much. A little downtime will refresh you and improve your attitude. Even half an hour a day will help. Fill the time with whatever relaxes you—reading, watching television, chatting on-line, playing a game or sport, walking, writing, or just doing nothing. Make downtime a priority.

Be flexible. Anytime, changes can result in priority shifts that jumble your schedule. On Monday, a homework assignment due in a week might be Priority 2; then, if you haven't gotten to it by Saturday, it becomes Priority 1. Perhaps more serious changes occur, such as a car problem or a job loss. Think of change as part of life, and you will be able to more effectively solve the dilemmas that come up. For some changes that occur frequently, you can think through a backup plan ahead of time. For others, the best you can do is to keep an open mind about possibilities and to remember to call on your resources in a pinch. Your problem-solving skills (see Chapter 6) will help you build your ability to adjust to whatever changes come your way.

No matter how well you schedule your time, you will have moments when it's hard to stay in control. Knowing how to identify and avoid procrastination and other time traps will help you get back on track.

WHY IS PROCRASTINATION A PROBLEM?

Procrastination occurs when you postpone tasks. People procrastinate for different reasons. If it is taken to the extreme, however, procrastination can develop into a habit that will cause problems at school, on the job, and at home. Jane B. Burka and Lenora M. Yuen, authors of *Procrastination: Why You Do It and What to Do About It,* say that habitual procrastinators create problems because "The performance becomes the only measure of the person; nothing else is taken into account. An outstanding performance means an outstanding person; a mediocre performance means a mediocre person. . . . As long as you procrastinate, you never have to confront the real limits of your ability, whatever those limits are."[4] For the procrastinator, the fear of failure prevents taking the risk that could bring success.

Antiprocrastination Strategies

Following are some ways to fight your tendencies to procrastinate:

Weigh the benefits (to you and others) of completing the task versus the effects of procrastinating. What rewards lie ahead if you get it done? What will be the effects if you continue to put it off? Which situation has better effects? Chances are you will benefit more in the long term from facing the task head-on.

Set reasonable goals. Plan your goals carefully, allowing enough time to complete them. Unreasonable goals can be so intimidating that you do nothing at all. "Pay off the credit card bill next month" could throw you. However, "pay off the credit card bill in 10 months" might inspire you to take action.

Break the task into smaller parts. Look at the task in terms of its parts. How can you approach it step-by-step? If you can concentrate on achieving one small goal at a time, the task may become less of a burden. In addition, setting concrete time limits for each task may help you feel more in control.

Get started whether or not you "feel like it." Going from doing nothing to doing something is often the hardest part of avoiding procrastination. Thinking about the long-term reasons why the task is important might help you take the first step. Once you start, you may find it easier to continue.

> The right time is any time that one is still so lucky as to have. . . . Live!
>
> HENRY JAMES

Ask for help with tasks and projects at school, work, and home. You don't always have to go it alone. For example, if you avoid a project because you dislike the employee with whom you have to work, talk to your supervisor about adjusting tasks or personnel. Once you identify what's holding you up, see who can help you face the task.

Don't expect perfection. No one is perfect. Most people learn by starting at the beginning and wading through plenty of mistakes and confusion. It's better to try your best than to do nothing at all.

Procrastination is natural, but it can cause you problems if you let it get the best of you. When it does happen, take some time to think about the causes. What is it about this situation that frightens you or puts you off? Answering that question can help you address what causes lie under-neath the procrastination. These causes might indicate a deeper issue that you can address.

J OURNAL ENTRY

To record your thoughts, use a separate sheet or journal.

Using the personal mission statement examples in the chapter as a guide, consider what you want out of your life and create your own per-sonal mission statement. You can write it in paragraph form, in a list of long-term goals, or in a visual format such as a think link (see Chapter 8 for information on think links). Take as much time as you need in order to be as complete as possible.

Critical and Creative Thinking

TAPPING THE POWER OF YOUR MIND

Your mind's powers can show in everything you do, from the smallest chores (comparing prices on cereals at the grocery store) to the most complex situations. Critical thinking and creative thinking enable your mind to process, store, and create with the facts and ideas it encounters. Understanding how your mind works is the first step toward critical thinking. When you have that understanding, you can perform the essential critical-thinking task: asking important questions about ideas, information, and media. This chapter will show you both the mind's basic actions and the thinking processes that incorporate them. You will explore how being an open-minded critical and creative thinker will promote your success in college, career, and life. As we note in Chapter 10, critical thinking is an important foundation that enables liberal arts graduates to be successful in the world of work.

In this chapter, you will explore answers to the following questions:

- What is critical thinking?
- How does critical thinking help you solve problems and make decisions?
- Why should you explore perspectives?
- Why plan strategically?
- How can you develop your creativity?
- What is media literacy?

WHAT IS CRITICAL THINKING?

Although you might figure that the word *critical* implies something difficult and negative, critical thinking is "critical" mainly in the sense of one definition of *critical*: "indispensable" and "important." You think critically every day, though you may not realize it.

Defining Critical Thinking

The following is one way to define critical thinking:

> Critical thinking is thinking that *goes beyond the basic recall of information* but depends on the information recalled. It focuses on the *important, or critical, aspects* of the information. Critical thinking means *asking questions.* Critical thinking means that you *take in information, question it,* and then *use it* to create new ideas, solve problems, make decisions, construct arguments, make plans, and refine your view of the world.

One way to clarify a concept is to look at its opposite. Not thinking critically means not examining important aspects through questioning. A person who does not think critically tends to accept or reject information or ideas without examining them. Table 6.1 compares how a critical thinker and a noncritical thinker might respond to particular situations.

Think about responses you or others have had to different situations. Consider when you have seen critical thinking take place, and when you haven't, and what resulted from each way of responding. This will help you begin to see what kind of an effect critical thinking can have on the way you live.

TABLE 6.1

Not thinking critically vs. thinking critically

YOUR ROLE	SITUATION	NON-QUESTIONING (UNCRITICAL) RESPONSE	QUESTIONING (CRITICAL) RESPONSE
Student	Instructor is lecturing on the causes of the Vietnam War.	You assume everything your instructor says is true.	You consider what the instructor says, write questions about issues you want to clarify, and discuss them with the instructor or classmates.
Spouse/ Partner	Your partner feels he/she does not have enough quality time with you.	You think he/she is wrong and defend yourself.	You ask your partner why he/she thinks this is happening, and together you decide how the situation can be improved.
Employee	Your supervisor is angry with you about something that happened.	You avoid your supervisor or deny responsibility for the incident.	You determine what caused your supervisor to place the blame on you; you talk with your supervisor about what happened and why.

The Path of Critical Thinking

Look at Figure 6.1 to see a visual representation of critical thinking. The path involves taking in information, questioning information, and then using information.

Taking In Information

Although most of this chapter focuses on questioning and using information, the first step of the process is just as crucial. The information you receive is your raw material that you will examine and mold into something new. If you take in information accurately and without judgment, you will have the best material with which to work as you think. Once you have the clearest, most complete information possible, you can begin to examine its important aspects through questioning.

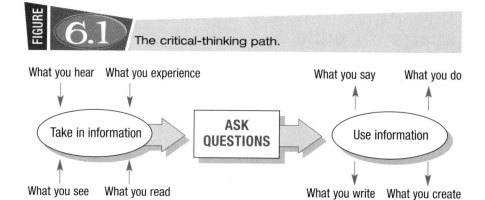

FIGURE **6.1** The critical-thinking path.

Questioning Information

A critical thinker asks many kinds of questions about a given piece of information, such as: *Where did it come from? What could explain it? In what ways is it true or false? How do I feel about it, and why? How is this information similar to or different from what I already know? Is it good or bad? What caused it, and what effects does it have?* Critical thinkers also try to transform information into something they can use. They ask whether information can help them solve a problem, make a decision, learn or create something new, or anticipate the future.

As an example of the questioning process, consider the following as your "information in": You encounter a number of situations—financial strain, parenting on your own, and being an older student—that seem to be getting in the way of your success at school. Whereas non-questioning thinkers may assume defeat, critical thinkers will examine the situation with proactive questions such as these:

> *What exactly are my obstacles?* Examples of my obstacles are a heavy work schedule, single parenting, being in debt, and returning to school after 10 years. *(recall)*

> *Are there other cases different from mine?* I do have one friend who is going through problems worse than mine, and she's getting by. I also know another guy who doesn't have too much to deal with that I can tell, and he's struggling just like I am. *(difference)*

> *Who has problems similar to mine?* Well, if I consider my obstacles specifically, my statement might mean that single parents and returning adult students will all have trouble in school. That is not necessarily true. People who have trouble in school may still become successful. *(similarity)*

What is an example of someone who has had success despite obstacles? What about Oseola McCarty, the cleaning woman who saved money all her life and raised $150,000 to create a college scholarship? She did it without a high-paying job or a college education. *(idea to example)*

What conclusion can I draw from my questions? From thinking about my friend and about Oseola McCarty, I conclude that people can successfully overcome their obstacles by working hard, focusing on their abilities, and concentrating on their goals. *(example to idea)*

Why am I worried about this? Maybe I am scared of the challenge of returning to school. Whatever the cause, one effect is that I don't work to the best of my abilities, which can hurt me and others who depend on me. *(cause and effect)*

How do I evaluate the effects of my worries? I think they're harmful. When we say that obstacles equal difficulty, we can damage our desire to try to overcome them. *(evaluation)*

Remember these types of questions. When you explore the seven mind actions later in the chapter, refer to these questions to see how they illustrate the different actions your mind performs.

Using Information

After taking in and examining information, critical thinkers try to transform it into something they can use. They use information to help them solve a problem, make a decision, learn or create something new, or anticipate what will happen in the future. This part of the critical-thinking path is where you benefit from the hard work of asking questions. This is where inventions happen, new processes are born, theories are created, and information interacts with your own thoughts to create something new.

The Value of Critical Thinking

Critical thinking has many positive effects, or benefits, including the following:

You will increase your ability to perform thinking processes. Critical thinking is a learned skill, just like shooting a basketball or using a word-processing program. As with any other skill, the more you use it, the better you become. The more you ask questions, the better you think. The better you think, the more effective you will be in school, work, and life situations.

You will produce knowledge rather than just reproduce it. The interaction of newly learned information with what you already know creates new knowledge. Its usefulness can be judged by your ability to apply it. For instance, it won't mean much for students studying education to quote the stages of child development on an exam unless they can evaluate children's needs when they begin working as teachers.

You will be a valuable employee. You won't be a failure if you follow directions. However, you will be even more valuable if you ask strategic questions—ranging from "Is there a better way to deliver phone messages?" to "How can we increase business?"—that will improve productivity. Employees who think critically are more likely to make progress in their careers than those who simply do what they are told.

Your mind has some basic moves, or actions, that it performs in order to understand relations between ideas and concepts. Sometimes it uses one action by itself, but most often it uses two or more in combination. These actions are the blocks you will use to build the critical-thinking processes you will explore later in the chapter.

Learning How Your Mind Works

Identify your mind's actions using a system originally conceived by educators Frank Lyman, Arlene Mindus, and Charlene Lopez[1] and developed by numerous other instructors. Based on their studies of how students think, they named seven basic building blocks of thought. These actions are not new to you, although some of their names may be. They represent the ways in which you think all the time.

Through exploring these actions, you can go beyond just thinking and learn *how* you think. This will help you take charge of your own thinking. The more you know about how your mind works, the more control you will have over thinking processes such as problem solving and decision making.

Following are explanations of each of the mind actions, including examples. As you read, write your own examples in the blank spaces. Icons representing each action will help you visualize and remember them.

Recall: *Facts, sequence, and description.* This is the simplest action. When you **recall** you name or describe facts, objects, or events, or put them into sequence. *Examples:*

- You name the steps of a geometry proof, in order.
- You remember your best friends' phone numbers.

Your example: Recall two important school-related events this month.

_____

_____

_____

 The icon: Capital R stands for recall or remembering.

Similarity: *Analogy, likeness, comparison.* This action examines what is **similar** about two or more things. You might compare situations, ideas, people, stories, events, or objects. *Examples:*

- You compare notes with another student to see what facts and ideas you both consider important.
- You analyze the arguments you've had with your partner this month and then see how they all seem to be about the same problem.

Your example: Tell what is similar about two of your best friends.

_____

_____

_____

 The icon: The Venn diagram illustrates the idea of similarity. The two circles represent the things being compared, and the shaded area of intersection indicates that they have some degree or element of similarity.

Difference: *Distinction, contrast.* This action examines what is **different** about two or more situations, ideas, people, stories, events, or objects, contrasting them with one another. *Examples:*

- You see how two instructors differ—one divides the class into small groups for discussions; the other keeps desks in place and delivers lectures.
- You contrast a day when you combine work and school with a day when you attend class only.

Your example: Explain how your response to a course you like differs from your response to a course you don't like as much.

_____

_____

_____

The icon: Here the Venn diagram is used again, to show difference. The nonintersecting parts of the circles are shaded, indicating that the focus is on what is not in common.

Cause and Effect: *Reasons, consequences, prediction.* Using this action, you look at what has **caused** a fact, situation, or event and/or what **effects**, or consequences, come from it. In other words, you examine what led up to something and/or what will follow because of it. *Examples:*

- Staying up late causes you to oversleep, which causes you to be late to class. This causes you to miss some material, which has the further effect of your having problems on the test.

- When you pay your phone and utility bills on time, you create effects such as a better credit rating, uninterrupted service, and a better relationship with your service providers.

Your example: Name what causes you to like your favorite class and the effects that class has on you.

_____

_____

_____

 The icon: The arrows, pointing toward each other in a circular pattern, show how a cause leads to an effect.

Example to Idea: *Generalization, classification, conceptualization.* From one or more **examples** (facts or events), you develop a general **idea** or ideas. Grouping facts or events into patterns may allow you to make a general statement about several of them at once. Classifying a fact or event helps you build knowledge. This mind action moves from the specific to the general. *Examples:*

- You have had trouble finding a baby-sitter. A classmate even brought her child to class once. Your brother drops his daughter at day care and doesn't like not seeing her all day. From these examples, you derive the idea that your school needs an on-campus day-care program.

- You see a movie, and you decide it is mostly about pride.

Your example: Name activities you enjoy. Using them, derive an idea of a class you want to take.

_____

_____

_____

The icon: The arrow and "Ex" pointing to a light bulb on their right indicate how an example or examples lead to the idea (the light bulb, lit up).

Idea to Example: *Categorization, substantiation, proof.* In a reverse of the previous action, you take an **idea** or ideas and think of **examples** (events or facts) that support or prove that idea. This mind action moves from the general to the specific. *Examples:*

- For a paper, you start with this thesis statement: "Computer knowledge is a must for the modern worker." To support that idea, you gather examples, such as the number of industries that use computers or the kinds of training employers are requiring.

- You talk to your advisor about changing your major, giving examples that support your idea, such as the facts that you have worked in the field you want to change to and you have fulfilled some of the requirements for that major already.

Your example: Name an admirable person. Give examples that show how that person is admirable.

_____

_____

_____

 The icon: In a reverse of the previous icon, this one starts with the light bulb and has an arrow pointing to "Ex." This indicates that you start with the idea and then move to the supporting examples.

Evaluation: *Value, judgment, rating.* Here you **judge** whether something is useful or not useful, important or unimportant, good or bad, or right or wrong by identifying and weighing its positive and negative effects (pros and cons). Be sure to consider the specific situation at hand (a cold drink might be good on the beach in August but not so good in the snowdrifts in January). With the facts you have gathered, you determine the value of something in terms of both predicted effects and your own needs. Cause-and-effect analysis always accompanies evaluation. *Examples:*

- For one semester, you schedule classes in the afternoons and spend nights working. You find that you tend to sleep late and lose your only study time. From this harmful effect, you evaluate that this schedule doesn't work for you. You decide to schedule earlier classes next time.

- Someone offers you a chance to cheat on a test. You evaluate the potential effects if you are caught. You also evaluate the long-term effects of not actually learning the material and of doing something ethically wrong. You decide that it isn't right or worthwhile to cheat.

Your example: Evaluate your mode of transportation to school.

_____

_____

_____

 The icon: A set of scales out of balance indicates how you weigh positive and negative effects to arrive at an evaluation.

You may want to use a *mnemonic device*—a memory tool, as explained in Chapter 9—to remember the seven mind actions. You can make a sentence of words that each start with a mind action's first letter, such as "Really Smart Dogs Cook Eggs In Enchiladas."

We do not live to think, but, on the contrary, we think in order that we may succeed in surviving.

JOSE ORTEGA Y GASSET

How Mind Actions Build Thinking Processes

The seven mind actions are the fundamental building blocks that indicate relation between ideas and concepts. You will rarely use one at a time in a step-by-step process, as they are presented here. You will usually combine them, overlap them, and repeat them, using different actions for different situations. For example, when a test question asks you to explain prejudice, you might give *examples, different* from one another, that show your *idea* of prejudice (combining difference with example to idea).

When you combine mind actions in working toward a goal, you are performing a thinking process. Following are explorations of some of the most important critical-thinking processes: solving problems, making decisions, recognizing perspectives, and planning strategically. Each thinking process helps to direct your critical thinking toward the achievement of your goals. Figure 6.4, which appears later in the chapter, reminds you that the mind actions form the core of the thinking processes.

HOW DOES CRITICAL THINKING HELP YOU SOLVE PROBLEMS AND MAKE DECISIONS?

Problem solving and decision making are probably the two most crucial and common thinking processes. Each one requires various mind actions. They overlap somewhat because every problem that needs solving requires you to make a decision. However, not every decision requires that you solve a problem (e.g., not many people would say that deciding what to order for lunch is a problem).

Although both of these processes have multiple steps, you will not always have to work through each step. As you become more comfortable with solving problems and making decisions, your mind will automatically click through the steps. Also, you will become more adept at evaluating which problems and decisions need serious consideration and which can be taken care of more quickly and simply.

Problem Solving

Life constantly presents problems to be solved, ranging from average daily problems (how to manage study time) to life-altering situations (how to design a child-custody plan during a divorce). Choosing a solution without thinking critically may have negative effects. If you use the steps of the following problem-solving process, however, you will maximize the number of possible solutions you generate and will explore each one as fully as possible.

Step 1. Identify the problem accurately. What are the facts? *Recall* the details of the situation. To define a problem correctly, focus on its causes rather than its effects. Consider the Chinese saying: "Give a man a fish, and he will eat for a day. Teach a man to fish, and he will eat for a lifetime." If you state the problem as "The man is hungry," giving him a fish seems like a good solution. Unfortunately, the problem returns—because hunger is an effect. Focusing on the cause brings a new definition: "The man does not know how to find food." Given that his lack of knowledge is the true cause, teaching him to fish will truly solve the problem.

Sample problem: A student is not understanding course material.

Step 2. Analyze the problem. Analyze, or break down into understandable pieces, what surrounds the problem. What *effects* of the situation concern you? What *causes* these effects? Are there hidden causes? Look at the causes and effects that surround the problem.

Sample problem: If some effects of not understanding include poor grades and lack of interest, some causes may include poor study habits, not listening in class, or lack of sleep.

Step 3. Brainstorm possible solutions. Brainstorming will help you to think of examples of how you solved similar problems, consider what is different about this problem, and come up with new possible solutions (see page 139 for more about brainstorming). Remember that to get to the

REAL WORLD PERSPECTIVE

John McLaughlin, *Whittier College, 1996, Major: Physics*

I graduated from Whittier College in 1996 with a major in physics. In September 1996, I was accepted into the Stanford graduate school of Engineering for a Masters in Manufacturing and Systems Engineering. I completed this degree in June 1997.

Certain humanities and social science courses from Whittier helped me in the Stanford program. A sociology course helped further my ability to read, comprehend, analyze, and discuss. This skill was very helpful when applied to science and engineering courses. A writing course was also very helpful in exploring creative thought. The process involved in writing creatively is very similar to the process of developing a product.

My first job after college was operations manager for the Diamond Bar Medical Clinic. Then, I joined my present employer, Wet Design, the world's biggest creator of water fountain designs—featured in *Forbes, USA Today,* and other magazines. Wet Design created the Bellagio fountain in Las Vegas. Long-term I'd like to be the chief operating officer of a 20 to 100 million dollar company.

The real value of a liberal education in my work is that it developed my ability to think and make the connections between different disciplines. For example, philosophy relates to physics in the real world. Our lives are governed by how we see things. Philosophy allows us to develop our own ideas about what is real. By looking at writers with different viewpoints, you come up with your own ideas.

Whittier encouraged me and other students to be open to ideas. This has helped me to manage people in the workplace because everyone has different ideas. You have to hear them and then bring them back together after they've expressed their differences. This happens in product development sessions where people are throwing around every idea they can think of. Openness to new concepts matters a lot here. You want to get as many thoughts as you can from everyone in the group. I learned that from my

(continued)

teachers at Whittier. Not stopping the discussion from going where I think it shouldn't go is a highly valuable skill.

I developed my critical-thinking skills at Whittier. I was helped by courses where we delved into texts that are controversial and then we had to back up our points of view with other sources.

After having completed one and one-half years at Whittier, I was a Mormon missionary for two years in Guatemala. There are people down there who have nothing but are very happy with what they have. People up here have TONS, but they always want more. I would recommend to anyone that they go out of the country for a few years.

People here should focus more on family and what's important rather than material things, things of this world. I'm not going to sacrifice my family for a career goal.

If you go through a program of liberal arts, you have a much better chance of loving learning because liberal arts fosters this, and because you study so many different things. The courses are taught in an open environment. You love the discussion. You love to challenge people and find information that backs up your point of view. A lot of success on the job is being able to present yourself and state your ideas confidently.

IF YOU CAN'T LEARN AND ACQUIRE NEW SKILLS,
THEY REPLACE YOU WITH SOMEONE ELSE.

My most lasting impression of a liberal education is that as you go through life, everything is about learning. If you can't learn and acquire new skills, you will be replaced with someone else.

In liberal arts, you're forced to challenge your views and then you're given the tools to think about these perspectives. You come out a better person. Students develop stronger convictions because they've tested their ideas against others. Because they're now able to back up their viewpoints, they're going to succeed.

The nice thing about a liberal arts college is that you are exposed to almost everything that's out there.

heart of a problem, you must base possible solutions on the most significant causes instead of putting a bandage on the effects.

Sample problem: Looking at his study habits, the student comes up with ideas like seeking help from his instructor or working with a study group.

Step 4. Explore each solution. Why might your solution work, or not? Might a solution work partially, or in a particular situation? *Evaluate* ahead of time the pros and cons (positive and negative effects) of each plan. Create a chain of causes and effects in your head, as far into the future as you can, to see where this solution might lead.

Sample problem: The student considers the effects of improved study habits, more sleep, tutoring, or dropping the class.

Step 5. Choose and execute the solution you decide is best. Decide how you will put your solution to work. Then, execute your solution.

Sample problem: The student decides on a combination of improved study habits and tutoring.

Step 6. Evaluate the solution that you acted upon, looking at its effects. What are the positive and negative *effects* of what you did? In terms of your needs, was it a useful solution or not? Could the solution use any adjustments to be more useful? Would you do the same again or not? In evaluating, you are collecting data.

Sample problem: Evaluating his choice, the student may decide that the effects are good but that his fatigue still causes a problem.

Step 7. Continue to evaluate and refine the solution. Problem solving is a process. You may have opportunities to apply the same solution again. Evaluate repeatedly, making changes that you decide make the solution better (i.e., more reflective of the causes of the problem).

Sample problem: The student may decide to continue to study more regularly but, after a few weeks of tutoring, could opt to trade in the tutoring time for some extra sleep. He may decide to take what he has learned from the tutor so far and apply it to his increased study efforts.

Using this process will enable you to solve school, work, and personal problems in a thoughtful, comprehensive way. The think link in Figure 6.2 demonstrates a way to visualize the flow of problem solving. Figure 6.3 shows how one person used this plan to solve a problem. It represents the same plan as Figure 6.2 but with space to write in so that it can be used in the problem-solving process.

Problem-solving plan.

FIGURE 6.2

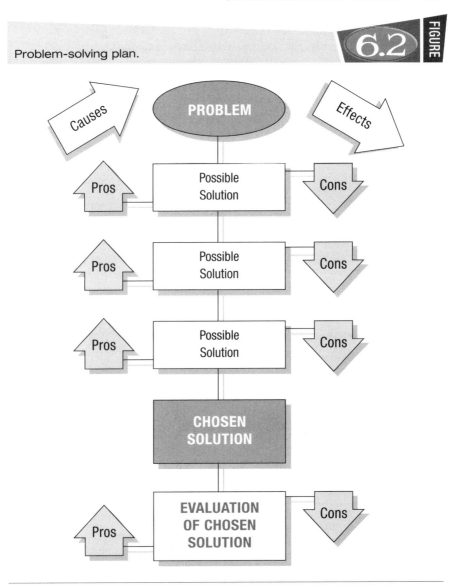

Decision Making

Although every problem-solving process involves making a decision (deciding on a solution), not all decisions involve problems. Decisions are choices. Making a choice, or decision, requires thinking critically through the possible choices and evaluating which will work best for you and for the situation.

How one student worked through a problem.

LIST CAUSES OF PROBLEM:

Must go to school to take classes

Can't have child with me in class

No one else at home to watch
    child

STATE PROBLEM HERE:

Need some way to
provide child-care
while I'm at school

LIST EFFECTS OF PROBLEM:

Missed exams and classes sometimes

Logistics take extra time, transport

Stress created for me and child

Lack of routine & comfort

Use boxes below to list | possible solutions:

**List potential POSITIVE
effects for each solution:**

Care is consistent

Reliable and familiar setting

Doesn't matter if child is sick

SOLUTION #1:

Have a nanny at
home

**List potential NEGATIVE
effects for each solution:**

Expensive

Hard to find someone to trust

Person must follow my schedule

SOLUTION #2:

Join child-care
co-op

Meet parents like myself

Child has playmates

Inexpensive

Must trust other parents

Sick child might get others sick

SOLUTION #3

Get school to provide
child care on campus

Close by to classes

Reliable care

No extra transport time

Costs school money

Need to find space & create facility

Restrictions & waiting lists

Now choose the solution | you think is best—and try it.

**List the actual POSITIVE
effects for this solution:**

CHOSEN SOLUTION

Join child-care co-op

**List the actual NEGATIVE
effects for this solution:**

Met some helpful people who understand me

My child likes the other three children

Low cost helps my budget

When it's my turn, I have to care for four children

Sometimes our schedules clash

Can't let a sick child participate

FINAL EVALUATION: Was it a good or bad choice?

All in all, I think this is the best I could do on my budget. There are times when I have to
stay home with a sick child, but I'm mostly able to stay committed to both parenting and school.

Before you begin the process, evaluate the decision. Some decisions are little day-to-day considerations that you can take care of quickly (what books to bring to class). Others require thoughtful evaluation, time, and perhaps the input of others you trust (whether to quit a good job). The following is a list of steps for thinking critically through the more complex kind of decision.

1. Decide on a goal. Why is this decision necessary? What result do you want from this decision, and what is its value? Considering the *effects* you want can help you formulate your goal.

   Sample decision: A student currently attends a small private college. Her goal is to become a physical therapist. The school has a good program, but her father has changed jobs and the family can no longer pay the tuition and fees.

2. Establish needs. *Recall* the needs of everyone (or everything) involved in the decision. Consider all who will be affected.

   Sample decision: The student needs a school with a full physical therapy program; she and her parents need to cut costs; she needs to be able to transfer credits.

3. Name, investigate, and evaluate available options. Brainstorm possible choices, and then look at the facts surrounding each. *Evaluate* the good and bad effects of each possibility. Weigh these effects and judge which is the best course of action.

   Sample decision: Here are some possibilities that the student might consider:

   - Continue at the current college. **Positive effects:** I wouldn't have to adjust to a new place or to new people. I could continue my course work as planned. **Negative effects:** I would have to find a way to finance most of my tuition and costs on my own, such as through loans, grants, or work. I'm not sure I could find time to work as much as I would need to, and I don't think I would qualify for as much aid as I now need.

   - Transfer to the state college. **Positive effects:** I could reconnect with people there that I know from high school. Tuition and room costs would be cheaper than at my current school. I could transfer credits. **Negative effects:** I would still have to work some or find minimal financial aid. The physical therapy program is small and not very strong.

   - Transfer to the community college. **Positive effects:** They have many of the courses I need to continue with the physical therapy curriculum. The school is close by, so I could live at home

REAL WORLD PERSPECTIVE

Bryan Gittings, *Whittier College, 1999,*
Major: Psychology, Minor: Political Science

I graduated from Whittier College in 1999 with a major in psychology and a minor in political science. Originally, I wanted to be a doctor like my mother. I was a combat medic for three years of active duty in the Army. I had enough of the health field. I got burned out. At that point I decided to join law enforcement.

I'm in an MBA program right now; I want a Ph.D. in Forensic Psychology in order to compile evidence to identify the type of criminal or behavior associated with the criminal who committed the offense.

My path to liberal arts began with lacrosse. I was recruited by friends to help the Whittier lacrosse team.

I got to Whittier and they didn't even know what a Scantron was—that's how all my tests were scored at UMBC. Every test was an essay exam. I was really being forced to think, make decisions, stand behind them, and prove what I said was the right answer. My grades dropped. I had my lowest semester ever. But I bounced back once I learned how to study.

I was captain of the lacrosse team, a resident advisor, and involved in several campus activities. I was able to do all of those things effectively because Whittier taught me how to think, how to prioritize, how to organize my time.

Back at UMBC, if I had to write a paper, I'd drop the class and pick one where I didn't have to write anything. If I was asked to do a five-page paper, I'd say, What is this? I can't do this. Now, at Whittier having a 30-page paper doesn't frighten me. I've learned how to knock them out.

In psychology, I've already written papers that require literature reviews. That's what they do in graduate school.

I had to take "The Western Mind I and II," courses that I never would have taken on my own. Those courses were excellent.

I also took the "Arabs and Muslims" class for a whole year. I had participated in the Gulf War. During the course, I realized that I had

(continued)

developed prejudices against people over there while in the military. But I learned the origins of the religion and the country and I understood them better. I listened to these various Muslim and Arab speakers and I said to myself, "They're just like us. They have conflicts between their own religious sects. They have conflicts between their own ethnicities."

At UMBC, courses like that would have been offered as electives and I never would have taken such a class. Western Mind? History and philosophy? Those are things I'm not interested in so I would not take those classes. At Whittier, you have to take such courses. They're requirements to graduate.

EVERY TEST WAS AN ESSAY TEST.
I WAS REALLY BEING FORCED TO THINK.

You can get a class at this school in every department. They push you to take electives here. This school WANTS you to take courses outside your major.

Liberal arts has helped my writing greatly. My writing on the job is important because the judge, the attorneys, and the jury have to understand clearly what I'm saying. I have to back up what I'm saying. I can't have a district attorney ripping up my report or a lawyer saying there's not enough information in this narrative.

Philosophy for me was just way out there because I was very factual and here they're asking, "How do you know if you exist?"

I presently work for Target Stores as a Theft Coordinator, and I plan to develop security systems for the company. These kinds of liberal arts courses help me on my job today; they encourage me to listen more closely to differences and conflicts among people where I work—the store workers and the customers.

My long-range career goals are to be employed by a federal or local police agency as an investigator dealing with career criminals and the factors that lead to a lifetime of deviant behavior.

and avoid paying housing costs. Credits will transfer. The tuition is extremely reasonable. **Negative effects:** I don't know anyone there. I would be less independent. The school doesn't offer a bachelor's degree.

4. Decide on a plan and take action. Make a choice based on your evaluation, and act on it.

   Sample decision: In this case, the student might decide to go to the community college for two years and then transfer back to a four-year school to earn a bachelor's degree in physical therapy. Although she might lose some independence and contact with friends, the positive effects are money saved, opportunity to spend time on studies rather than working to earn tuition, and the availability of classes that match the physical therapy program requirements.

5. Evaluate the result. Was it useful? Not useful? Some of both? Weigh the positive and negative effects. If the student decides to transfer, she may find that it can be hard being back at home, although her parents are adjusting to her independence and she is trying to respect their concerns. Fewer social distractions result in her getting more work done. The financial situation is favorable. All things considered, she evaluates that this decision was a good one.

Making important decisions can take time. Think through your decisions thoroughly, considering your own ideas as well as those of others you trust, but don't hesitate to act once you have your plan. You cannot benefit from your decision until you follow through on it.

WHY SHOULD YOU EXPLORE PERSPECTIVES?

Perspective is complex. Each individual has her own way of looking at the world. However, seeing the world *only* from your perspective—and resisting any challenges to that perspective—can be inflexible, limiting, and frustrating to both you and others.

Evaluating Perspective

The most effective way to evaluate perspectives involves taking in information, evaluating it with questions, and then acting upon it in whatever way seems appropriate. Exploring perspectives critically will introduce you to new ideas, improve your communication with others, and encourage mutual respect.

Take In New Information

The first step is to take in new perspectives and simply acknowledge that they exist without immediately judging, rejecting, or even accepting them. It's easy to feel so strongly about a topic—for example, whether the government should allow capital punishment—that you don't even give a chance to anyone with an opposing view. Resist your own strong opinions and listen. A critical thinker is able to allow for the existence of perspectives that differ from, and even completely negate, his own.

> The world of reality has its limits. The world of imagination is boundless.
> **JEAN-JACQUES ROUSSEAU**

Evaluate the Perspective

Asking questions will help you maintain flexibility and openness.

- What is similar and different about this perspective and my own perspective and about this person and me? What personal experiences have led to our particular perspectives?

- What examples, evidence, or reasons could be used to support or justify this perspective? Do some reasons provide good support even if I don't agree with the reasons?

- What effects may come from this way of being, acting, or believing? Are the effects different on different people and in different situations? Even if this perspective seems to have negative effects for me, how might it have positive effects for others and therefore have value?

- What can I learn from this different perspective? Is there anything I could adopt that would improve my life? Is there anything I wouldn't do but that I can still respect and learn from?

Accept and Perhaps Take Action

On the one hand, perhaps your evaluation will lead you simply to a recognition and appreciation of the other perspective, even if you decide that it is not right for you. On the other hand, thinking through the new perspective may lead you to feel that it would be worthwhile to try it out or to adopt it as your own.

The Value of Seeing Other Perspectives

Seeing beyond one's own perspective can be difficult, but there are some real benefits of being able to see and consider other perspectives.

FIGURE 6.4 The wheel of thinking.

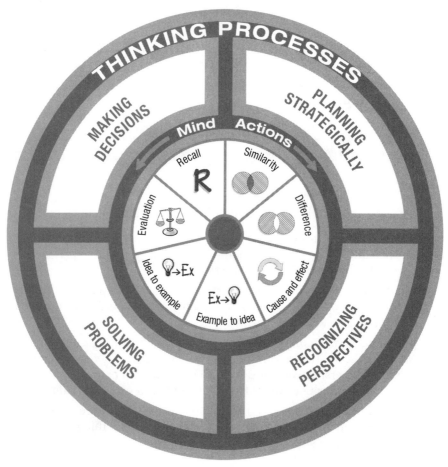

Improved communication. When you consider another perspective, you open lines of communication. For example, if you want to drop a course and your advisor says it's impossible before listening to you, you might not feel much like explaining. But if your advisor asks to hear your perspective, you may sense that your needs are respected and be ready to talk.

Mutual respect. When someone takes the time and energy to understand how you feel about something, you probably feel respected and in return offer respect to the person who made the effort. When people respect one another, relationships become stronger and more productive, whether they are personal, work-related, or educational.

Continued learning. Every time you shift your perspective, you can learn something new. There are worlds of knowledge and possibilities outside your experience. You may find different yet equally valid ways of living. Above all else, you may see that each person is entitled to her own perspective, no matter how foreign it may be to you.

By being able to recognize perspectives, the connection that you foster with others may mean the difference between success and failure in today's world. This becomes more true as the Information Age introduces you to an increasing number of perspectives every day.

HY PLAN STRATEGICALLY?

If you've ever played a game of chess, participated in a martial arts match, or made a detailed plan of how to reach a particular goal, you have had experience with strategy. Strategy is the plan of action, that is, the method or the "how," behind any goal you want to achieve.

Strategic planning means looking at the next week, month, year, or 10 years and exploring the future positive and negative effects that current choices and actions may have. As a student, you have planned strategically by deciding that the effort of school is a legitimate price to pay for the skills and opportunities you will receive. Being strategic means using decision-making skills to choose how to accomplish tasks. It means asking questions.

Strategy and Critical Thinking

In situations that demand strategy, think critically by asking questions like these:

- If you aim for a certain goal, what actions may cause you to achieve that goal?

- What are the potential effects, positive or negative, of different actions or choices?

- What can you learn from previous experiences that may inspire similar or different actions?

- What can you recall about what others have done in similar situations?

- Which set of effects would be most helpful or desirable to you?

For any situation that would benefit from strategic planning, from getting ready for a study session to aiming for a career, these steps will help you make choices that bring about the most positive effects.

1. Establish a goal. What do you want to achieve? When do you want to achieve it?
2. Brainstorm possible plans. What are some ways that you can get where you want to go? What steps toward your goal will you need to take 1 year, 5 years, 10 years, or 20 years from now?
3. Anticipate all possible effects of each plan. What positive and negative effects may occur, both soon and in the long term? What approach may best help you to achieve your goal?
4. Put your plan into action. Act on the decision you have made.
5. Evaluate continually. Your strategies might not have the effects you predicted. If you discover that things are not going the way you planned, for any reason, reevaluate and change your strategy.

The most important critical-thinking question for successful strategic planning begins with "how." *How* do you remember what you learn? *How* do you develop a productive idea at work? The process of strategic planning, in a nutshell, helps you find the best answer.

Benefits of Strategic Planning

Strategic planning has many important positive effects, including the following:

School and work success. A student who wants to do well in a course needs to plan study sessions. A lawyer needs to anticipate how to respond to points raised in court. Strategic planning creates a vision into the future that allows the planner to anticipate possibilities and to be prepared for them.

Successful goal setting. Thinking strategically helps you to see how to achieve goals over time. For example, a student might have a part-time job to work toward the goal of paying tuition.

Keeping up with technology. Technological developments have increased workplace change. Thinking strategically about job opportunities may lead you to a broader range of courses or a major and career in a growing career area, making it more likely that your skills will be in demand when you graduate.

Strategic planning means using critical thinking to develop a vision of your future. Although you can't predict with certainty what will happen, you can ask questions about the potential effects of your actions. With what you learn, you can make plans that will bring the best possible effects for you and others.

HOW CAN YOU DEVELOP YOUR CREATIVITY?

Everyone is creative. Although the word *creativity* may inspire images of art and music, creativity comes in many other forms. A creation can be a solution, idea, approach, tangible product, work of art, system, or program. Creative innovations introduced by all kinds of people continually expand and change the world. Here are some that have had an impact:

- Rosa Parks refused to give up her seat on the bus to a white person, setting off a chain of events that gave rise to the civil rights movement.
- Jody Williams and the group she founded, International Campaign to Ban Landmines, have convinced nearly 100 countries to support a treaty that would end land mine production and sales.
- Art Fry and Spencer Silver invented the Post-it™ in 1980, enabling people to save paper and protect documents by using removable notes.

Even though these particular innovations had wide-ranging effects, the characteristics of these influential innovators can be found in all people who exercise their creative capabilities. Creativity can be as down-to-earth as planning how to coordinate your work and class schedules.

Characteristics of Creative People

Creative people combine ideas and information in ways that form new solutions, ideas, processes, or products. "I've found that the hallmark of creative people is their mental flexibility," says creativity expert Roger van Oech. "Like race-car drivers who shift in and out of different gears depending on where they are on the course, creative people are able to shift in and out of different types of thinking depending on the needs of the situation at hand."[2] See Table 6.2 for some primary characteristics of creative people.

Enhancing Your Creativity

Following are some ways to enhance your natural creativity, adapted from material by J. R. Hayes.[3]

Take the broadest possible perspective. At first, a problem may look like "My child won't stay quiet when I study." If you take a wider look, you may discover hidden causes or effects of the problem, such as "We haven't had time together, so he feels lonely."

| TABLE **6.2** | Characteristics of creative people. |

CHARACTERISTIC	EXAMPLE
Willingness to take risks	Taking a difficult, high-level course.
Tendency to break away from limitations	Entering a marathon race.
Tendency to seek new challenges and experiences	Taking on an internship in a high-pressure workplace.
Broad range of interests	Inventing new moves on the basketball court and playing guitar on open-mike night.
Ability to make new things out of available materials	Making curtains out of bedsheets.
Tendency to question norms and assumptions	Adopting a child of different ethnic background than the family's.
Willingness to deviate from popular opinion	Working for a small, relatively unknown political party.
Curiosity and inquisitiveness	Wanting to know how a computer program works.

Source: Adapted from T. Z. Tardif and R. J. Sternberg, "What Do We Know About Creativity?" in *The Nature of Creativity,* ed., R. J. Sternberg (London: Cambridge University Press, 1988).

Give yourself time. Rushing can stifle your creative ability. When you allow time for thoughts to percolate or you take breaks when figuring out a problem, you may increase your creative output.

Gather varied input. The more information and ideas you gather as you think, the more material you have to build a creative idea or solution. Every new piece of input offers a new perspective.

Here are a few additional creativity tips from van Oech:[4]

Don't get hooked on finding the one right answer. There can be lots of "right answers" to any question. The more possibilities you generate, the better your chance of finding the best one.

Let yourself play. People often hit upon their most creative ideas when they are exercising or just relaxing. Often when your mind switches into play mode, it can more freely generate new thoughts.

Don't fear failure. Even Michael Jordan got cut from the basketball team as a high school sophomore in Wilmington, North Carolina. If you insist on getting it right all the time, you may miss out on the creative path—often paved with failures—leading to the best possible solution.

Brainstorming combines many of these strategies. Use brainstorming for problem solving, decision making, writing a paper, or whenever you need to free your mind for new possibilities.

> Learning to let yourself create is like learning to walk. . . . Progress, not perfection, is what we should be asking of ourselves.
>
> JULIA CAMERON

Brainstorming Toward a Creative Answer

You are brainstorming when you approach a problem by letting your mind free-associate and come up with as many possible ideas, examples, or solutions as you can, without immediately evaluating them as good or bad. Brainstorming is also referred to as *divergent thinking;* you start with the issue or problem and then let your mind diverge, or go in as many different directions as it wants, in search of ideas or solutions. Following are two general guidelines for successful brainstorming:[5]

Don't evaluate or criticize an idea right away. Write down your ideas so that you remember them. Evaluate them later, after you have had a chance to think about them. Try to avoid criticizing other people's ideas as well. Students often become stifled when their ideas are evaluated during brainstorming.

Focus on quantity; don't worry about quality until later. Generate as many ideas or examples as you can. The more thoughts you generate, the better the chance that one may be useful. Brainstorming works well in groups. Group members can become inspired by, and make creative use of, one another's ideas.

Remember, creativity can be developed if you have the desire and patience. Nurture your creativity by being accepting of your own ideas. Your creative expression will become more free with practice.

Creativity and Critical Thinking

Critical thinking is inherently creative because it requires you to use given information to come up with ideas or solutions to problems. For example, if you were brainstorming to generate possible causes of fatigue in afternoon classes, you might come up with lack of sleep, too much morning caffeine, or an instructor who doesn't inspire you. Through your consideration of causes and solutions, you have been thinking both creatively and critically.

Creative thinkers and critical thinkers have similar characteristics—both consider new perspectives, ask questions, don't hesitate to question accepted assumptions and traditions, and persist in the search for answers. You use critical-thinking mind actions throughout everything you do in school and in your daily life. In this chapter and in some of the other study skills chapters, you will notice mind action icons placed where they can help you to understand how your mind is working.

One particularly important area in which you will benefit from thinking critically is in how you approach the media that you encounter on a daily basis.

WHAT IS MEDIA LITERACY?

Do you believe everything you read, see on television, or find on the Internet? Think about it for a moment. If you trusted every advertisement, for example, you would believe that at least four fast-food restaurants serve "the best burger available." It is impossible to believe it all without becoming completely confused about what is real.

If literacy refers to the ability to read, media literacy can be seen as the ability to read the media. Media literacy—the ability to respond with critical thinking to the media that you encounter—is essential for a realistic understanding of the information that bombards you daily. It means that instead of accepting anything a newspaper article, TV commercial, or Internet site says is fact, you take time to question the information, using your mind actions and critical-thinking processes.

The people who founded the Center for Media Literacy work to encourage others to think critically about the media. They have put forth the following, which they call the "Five Core Concepts of Media Literacy":[6]

All media are constructions. Any TV show or advertisement, for example, is not a view of actual life or fact but rather a carefully constructed presentation that is designed to have a particular effect on the viewer—to encourage you to feel a certain emotion, develop a particular opinion, or buy the product advertised.

Media use unique "languages." The people who produce media carefully choose wording, background music, colors, images, timing, and other factors to produce a desired effect. When watching a movie, listen to the music that plays behind an emotional scene or a high-speed chase.

Different audiences understand the same media message differently. Individual people understand media in the context of their own unique experiences. For this reason, people may often interpret media quite differently. A child who has not experienced violence personally may not understand that it brings pain and suffering. In contrast, a child who has witnessed or experienced violence firsthand may react to TV violence with fear for his or her personal safety.

Media have commercial interests. Media are driven by the intent to sell you something, not by the need to tell the truth. Television and radio stations, newspapers, magazines, and commercial Web sites choose advertising that appeals to those most likely to encounter that particular kind of media.

Media have embedded values and points of view. Any media product carries the values of the people who created it. For example, even by choosing the topics on which to write articles, a magazine's editor conveys an opinion that those topics are important. *Runner's World* thinks that how to stay warm on a winter run is important, for example.

To be media literate is to approach what you see, hear, and read with thought and consideration. Use your critical-thinking processes to analyze the media and develop an informed opinion.

Ask questions based on the mind actions. Is what you read in a newspaper similar to something you already know to be true? Do you evaluate a magazine article to be useful or not? Do you agree with the causes or effects that are cited?

Recognize perspective. It is just as important to avoid rejecting the media automatically as it is to avoid accepting them automatically. Any media offering has its own particular perspective, coming from the person or people who created it. Explore this perspective, asking what positive and negative effects it might have.

Becoming media literate will help you become a smart consumer of the media, one who ultimately is responsible for his actions. Don't let a TV ad or a Web banner tell you what to do. Evaluate the message critically and make your own decision. Media literacy is a key to a responsible, self-powered life.

JOURNAL ENTRY

To record your thoughts, use a separate sheet or journal.

Choose a magazine you read, a Web site you visit, a TV program you watch, or any other media source with which you come into contact. Evaluate this media source according to what you know about media literacy. What effect does this media intend to have on you? Does it use particular language or images to create that effect? Is it trying to sell something? What values does it convey? And most importantly, how do you feel about its intentions and effects?

Reading and Studying

This chapter is an expression of the philosophy in Chapter 1, "Why Liberal Arts?," which states that all learning is valuable and "learning to learn" is an overarching purpose of being in college. Because so much of learning involves reading, this chapter proposes that learning how to read effectively will elevate your entire college education.

Your reading background—your past as a reader—may not necessarily prepare you for the new challenges of college reading. In high school, you generally had more time to read less material, with less necessity for deep-level understanding. In college, however, your reading will often be complex, and you may experience an overload of assignments. College reading and studying require a step-by-step approach aimed at the construction of meaning and knowledge. The material in this chapter will present techniques that can help you read and study as efficiently as possible while still having time left over for other things. Using the library is also a focus of this chapter. Through informed use of the library, you will be able to access resources that can help you learn and reach your potential.

In this chapter, you will explore answers to the following questions:

- What are some challenges of reading?
- Why define your purpose for reading?
- How can SQ3R help you own what you read?
- How can you respond critically to what you read?
- How and why should you study with others?
- How can you make the most of the library?

WHAT ARE SOME CHALLENGES OF READING?

Everyone has reading challenges, such as difficult texts, distractions, a lack of speed and comprehension, or insufficient vocabulary. Following are some ideas about how to meet these challenges. Note that if you have a reading disability, if English is not your primary language, or if you have limited reading skills, you may need additional support. Most colleges provide services for students through a reading center or tutoring program. Take the initiative to seek help if you need it. Many accomplished learners have benefited from help in specific areas.

Working Through Difficult Texts

Although many textbooks are useful learning tools, some may be poorly written and organized, perhaps written by experts who may not explain information in the friendliest manner for nonexperts. Because texts are often written to challenge the intellect, even well-written texts may be difficult to read.

Generally, the further you advance in your education, the more complex your required reading is likely to be. Assignments can also be difficult when the required reading is from *primary sources*—original documents rather than another writer's interpretation of these documents—or from academic journal articles and scientific studies that don't define basic terms or supply a wealth of examples. Primary sources include:

- historical documents
- works of literature (novels, poems, and plays)
- scientific studies, including lab reports and accounts of experiments
- journal articles

No barrier of the senses shuts me out from the sweet, gracious discourse of my book friends. They talk to me without embarrassment or awkwardness.

HELEN KELLER

The following strategies may help you make your way through difficult reading material:

Approach your reading assignments head-on. Be careful not to prejudge them as impossible or boring before you even start to read.

Accept the fact that some texts may require some extra work and concentration. Set a goal to make your way through the material and learn, whatever it takes.

When a primary source does not explain concepts, define them on your own. Ask your instructor or other students for help. Consult reference materials in that subject area, other class materials, dictionaries, and encyclopedias.

Look for order and meaning in seemingly chaotic reading materials. The information you will find in this chapter on the SQ3R reading technique and on critical reading will help you discover patterns and achieve a greater depth of understanding. Finding order within chaos is an important skill, not just in the mastery of reading but also in life. This skill can give you power by helping you "read" (think through) work dilemmas, personal problems, and educational situations.

Managing Distractions

With so much happening around you, it's often hard to focus on your reading. Some distractions are external: the telephone or a child who needs attention. Other distractions come from within, as thoughts arise about various topics; for example, a paper due in art history or a Web site that you want to visit.

REAL WORLD PERSPECTIVE

Julia Breitman, *Whittier College, 1990, Major: Social Science*

I'm a 1990 graduate of Whittier College who majored in social science.

After Whittier, I pursued my dream job, which was being a pharmaceutical sales representative. I think I got the job because they were impressed with the independence I had shown traveling and studying abroad, plus my liberal arts background.

Even in college, I knew that I wanted to obtain an advanced degree. I became interested in health law while working as a pharmaceutical sales associate. During this time, I called on doctors who worked at HMOs and learned of their frustration with having the administration dictate which drugs they would prescribe to their patients. I left the pharmaceutical profession in the hope of making a difference by using my legal knowledge.

I resigned from the pharmaceutical job in 1992 and went to Whittier Law School. I have been practicing since 1995. I decided to go into litigation. Working with powerful doctors in the pharmaceutical field gave me the strength and confidence to go into business litigation. I represent business clients to people who have not paid their bills.

I see how liberal arts has helped me. Taking Russian courses inspired me to go to Denmark on an exchange program. My studies abroad have been very beneficial in my work and life. I'm a Republican girl from Orange County and I needed to get away from my own culture. As a result of study abroad and travel, I'm more open-minded overall to other people and their ways of life.

Conversations in Denmark were more open. For example, at the dinner table, my Danish family talked with their children about sex education. In my family, we would never even mention the word.

I use my liberal education every day in my work. For example, I had a patent infringement case. If I had not taken science courses, I would have been lost.

(continued)

Liberal arts enables me to take on topics that might look daunting at first, but then I say, "I can handle this. I can even handle engineering concepts when necessary."

Liberal arts helps both on the intellectual side (the confidence I have that I can learn something new) and the personal side—understanding clients who are very impassioned about their case and their work.

Whittier required me to take some courses I never would have considered, and these courses helped me a lot. For example, courses called "Ethnicity" and "Latin American Literature/Spanish" (the latter is a combination course) helped me to understand differences between people much better.

It reflects life too—I don't just have lawyer friends. I have engineer friends, computer graphics friends, artsy friends, serious friends, and middle-of-the-road friends. In business as well, you don't just go into one area and stick with that area.

Managers who can relate to a wide variety of people, not just those in their specialty, are the ones who will go on to become senior managers.

I'M A REPUBLICAN GIRL FROM ORANGE COUNTY AND I NEEDED TO GET AWAY FROM MY OWN CULTURE.

Each case that I take on requires different knowledge. I need to become a sort of specialist for each case in order to adequately represent my clients with their problems. Liberal arts has helped to prepare me with knowledge of multiple topics of interest and to use this knowledge, as well as the research skills I learned, to research new, complex issues.

Liberal arts also gives you greater flexibility in your career. If you major in business, what happens if your company lays you off some years down the road? You don't have that broader background to rely on. If you major in liberal arts, you can do the business and you have all that other knowledge.

Liberal arts paves the way for changes in life. Most people do not have the same career their whole lives.

Identify the Distraction and Choose a Suitable Action

Pinpoint what's distracting you before you decide what to do. If the distraction is *external* and *out of your control,* such as outside construction or a noisy group in the library, try to move away from it. If the distraction is *external* but *within your control,* such as the television or telephone, take action; for example, turn off the television or let the answering machine answer the phone. Figure 7.1 explores some ways that parents or other people caring for children may be able to maximize their study efforts.

If the distraction is *internal,* different strategies may help you clear your mind. You may want to take a study break and tend to one of the issues that worries you. Physical exercise may relax and refocus you. For some people, studying while listening to music helps to quiet a busy mind. For others, silence may do the trick.

Find a Study Place and Time That Promote Success

Any reader needs focus and discipline in order to concentrate on the material. Finding a place and time to study that minimizes outside distractions will help you achieve that focus. Here are some suggestions:

Read alone unless you are working with other readers. Family members, friends, or others who are not in a study mode may interrupt your concentration. If you prefer to read alone, establish a relatively interruption-proof place and time, such as an out-of-the-way spot at the library or an after-class hour in an empty classroom.

Find a comfortable location. Many students study at a library desk. Others prefer an easy chair at the library or at home, or even the floor. Choose a spot comfortable enough for hours of reading but not so cushy that you fall asleep. Make sure that you have adequate lighting and aren't too hot or cold.

Choose a regular reading place and time. Choose a spot or two that you like, and return often. Also, choose a time when you feel alert and focused. Try reading just before or after the class for which the reading is assigned, if you can. Eventually, you will associate preferred places and times with focused reading.

Turn off the television. For most people, reading and television don't mix.

Building Comprehension and Speed

Most students lead busy lives, carrying heavy academic loads while perhaps working a job or even caring for a family. It's difficult to make time to study at all, let alone handle the reading assignments for your classes.

Exploring options and solutions.

MANAGING CHILDREN WHILE STUDYING

Keep them up-to-date on your schedule.

Let them know when you have a big test or project due and when you are under less pressure, and what they can expect of you in each case.

Explain what your education entails.

Tell them how it will improve your life and theirs. This applies, of course, to older children who can understand the situation and compare it to their own schooling.

Find help.

Ask a relative or friend to watch your children or arrange for a child to visit a friend's house. Consider trading baby-sitting hours with another parent, hiring a sitter to come to your home, or using a day-care center that is private or school-sponsored.

Keep them active while you study.

Give them games, books, or toys to occupy them. If there are special activities that you like to limit, such as watching videos on TV, same them for your study time.

Study on the phone.

You might be able to have a study session with a fellow student over the phone while your child is sleeping or playing quietly.

Offset study time with family time and rewards.

Children may let you get your work done if they have something to look forward to, such as a movie night, a trip for ice cream, or something else they like.

SPECIAL NOTES FOR INFANTS

Study at night if your baby goes to sleep early, or in the morning if your baby sleeps late.

Study during nap times if you aren't too tired yourself.

Lay your notes out and recite information to the baby. The baby will appreciate the attention, and you will get work done.

Put baby in a safe and fun place while you study, such as a playpen, motorized swing, or jumping seat.

Increasing your reading comprehension and speed will save you valuable time and effort. Because greater comprehension is the primary goal and actually promotes faster reading, make comprehension your priority over speed.

Methods for Increasing Reading Comprehension

Following are some specific strategies for increasing your understanding of what you read:

Continually build your knowledge through reading and studying. What you already know before you read a passage will determine your ability to understand and remember important ideas. Previous knowledge, including vocabulary, facts, and ideas, gives you a *context* for what you read.

Establish your purpose for reading. When you establish what you want to get out of your reading, you will be able to determine what level of understanding you need to reach and, therefore, on what you need to focus. A detailed discussion of reading purposes follows later in this chapter.

Remove the barriers of negative self-talk. Instead of telling yourself that you cannot understand, think positively. Tell yourself: *I can learn this material. I am a good reader.*

Think critically. Ask yourself questions. Do you understand the sentence, paragraph, or chapter you just read? Are ideas and supporting examples clear? Could you explain what you just read to someone else? Take in the concepts that titles, headings, subheadings, figures, and photographs communicate to you.

Methods for Increasing Reading Speed

The average American adult reads between 150 and 350 words per minute, and faster readers can be capable of speeds up to 1,000 words per minute.[1] However, the human eye can only move so fast; reading speeds in excess of 350 words per minute involve "skimming" and "scanning" (see page 153). The following suggestions will help increase your reading speed:

- Try to read groups of words rather than single words.
- Avoid pointing your finger to guide your reading because this will slow your pace.
- When reading narrow columns, focus your eyes in the middle of the column. With practice, you'll be able to read the entire column width as you read down the page.

- Avoid *vocalization*—speaking the words or moving your lips—when reading.
- Avoid thinking each word to yourself as you read it, a practice known as *subvocalization*.

Facing the challenges of reading is only the first step. The next important step is to examine why you are reading any given piece of material.

WHY DEFINE YOUR PURPOSE FOR READING?

As with other aspects of your education, asking questions will help you make the most of your efforts. When you define your purpose, you ask yourself *why* you are reading a particular piece of material. One way to do this is by completing this sentence: "In reading this material, I intend to define/learn/answer/achieve . . ." With a clear purpose in mind, you can decide how much time and what kind of effort to expend on various reading assignments.

Achieving your reading purpose requires adapting to different types of reading materials. Being a flexible reader—adjusting your reading strategies and pace—will help you to adapt successfully.

Purpose Determines Reading Strategy

When you know why you are reading something, you can decide how best to approach it. Following are four reading purposes. You may have one or more for any "reading event."

Purpose 1: Read for understanding. In college, studying involves reading for the purpose of comprehending the material. The two main components of comprehension are *general ideas* and *specific facts or examples*. These components depend on each other. Facts and examples help to explain or support ideas, and ideas provide a framework that helps the reader to remember facts and examples.

> *General ideas.* Reading for a general idea is rapid reading that seeks an overview of the material. You search for general ideas by focusing on headings, subheadings, and summary statements.

> *Specific facts or examples.* At times, readers may focus on locating specific pieces of information—for example, the stages of intellectual development in children. Often, a reader may search for examples that support or explain general ideas—for example, the causes of

economic recession. Because you know exactly what you are looking for, you can skim the material quickly.

Purpose 2: Read to evaluate critically. Critical evaluation involves understanding. It means approaching the material with an open mind, examining causes and effects, evaluating ideas, and asking questions that test the writer's argument and search for assumptions. Critical reading brings an understanding of material that goes beyond basic information recall (see page 157 for more on critical reading).

Purpose 3: Read for practical application. A third purpose for reading is to gather usable information that you can apply toward a specific goal. When you read a computer manual or an instruction sheet for assembling a gas grill, your goal is to learn how to do something. Reading and action usually go hand in hand. Remembering the specifics requires a certain degree of general comprehension.

Purpose 4: Read for pleasure. Some materials you read for entertainment, such as *Sports Illustrated* magazine or the latest John Grisham courtroom thriller.

Purpose Determines Pace

George M. Usova, senior education specialist and graduate professor at Johns Hopkins University, explains: "Good readers are flexible readers. They read at a variety of rates and adapt them to the reading purpose at hand, the difficulty of the material, and their familiarity with the subject area."[2] For example, you may need to read academic and/or unfamiliar materials more slowly, whereas you will increase reading speed for journalism, nonfiction and fiction books, magazines, and on-line publications.

So far, this chapter has focused on reading as a deliberate, purposeful process of meaning construction. Recognizing obstacles and defining reading purposes lay the groundwork for effective studying—the process of mastering the concepts and skills contained in your texts.

HOW CAN SQ3R HELP YOU OWN WHAT YOU READ?

When you study, you take ownership of the material you read. You learn it well enough to apply it to what you do. For example, by the time students studying to be computer-hardware technicians complete their course work, they should be able to analyze hardware problems that lead to malfunctions. On-the-job computer technicians use the same study technique to keep up with changing technology. Studying to understand and learn also gives you mastery over concepts. For example, a dental hygiene student learns the causes of gum disease, and a business student learns about marketing.

SQ3R is a technique that will help you grasp ideas quickly, remember ideas, and review effectively for tests. SQ3R stands for *survey, question, read, recite,* and *review*—all steps in the studying process. Developed in the 1940s by Francis Robinson, the technique is still being used today because it works.[3] It is particularly helpful for studying all kinds of textbooks.

Moving through the stages of SQ3R requires that you know how to skim and scan. *Skimming* involves rapid reading of chapter elements, including introductions, conclusions, and summaries; the first and last lines of paragraphs; boldfaced or italicized terms; pictures, charts, and diagrams. The goal of skimming is a quick construction of the main ideas. In contrast, *scanning* involves the careful search for specific facts and examples. You might use scanning during the review phase of SQ3R when you need to locate particular information (such as a formula in a chemistry text).

Survey

When reading textbooks, surveying can help you learn. *Surveying* refers to the process of previewing, or pre-reading, a book before you actually study it. Most textbooks include devices that give students an overview of the text as a whole, as well as of the contents of individual chapters. As you look at Figure 7.2, think about how many of these devices you already use when you read.

Question

Your next step is to examine the chapter headings and, on a separate piece of paper, to write *questions* linked to them. If your reading material has no headings, develop questions as you read. These questions focus your attention and increase your interest, helping you build comprehension and relate new ideas to what you already know. You can take questions from the textbook or from your lecture notes, or come up with them on your own when you survey, based on what ideas you think are most important.

Here is how this technique works. In Table 7.1, the column on the left contains primary-level headings from a section of *Business,* a text by Ricky W. Griffin and Ronald J. Ebert (Prentice Hall, 1996). The column on the right rephrases these headings in question form.

FIGURE 7.2   Text and chapter previewing devices.

AT THE BEGINNING OF THE TEXT OR CHAPTERS

- Text preface
- Table of contents
- Chapter summaries

IN THE MIDDLE, LINKED TO SPECIFIC CHAPTERS

- Part openers (if text chapters are divided into sections)
- Chapter titles
- Lists of objectives
- Chapter outlines
- Tables and figures
- Opening stories that set the stage for the chapter discussion
- Major and minor chapter headings
- Special learning tools
- End-of-chapter review questions, exercises, and problems
- Bold and italicized words and phrases
- Internal chapter progress checks
- Notes in the margins
- Photo illustrations
- End-of-chapter key terms and concepts

AT THE END OF THE TEXT

- End-of-text glossary
- Text index
- Text bibliography

There is no "correct" set of questions. Given the same headings, you could create your own particular set of questions. The more useful kinds of questions engage the critical-thinking mind actions and processes found in Chapter 6.

Read

Your questions give you a starting point for *reading,* the first R in SQ3R. Read the material with the purpose of answering each question you raised. Pay special attention to the first and last lines of every paragraph, which should tell you what the paragraph is about. As you read, record key terms, phrases, and concepts in your notebook. Some students divide the notebook into two columns, writing questions on the left and

Rephrasing in the form of a question.

1. The Consumer Buying Process	1. What Is the Consumer Buying Process?
A. Problem/Need Recognition	A. Why must consumers first recognize a problem or need before they buy a product?
B. Information Seeking	B. What is information seeking and who answers consumers' questions?
C. Evaluation of Alternatives	C. How do consumers evaluate different products to narrow their choices?
D. Purchase Decision	D. Are purchasing decisions simple or complex?
E. Postpurchase Evaluations	E. What happens after the sale?

answers on the right. This method is called the Cornell note-taking system (see Chapter 8).

If you own the textbook, marking it up will help you to make sense of the material. You may want to write notes in the margins, circle key ideas, or highlight key sections. Selective highlighting may help you pinpoint material to review before an exam, although excessive highlighting may actually interfere with comprehension. Here are some tips on how to strike a balance.

Mark the text after you read the material through once. If you do it on the first reading, you may mark less important passages.

Highlight key terms and concepts. Mark the examples that explain and support important ideas. You might try highlighting ideas in one color and examples in another.

Highlight figures and tables. They are especially important if they summarize text concepts.

Avoid overmarking. A phrase or two in any paragraph is usually enough. Set off long passages with brackets rather than marking every line.

Write notes in the margins. Comments like "main point" and "important definition" will help you find key sections later on.

Be careful not to mistake highlighting for learning. You will not learn what you highlight unless you review it carefully. Additional benefit will come from writing the highlighted information into your notes.

One critical step in the reading phase is to divide your reading into digestible segments. Pace your reading so that you understand as you go. If you find you are losing the thread of the ideas you are reading, you may want to try smaller segments, or you may need to take a break and come back to it later. Try to avoid reading in mere sets of time—such as, "I'll read for 30 minutes and then quit"—or you may destroy the meaning by stopping in the middle of a key explanation.

Recite

Once you finish reading a topic, stop and answer the questions you raised in the Q stage of SQ3R. You may decide to *recite* each answer aloud, silently speak the answers to yourself, tell the answers to another person as though you were teaching her, or write your ideas and answers in brief notes. Writing is often the most effective way to solidify what you have read because writing from memory checks your understanding. Use whatever techniques best suit your learning styles (see Chapter 4).

After you finish one section, read the next. Repeat the question-read-recite cycle until you complete the entire chapter. If during this process you find yourself fumbling for thoughts, you may not yet "own" the ideas. Reread the section that's giving you trouble until you master its contents. Understanding each section as you go is crucial because the material in one section often forms a foundation for the next.

Review

Review soon after you finish a chapter. Here are some techniques for reviewing.

- Skim and reread your notes. Then, try summarizing them from memory.
- Answer the text's end-of-chapter review, discussion, or application questions.
- Quiz yourself using the questions you raised in the Q stage. If you can't answer one of your own or one of the text's questions, go back and scan the material for answers.
- Review and summarize in writing the sections and phrases you have highlighted or bracketed.
- Create a chapter outline in standard outline form or as a think link.

- Reread the introduction, headings, tables, and summary.

- Recite important concepts to yourself, or record important information on a cassette tape and play it on your car's tape deck or your
portable cassette player.

- Make flash cards that have an idea or word on one side and examples,
a definition, or other related information on the other. Test yourself.

- Think critically: Break ideas down into examples, consider similar or
different concepts, recall important terms, evaluate ideas, and explore
causes and effects.

- Make think links that show how important concepts relate to one
another.

If you need help clarifying your reading material, ask your instructor.
Pinpoint the material you want to discuss, schedule a meeting with him or
her during office hours, and bring a list of questions.

Repeating the review process renews and solidifies your knowledge.
Set up regular review sessions, for example, once a week. As you review,
remember that refreshing your knowledge is easier and faster than learning it the first time. Reviewing in as many different ways as possible
increases the likelihood of retention.

As you can see in Figure 7.3, using SQ3R is part of being an active
reader. Active reading involves the specific activities that help you retain
what you learn.

HOW CAN YOU RESPOND CRITICALLY TO WHAT YOU READ?

Textbook features often highlight important ideas and help you
determine study questions. As you advance in your education, however,
many reading assignments—especially primary sources—will not be so
clearly marked. You will need critical-reading skills to select important
ideas, identify examples that support them, and ask questions about the
text without the aid of any special features.

Critical reading enables you to develop a thorough understanding of
reading material. A critical reader is able to discern the central idea of a
piece of reading material, as well as identify what in that piece is true or
accurate, such as when choosing material as a source for an essay. A critical reader can also compare one piece of material to another and evaluate
which makes more sense, which proves its thesis more successfully, or
which is more useful for the reader's purposes.

Engage your critical-thinking processes by using the following suggestions for critical reading.

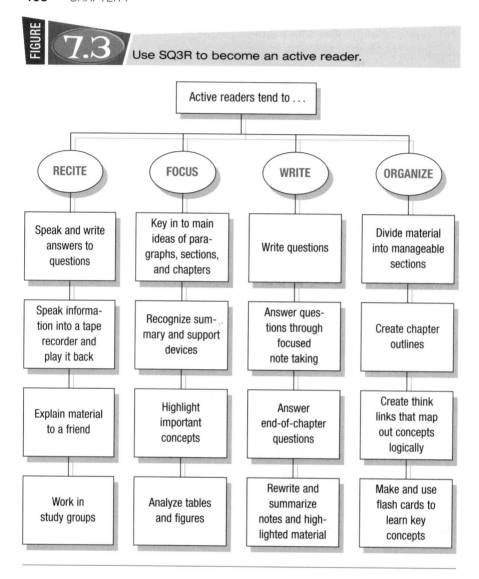

FIGURE 7.3 Use SQ3R to become an active reader.

Active readers tend to . . .

RECITE	FOCUS	WRITE	ORGANIZE
Speak and write answers to questions	Key in to main ideas of paragraphs, sections, and chapters	Write questions	Divide material into manageable sections
Speak information into a tape recorder and play it back	Recognize summary and support devices	Answer questions through focused note taking	Create chapter outlines
Explain material to a friend	Highlight important concepts	Answer end-of-chapter questions	Create think links that map out concepts logically
Work in study groups	Analyze tables and figures	Rewrite and summarize notes and highlighted material	Make and use flash cards to learn key concepts

Use SQ3R to "Taste" Reading Material

Sylvan Barnet and Hugo Bedau, authors of *Critical Thinking, Reading, and Writing: A Brief Guide to Argument,* suggest that the active reading of SQ3R will help you form an initial idea of what a piece of reading material is all about. Through surveying, skimming for ideas and examples, highlighting and writing comments and questions in the margins, and reviewing, you can develop a basic understanding of its central ideas and contents.[4]

Summarizing, part of the SQ3R review process, is one of the best ways to develop an understanding of a piece of reading material. To construct a summary, focus on the central ideas of the piece and the main examples that support them. A summary does not contain any of your own ideas or your evaluation of the material. It simply condenses the material, making it easier to focus on the structure and central ideas of the piece when you go back to read more critically. At that point, you can begin asking questions, evaluating the piece, and introducing your own ideas.

Ask Questions Based on the Mind Actions

The essence of critical reading, as with critical thinking, is asking questions. Instead of simply accepting what you read, seek a more thorough understanding by questioning the material as you go along. Using the mind actions to formulate your questions will help you understand the material. What parts of the material you focus on will depend on your purpose for reading. For example, if you are writing a paper on the causes of World War II, you might look at how certain causes fit your thesis.

You can question any of the following components of reading material:

- the central idea of the entire piece
- a particular idea or statement
- the examples that support an idea or statement
- the proof of a fact
- the definition of a concept

Following are some ways to critically question reading material. Apply them to any component you want to question by substituting the component for the words *it* and *this*.

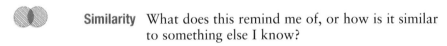

Similarity What does this remind me of, or how is it similar to something else I know?

Difference What different conclusions are possible?

How is this different from my experience?

Cause and Effect Why did this happen, or what caused this?

What are the effects or consequences of this?

What effect does the author want to have, or what is the purpose of this material?

What effects support a stated cause?

Example to Idea   How would I classify this, or what is the best idea to fit this example?

How would I summarize this, or what are the key ideas?

What is the thesis or central idea?

Idea to Example   What evidence supports this, or what examples fit this idea?

Evaluation   How would I evaluate this? Is it useful or well constructed?

Does this example support my thesis or central idea?

Is this information or point of view important to my work? If so, why?

Recognize Perspective

This critical-thinking process will help you understand that many reading materials are written from a particular perspective. For example, if both a recording artist and a music censorship advocate were to write a piece about a controversial song created by that artist, their different perspectives would result in two very different pieces of writing.

To analyze perspective, ask questions like the following:

What perspective is guiding this? What are the underlying ideas that influence this material?

Who wrote this and with what intent? For example, promotional materials on a new drug, written by the manufacturer, may differ from a doctor's or consumer advocate's evaluation of the drug.

How does the material's source affect its perspective? For example, an article on health maintenance organizations (HMOs) published in an HMO newsletter may be more favorable than one published in the *New York Times*.

Be Media Literate

Everything that you learned about media literacy in Chapter 6 applies to your college reading material. Even seemingly objective textbooks are written by a person or persons who have particular points of view, which may influence the information they include or how they include it. In all your reading, especially primary sources, remember the following:

- Your reading materials are created by people who have particular perspectives.
- Authors may use wording or tone to create an effect on a reader.
- Different readers may have different interpretations of a piece of reading material, depending on individual perspective and experience.
- Users of media may intend to market a product to you.
- Any written material is influenced, to varying degrees, by the values, perspectives, and intents of the authors.

As a media literate reader, you have the ability to stay aware of these realities and to sift through your materials critically so that you gain from them what is most useful to you.

> In books, I could travel anywhere, be anybody, understand worlds long past and imaginary colonies in the future.
>
> **RITA DOVE**

Seek Understanding

The fundamental purpose of all college reading is to understand the material. Reading critically allows you to reach the highest possible level of understanding. Think of your reading process as an archaeological dig. The first step is to excavate a site and uncover the artifacts, which corresponds to your initial survey and reading of the material. As important as the excavation is, the process would be incomplete if you took home a bunch of dirt-covered items and stopped there. The second half of the process is to investigate each item, evaluate what each one means, and derive new knowledge and ideas from what you discover. Critical reading allows you to complete that crucial second half of the process.

Remember that critical reading takes time and focus. Give yourself a chance to be a successful critical reader by finding a time, place, and purpose for your reading. Take advantage of the opportunity to learn from others by working in pairs or groups whenever you can.

H OW AND WHY SHOULD YOU STUDY WITH OTHERS?

Everything you know and will learn comes from your interaction with the outside world. Often this interaction takes place between you and one or more people. You learn from listening to them, reading what they write, observing them, and modeling yourself after the behavior and ideas of those whom you most trust and respect. Studying with others helps maximize your learning.

Strategies for Study Group Success

Certain general strategies will help any kind of study group.

Choose a leader for each meeting. Rotating the leadership helps all members take ownership of the group.

Set meeting goals. At the start of each meeting, compile a list of questions you want to address.

Adjust to different personalities. Respect and communicate with others. The art of getting along will serve you well in the workplace, where you don't often choose your coworkers.

Set general goals and a schedule. Determine what the group wants to accomplish over the course of a semester.

Meet on a regular basis. Try every week, every two weeks, or whatever the group can manage.

Create study materials. Have each member find information to compile, photocopy, and review for the other group members.

Help each other learn. Have group members teach certain pieces of information; make up quizzes for each other; go through flash cards together.

Pool your note-taking resources. Compare notes with your group members and fill in the gaps.

Benefits of Working with Others

If you apply this information to your schoolwork, you will see that studying with a partner or in a group can enhance your learning in many ways. You will benefit from shared knowledge, solidified knowledge, increased motivation, and increased teamwork ability.

Shared knowledge. Students can learn from one another. To have individual students pass on their knowledge to each other in a study group requires less time and energy than for each of those students to learn all of the material alone.

Solidified knowledge. When you discuss concepts or teach them to others, you reinforce what you know and strengthen your critical thinking.

Increased motivation. When you study by yourself, you are accountable to yourself alone. In a study group, however, others will see your level of work and preparation, which may increase your motivation.

Increased teamwork ability. The more you understand how to work with a group and the more experience you have at it, the more you will build your ability to work well with others. This is an invaluable skill for the workplace.

No matter where or how you prefer to study, your school's library (or libraries) can provide many useful services to help you make the most of classes, reading, studying, and assignments.

OW CAN YOU MAKE THE MOST OF THE LIBRARY?

A library is a home for information; consider it the "brain" of your college. Libraries contain a world of information—your job is to find what you need as quickly and efficiently as you can.

Start with a Road Map

Most college libraries are bigger than high school and community libraries. You may feel lost on your first visit, or even a few visits after that. Make your life easier right away by learning how your library is organized. Although every library has a different layout, all libraries have certain areas in common.

> **Reference area.** Here you'll find reference books, including encyclopedias, public- and private-sector directories, dictionaries, almanacs, and atlases. You'll also find librarians and/or other library employees who can help direct you to the information you need. Computer terminals, containing the library's catalog of holdings as well as on-line bibliographic and full-text databases, are usually part of the reference area.

> **Book area.** Books—and, in many libraries, magazines and journals in bound or boxed volumes—are stored in the stacks. A library with "open stacks" will allow you to search for materials on your own. In a "closed-stack" system, a staff member will retrieve materials for you.

> **Periodicals area.** Here you'll find recent issues of popular and scholarly magazines, journals, and newspapers. Most college libraries collect periodicals, ranging from *Time* to *Advertising Age* to the *New England Journal of Medicine*.

Audiovisual materials areas. Many libraries have specialized areas for video, art, photographic, and recorded music collections.

Computer areas. Computer terminals, linked to databases and the Internet, are increasingly found in libraries and may be scattered throughout the building or set off in special areas. You may be able to access these databases and the Internet from the college's computer labs and writing centers, or even from your own computer if you have one.

Microform areas. Most libraries have microform reading areas or rooms. Microforms are materials printed on film, either microfilm or microfiche, that is read through special viewing machines. Many microform reading machines can print hard copies of stored images and text.

To learn about your college library, take a library tour or a training session. Almost all college libraries offer some kind of orientation on how to use their books, periodicals, databases, and Internet hookups. You might also ask for a pamphlet that describes the layout, and then take some time for a self-tour.

Learn How to Conduct an Information Search

The most successful library research involves following a *search strategy*—a step-by-step method for finding information. Starting with general sources usually works best because they provide an overview of your research topic and can lead you to more specific information and sources. For example, an encyclopedia article on the Dead Sea Scrolls—manuscripts written between 250 B.C. and A.D. 68 that trace the roots of Judaism and Christianity—may mention an important book on the subject, *Understanding the Dead Sea Scrolls,* edited by Hershel Shanks (New York: Random House, 1992). This book, in turn, will lead you to 13 experts, the authors who wrote chapters in the book.

Defining your exact topic is critical to the success of your search. Although "the Dead Sea Scrolls" may be too broad for your research paper, an example of a narrower topic is "the process archaeologists used to reconstruct scroll fragments."

Conducting a Keyword Search

A *keyword search*—a search for information through the use of specific words and phrases associated with your search subject—will help you narrow your topic. Use your library's computer database for keyword searches. For example, instead of searching through the broad category *art,* use a keyword search to narrow your focus to *French art* or more specifically to *French art in the nineteenth century.*

How to perform an effective keyword search.

IF YOU ARE SEARCHING FOR . . .	DO THIS	EXAMPLE
A word	Type the word normally	aid
A phrase	Type the phrase in its normal word order order (use regular word spacing) or surround the phrase with quotation marks	financial aid or "financial aid"
Two or more keywords without regard to word order	Type the words in any order, surrounding the words with quotation marks (use *and* to separate the words)	"financial aid" and "scholarships"
Topic A or topic B	Type the words in any order, surrounding the words with quotation marks (use *or* to separate the words)	"financial aid" or "scholarships"
Topic A but not topic B	Type topic A first, within quotation marks, and then topic B, within quotation marks (use *not* to separate the words)	"financial aid" not "scholarships"

Keyword searches are relatively easy because you use natural language rather than specialized classification vocabulary. Table 7.2 includes some tips that will help you use the keyword system.

As you search, keep in mind that

- Quotation marks around a word or phrase will locate the term exactly as you entered it ("financial aid").

- Using upper or lower case will not affect the search (*Scholarships* will find *scholarships*).

- Singular terms will find the plural (*scholarship* will find *scholarships*).

Conduct Research Using a Search Strategy

Knowing where to look during each phase of your search will help you find information efficiently. A successful search strategy often starts with general reference works, then moves to more specific reference works, books, periodicals, and electronic sources, including the Internet (see Figure 7.4).

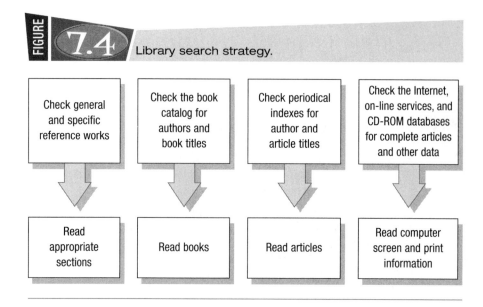

FIGURE 7.4 Library search strategy.

Use General Reference Works

Begin your research with *general reference works*. These works cover hundreds—and sometimes thousands—of different topics in a broad, non-detailed way. General reference guides are often available on-line or on CD-ROM.

General reference works include:

- encyclopedias such as the multivolume *Encyclopedia Americana*
- almanacs such as the *World Almanac and Book of Facts*
- yearbooks such as the *McGraw-Hill Yearbook of Science and Technology*
- dictionaries such as *Webster's New World College Dictionary*
- biographical reference works such as *American Writers* and *Who's Who*
- bibliographies such as *Books in Print* (especially the *Subject Guide to Books in Print*)

Scan these sources for an overview of your topic. Bibliographies at the end of encyclopedia articles may also lead to other important sources.

Search Specialized Reference Works

After you have an overview of your topic, specialized reference works will help you find more specific facts. The short summaries you will find in such works focus on critical ideas and on the keywords you will need to research further. Bibliographies that accompany the articles point to the names and works of recognized experts. Examples of specialized reference works, organized by subject, include the following:

- history, such as the *Encyclopedia of American History*
- science and technology, such as the *Encyclopedia of Computer Science and Technology*
- social sciences, such as the *Dictionary of Education*
- current affairs, such as the *Social Issues Resources Series (SIRS)*

Browse Through Books on Your Subject

Use the library catalog to find books and other materials on your topic. Most card catalogs have been replaced by on-line computerized catalogs. The library catalog contains a list of every library holding, searchable by author, title, and subject. For example, a library that owns *The Artist's Way: A Spiritual Path to Higher Creativity* by Julia Cameron may list the book in the author catalog under Cameron, Julia (last name first); in the title catalog, under *Artist's Way* (articles such as *the, a,* and *an* are dropped from the beginnings of titles and subjects); and in the subject catalog under "Creative Ability—problems, exercises, etc."

Library Classification Systems

Each catalog listing refers to the library's classification system, which tells you exactly where the publication can be found. The Dewey decimal and Library of Congress systems are among the most common classification systems.

The *Dewey decimal system* classifies materials into 10 major subject categories and assigns each library holding a specific *call number.* For example, publications with call numbers from 100 to 199 deal with philosophy. Successive numbers and decimal points divide each major category into subcategories.

The *Library of Congress system* uses a letter-based classification system to divide library holdings according to subject categories (Figure 7.5 shows the call letters that correspond to each category). Each category is divided further into specialized subgroups through the addition of letters and numbers.

Use Periodical Indexes to Search for Periodicals

Because of their frequent publication, periodicals are a valuable source of current information. *Journals* are periodicals written for readers with special knowledge and expertise. Whereas *Newsweek* magazine may run

FIGURE 7.5   Library of Congress subject classification system.

CALL LETTER	MAIN CLASSIFICATION CATEGORY	CALL LETTER	MAIN CLASSIFICATION CATEGORY
A	General works	N	Fine arts
B	Philosophy and religion	P	Language - Literature (nonfiction)
C	History - Auxiliary sciences	Q	Sciences
D	History - Topography	R	Medicine
E–F	American history - Topography	S	Agriculture
G	Geography - Anthropology	T	Technology
H	Social sciences	U	Military science
J	Political sciences	V	Naval science
K	Law	Z	Bibliography and library science
L	Education	P–Z	Literature (fiction)
M	Music		

a general-interest article on AIDS research, the *Journal of the American Medical Association* may print the original scientific study and direct the article to physicians and scientists. Many libraries display periodicals that are up to a year or two old and convert older copies to microfilm or microfiche. Many full-text articles are also available on computer databases.

Periodical indexes lead you to specific articles. The *Reader's Guide to Periodical Literature,* available on CD-ROM and in book form, provides general information. The *Reader's Guide* indexes articles in more than 240 general-interest magazines and newspapers. Many libraries also carry the *Reader's Guide Abstracts,* which include article summaries. Look in the *Infotrac* family of databases, on-line or on CD-ROM, for other periodical indexes such as *Health Reference Center* and *General Business File.*

In addition, journals not found in your library or on-line may be available through *interlibrary loan.* Interlibrary loan is a process by which you can have your library request materials from another library. You can then use the materials at your library, but you must return them by a specified date. Interlibrary loans can be helpful, but the amount of time you will have to wait for the materials can be unpredictable and may stretch out for weeks.

Search the Internet

In many ways, the Internet is a researcher's dream come true. You'll find sites that teach you how to write a business plan; others that list job openings at major companies; others that provide health, wellness, and nutritional information; and still others that analyze different theories of child development. Navigating the constantly changing Internet can be challenging. Consult one of the guides mentioned in the Bibliography for advice on how to find the information you need.

Ask the Librarian

Librarians are information experts who can help you locate unfamiliar or hard-to-find sources as well as navigate computer catalogs and databases. Note that librarians are not the only helpful people in the library. For simplicity's sake, this book will use the word *librarian* to refer to both librarians and other staff members who are trained to help.

Among the specific services librarians provide are the following:

Search services. Here are some tips on getting the best advice:

- Be prepared. Know what you're looking for. Instead of asking for information on the American presidency, focus on your paper's specific topic, for example, how President Franklin D. Roosevelt's physical disability may have affected his leadership during World War II.
- Be willing to reach out. You don't have to do it all yourself. Librarians will help you with sources or more difficult problems. Asking questions is a sign of willingness to learn, not weakness.
- Ask for help when you can't find a specific source. For example, when a specific book is not on the shelf, the librarian may direct you to another source that will work just as well.

> With one day's reading a man may have the key in his hands.
> — EZRA POUND

Information services. Most libraries answer phone inquiries that can be quickly researched. For example, if you forget to write down the publisher and date of publication of Renee Blank and Sandra Slipp's book, *Voices of Diversity: Real People Talk about Problems and*

Solutions in a Workplace Where Everyone Is Not Alike, call a staff member and tell them the title and author, and they can look it up for you.

Interlibrary loans. If a publication is not available in your library, the librarian can sometimes arrange for an interlibrary loan.

Use Critical Thinking to Evaluate Every Source

If all information were equal, you could trust the accuracy of every book and article, and information from the Internet home page of the National Aeronautics and Space Administration (NASA) would have the same value as information from "Bob's Home Page on Aliens and Extraterrestrials." Because that isn't the case, use critical-thinking skills to evaluate research sources. Here are some critical-thinking questions to ask about every source:

Is the author a recognized expert? A journalist who writes his or her first article on child development may not have the same credibility as an author of three child development texts.

Does the author write from a particular perspective? An article evaluating liberal democratic policies written by a Republican conservative would almost certainly have a bias.

Is the source recent enough for your purposes? Whereas a history published in 1990 on the U.S. Civil War will probably be accurate in the year 2005, a 1990 analysis of current computer technology would be hopelessly out of date long before then.

Are the author's sources reliable? Where did the author get the information? Check bibliography and footnotes for the number of sources listed and for their quality. Find out whether they are reputable, established publications.

Critical-thinking skills are especially important when using the Internet. Accepting information you find there on face value—no matter what the source—is often a mistake and may lead to incorrect conclusions. Anyone, without being screened or evaluated, can post any kind of information on the Internet. It is up to you to discern whether the information you find is accurate, from a reliable source, and useful.

The library is one of your college's most valuable resources, so take advantage of it. Your library research and critical-thinking skills will give you the ability to collect information, weigh alternatives, and make decisions. These skills will last a lifetime.

JOURNAL ENTRY

To record your thoughts, use a separate sheet or journal.

What is your most difficult college reading challenge? A challenge might be a particular kind of reading material, a reading situation, or the achievement of a reading goal. Considering the tools that this chapter presents, make a plan that addresses this challenge. What techniques might be able to help, and how will you test them? What positive effects do you anticipate they may have?

Note Taking and Writing

HARNESSING THE POWER OF WORDS AND IDEAS

This chapter extends one of the key messages of Chapter 2, "Liberal Arts Courses," which says that writing is a skill you should seek to develop in many of your college courses. Writing skills are also emphasized in Chapter 10, because career opportunities across the world of work often depend heavily on the ability to write clearly and persuasively.

Words, joined to form ideas, are tools that have enormous power. Whether you write an essay, a memo to a supervisor, or a love letter sent by e-mail, words allow you to take your ideas out of the realm of thought and give them a form that other people can read and consider. Set a goal for yourself: Strive continually to improve your knowledge of how to use words to construct understandable ideas. This chapter will teach you the note-taking skills you need to record information successfully. It will show you how to express your written ideas completely and how good writing is linked to clear thinking. In class or at work, taking notes and writing well will help you truly understand what you learn.

In this chapter, you will explore answers to the following questions:

- How can you make the most of note taking?
- Which note-taking system should you use?
- How can you write faster when taking notes?
- Why does good writing matter?
- What are the elements of effective writing?
- What is the writing process?

HOW CAN YOU MAKE THE MOST OF NOTE TAKING?

Notes help you learn when you are in class, doing research, or studying. Because it is virtually impossible to take notes on everything you hear or read, the act of note taking encourages you to decide what is worth remembering, and it has many more positive effects:

- Your notes provide material that helps you study information and prepare for tests.
- When you take notes, you listen better and become more involved in class.
- Notes help you think critically and organize ideas.
- The information you learn in class may not appear in any text; you will have no way to study it without writing it down.
- If it is difficult for you to process information while in class, having notes to read can help you process and learn the information.
- Note taking is a skill for life that you will use on the job, in community activities, and in your personal life.

Recording Information in Class

Your notes have two purposes: First, they should reflect what you heard in class, and second, they should be a resource for studying, writing, or comparing with your text material.

Omit needless words. . . . This requires not that the writer make all his sentences short, or that he avoid all detail and treat his subjects only in outline, but that every word tell.

WILLIAM STRUNK, JR.

Preparing to Take Class Notes

Taking good class notes depends on good preparation.

- Preview the text (or any other assigned reading material) to become familiar with the topic and any new concepts that it introduces. Visual familiarity helps note taking during lectures.

- Use separate pieces of 8.5 × 11-inch paper for each class. If you use a three-ring binder, punch holes in handouts and insert them immediately following your notes for that day.

- Find a comfortable seat where you can easily see and hear—sitting near the front may be your best bet. Be ready to write as soon as the instructor begins speaking.

- Choose a note-taking system that helps you handle the instructor's style. (You'll probably be able to determine this style after a few classes.) For example, whereas one instructor may deliver organized lectures at a normal speaking rate, another may jump from topic to topic or talk very quickly.

- For each class, set up a support system with two students. That way, when you are absent, you can get the notes you missed (having two "buddies" instead of one helps make it likely that at least one person will be in class on any given day).

What to Do During Class

Because no one has time to write down everything he or she hears, the following strategies will help you choose and record what you feel is important in a format that you can read and understand later. This is not a list of "musts." Rather, it is a list of ideas to try as you work to find the note-taking system that works best for you. Remember that the first step in note taking is to listen actively; you can't write down something that you don't hear.

- Date and identify each page. When you take several pages of notes during a lecture, add an identifying letter or number to the date on each page: for example, 11/27 A, 11/27 B, or 11/27—1 of 3, 11/27—2 of 3. This will help you keep track of the order of your pages.

- If your instructor jumps from topic to topic during a single class, try starting a new page for each new topic.

- Ask yourself critical-thinking questions as you listen: Do I need this information? Is the information important or just a digression? Is the source of the information reliable?

- Record whatever an instructor emphasizes (see Figure 8.1 for specifics on how an instructor might call attention to particular information).

- Continue to take notes during class discussions and question-and-answer periods. What your fellow students ask about may help you as well.

- Leave one or more blank spaces between points. This white space will help you review your notes because information will appear in self-contained sections.

- Draw pictures and diagrams that help illustrate ideas.

- Indicate material that is especially important with a star, with underlining, with a highlighting marker, or by writing words in capital letters.

- If you don't understand something, leave space and place a question mark in the margin. Then take advantage of your resources—ask the instructor to explain it after class, discuss it with a classmate, or consult your textbook—and fill in the blank when the idea is clear.

- Take notes until the instructor stops speaking. If you stop writing a few minutes before the class is over, you might miss critical information.

- Make your notes as legible and organized as possible—you can't learn from notes that you can't read or understand.

Make Notes a Valuable Reference: Review and Revise Your Notes

Class notes are a valuable study tool when you review them regularly. Begin your review within a day of the lecture. Review the notes to learn information, clarify points, write out abbreviations, fill in missing information, and underline or highlight key ideas. Try to review each week's notes again at the end of the week. Think critically about the material in writing, in study group discussions, or during reflective thought. You might also try revising and adding to your notes using material from your print sources.

You can take notes in many ways. Different note-taking systems suit different people and situations. Explore each system and choose what works for you.

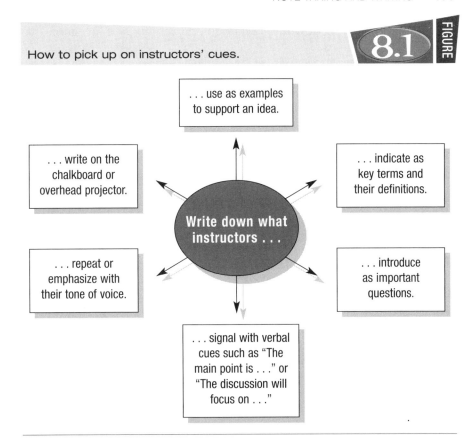

FIGURE 8.1

How to pick up on instructors' cues.

... use as examples to support an idea.

... write on the chalkboard or overhead projector.

... indicate as key terms and their definitions.

Write down what instructors . . .

... repeat or emphasize with their tone of voice.

... introduce as important questions.

... signal with verbal cues such as "The main point is . . ." or "The discussion will focus on . . ."

WHAT NOTE-TAKING SYSTEM SHOULD YOU USE?

You will benefit most from the system that feels most comfortable to you and makes the most sense for the type of content covered in any given course. For example, you might take notes in a different style for a history class than for a foreign language class. The most common note-taking systems include outlines, the Cornell system, and think links. As you consider each system, take your learning styles into account.

Taking Notes in Outline Form

When a reading assignment or lecture seems well organized, you may choose to take notes in outline form. When you use an outline, you construct a line-by-line representation, with certain phrases set off by varying indentations, showing how ideas relate to one another and are supported by facts and examples.

Formal outlines indicate ideas and examples using Roman numerals, capital and lowercase letters, and numbers. When you are pressed for time, such as during class, you can use an informal system of consistent indenting and dashes instead. Formal outlines also require at least two headings on the same level—that is, if you have a IIA you must also have a IIB. Figure 8.2 shows an outline on civil rights legislation.

Guided Notes

From time to time, an instructor may give you a guide, usually in the form of an outline, to help you take notes in the class. This outline may be on a page that you receive at the beginning of the class, on the board, or on an overhead projector.

Although guided notes help you follow the lecture and organize your thoughts, they do not replace your own notes. Because they are more of a basic outline of topics than a comprehensive coverage of information, they require that you fill in what they do not cover in detail. If your mind wanders because you think that the guided notes are all you need, you may miss important information.

When you receive guided notes on paper, write directly on the paper if there is room. If not, use a separate sheet and copy the outline categories that the guided notes suggest. If the guided notes are on the board or overhead, copy them, leaving plenty of space in between for your own notes.

Using the Cornell Note-Taking System

The Cornell note-taking system, also known as the T-note system, was developed more than 45 years ago by Walter Pauk at Cornell University.[1] The system is successful because it is simple—and because it works. It consists of three sections on ordinary notepaper:

- *Section 1*, the largest section, is on the right. Record your notes here in informal outline form.

- *Section 2*, to the left of your notes, is the *cue column*. Leave it blank while you read or listen; then fill it in later as you review. You might fill it with comments that highlight main ideas, clarify meaning, suggest examples, or link ideas and examples. You can even draw diagrams.

- *Section 3*, at the bottom of the page, is the *summary area*, where you use a sentence or two to summarize the notes on the page. When you review, use this section to reinforce concepts and provide an overview.

Sample formal outline.

FIGURE 8.2

Civil Rights Legislation: 1860–1968

I. Post-Civil War Era
   A. Fourteenth Amendment, 1868: equal protection of the law
      for all citizens
   B. Fifteenth Amendment, 1870: constitutional rights of citizens
      regardless of race, color, or previous servitude
II. Civil Rights Movement of the 1960s
   A. National Association for the Advancement of Colored People (NAACP)
      1. Established in 1910 by W.E.B. DuBois and others
      2. Legal Defense and Education fund fought school segregation
   B. Martin Luther King Jr., champion of nonviolent civil rights action
      1. Led bus boycott: 1955-1956
      2. Marched on Washington, D.C.: 1963
      3. Awarded NOBEL PEACE PRIZE: 1964
      4. Led voter registration drive in Selma, Alabama: 1965
   C. Civil Rights Act of 1964: prohibited discrimination in voting,
      education, employment, and public facilities
   D. Voting Rights Act of 1965: gave the government power to enforce
      desegregation
   E. Civil Rights Act of 1968: prohibited discrimination in the sale
      or rental of housing

When you use the Cornell system, create the note-taking structure before class begins. Picture an upside-down letter T and use Figure 8.3 as your guide. Make the cue column about 2.5 inches wide and the summary area 2 inches tall. Figure 8.3 shows how a student used the Cornell system to take notes in an introductory business course.

Creating a Think Link

A *think link*, also known as a mind map, is a visual form of note taking. When you draw a think link, you diagram ideas by using shapes and lines

FIGURE **8.3** Sample Cornell System notes.

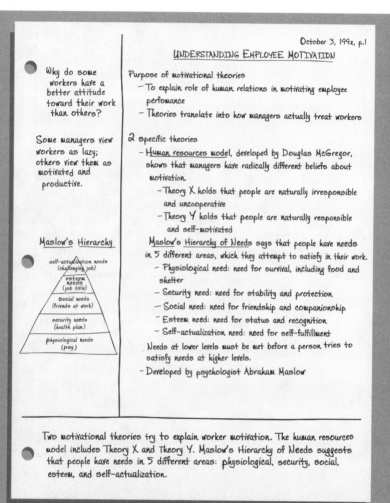

that link ideas and supporting details and examples. The visual design makes the connections easy to see, and the use of shapes and pictures extends the material beyond just words. Many learners respond well to the power of *visualization*. You can use think links to brainstorm ideas for paper topics as well.

One way to create a think link is to circle your topic in the middle of a sheet of paper. Next, draw a line from the circled topic and write the

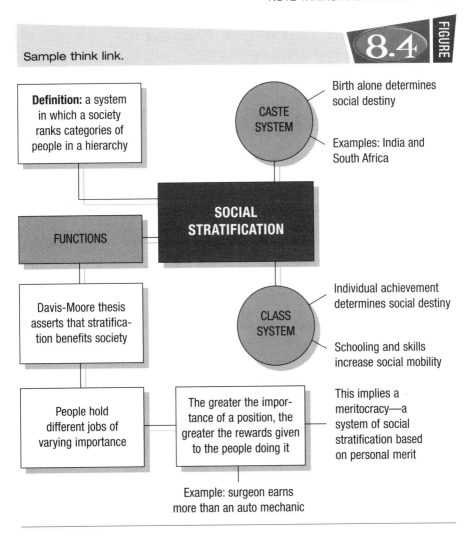

FIGURE 8.4

Sample think link.

Definition: a system in which a society ranks categories of people in a hierarchy

CASTE SYSTEM

Birth alone determines social destiny

Examples: India and South Africa

SOCIAL STRATIFICATION

FUNCTIONS

Davis-Moore thesis asserts that stratification benefits society

CLASS SYSTEM

Individual achievement determines social destiny

Schooling and skills increase social mobility

People hold different jobs of varying importance

The greater the importance of a position, the greater the rewards given to the people doing it

This implies a meritocracy—a system of social stratification based on personal merit

Example: surgeon earns more than an auto mechanic

name of one major idea at the end of the line. Circle that idea also. Then jot down specific facts related to the idea, linking them to the idea with lines. Continue the process, connecting thoughts to one another by using circles, lines, and words. Figure 8.4 shows a think link on a sociology concept called social stratification. This is only one of many think link styles; other examples include stair steps (showing connecting ideas that build to a conclusion) and a tree shape (roots as causes and branches as effects). You can design any think link that makes sense to you.

A think link may be tough to construct in class, especially if your instructor talks quickly. In this case, use another note-taking system during class. Then make a think link as you review your notes.

H OW CAN YOU WRITE FASTER WHEN TAKING NOTES?

When taking notes, many students feel that they can't keep up with the instructor. Using some personal shorthand (not standard secretarial shorthand) can help you push your pen faster. *Shorthand* is writing that shortens words or replaces them with symbols. Because you are the only intended reader, you can misspell and abbreviate words in ways that only you understand.

The only danger with shorthand is that you might forget what your writing means. To avoid this problem, review your shorthand notes while your abbreviations and symbols are fresh in your mind. If there is any confusion, spell out words as you review.

Here are some suggestions that will help you master this important skill:

1. Use the following standard abbreviations in place of complete words:

w/	with	cf	compare, in comparison to
w/o	without	ff	following
→	means; resulting in	Q	question
←	as a result of	p.	page
↑	increasing	*	most importantly
↓	decreasing	<	less than
∴	therefore	>	more than
∵	because	=	equals
≈	approximately	%	percent
+ or &	and	Δ	change
−	minus; negative	2	to; two; too
NO. or #	number	vs	versus; against
i.e.	that is	e.g.	for example
etc.	and so forth	c/o	care of
ng	no good	lb	pound

2. Shorten words by removing vowels from the middle of words:

prps	=	purpose
lwyr	=	lawyer
cmptr	=	computer

3. Substitute word beginnings for entire words:

assoc	=	associate; association
info	=	information
subj	=	subject

4. Form plurals by adding "s" to shortened words:

prblms	=	problems
drctrys	=	directories
prntrs	=	printers

5. Make up your own symbols and use them consistently:

b/4	=	before
4tn	=	fortune
2thake	=	toothache

6. Use key phrases instead of complete sentences ("German: nouns capitalized" instead of "In the German language, all nouns are capitalized.")

Although note taking focuses on taking in ideas, writing focuses on expressing them. Next you will explore the roles that writing can play in your life.

Clear a space for the writing voice . . . you cannot will this to happen. It is a matter of persistence and faith and hard work. So you might as well just go ahead and get started.

ANNE LAMOTT

WHY DOES GOOD WRITING MATTER?

Almost any course will require you to communicate your knowledge and thought processes by writing essays or papers. To express yourself successfully, you need good writing skills. Knowing how to express your ideas in writing is essential outside of school as well. People who see your writing judge your thinking ability based on what you write and how you write it. Over the next few years you may write papers, essays, answers to essay test questions, job application letters, resumes, business proposals and reports, memos to coworkers, and letters to customers and suppliers. Good writing skills will help you achieve the goals you set out to accomplish with each writing task.

Good writing depends on and reflects clear thinking. Therefore, a clear thought process is the best preparation for a well-written document, and a well-written document shows the reader a clear thought process. Good writing also depends on reading. Exposing yourself to the work of other writers helps you learn words, experience concepts, and discover different ways to express ideas. In addition, critical reading generates new ideas you can use in your writing. The processes of reading and writing are interrelated; the skills in one process tend to enhance the skills in the other.

WHAT ARE THE ELEMENTS OF EFFECTIVE WRITING?

Every writing situation is different, depending on three elements. Your goal is to understand each element before you begin to write:

- **Your purpose:** What do you want to accomplish with this particular piece of writing?
- **Your topic:** What is the subject about which you will write?
- **Your audience:** Who will read your writing?

Figure 8.5 shows how these elements depend on one another. As a triangle needs three points to be complete, a piece of writing needs these three elements. Consider purpose and audience even before you begin to plan. Topic will come into play during the planning stage (the first stage of the writing process).

Writing Purpose

Writing without having a clear purpose is like driving without deciding where you want to go. You'll get somewhere, but chances are it won't be the right place. Therefore, when you write, always decide what you want to accomplish before you start. Although there are many different writing purposes, the two you will most commonly use for school and on the job are to inform and to persuade.

The purpose of *informative writing* is to present and explain ideas. A research paper on how hospitals use donated blood to save lives informs

FIGURE **8.5** The three elements of writing.

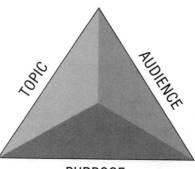

PURPOSE

readers without trying to mold opinions. The writer presents facts in an unbiased way without introducing a particular point of view. Most newspaper articles, except on the opinion and editorial pages, are examples of informative writing.

Persuasive writing has the purpose of convincing readers to adopt your point of view. For example, as a member of the student health committee, you write a newspaper column attempting to persuade readers to give blood. Examples of persuasive writing include newspaper editorials, business proposals, and books and magazine articles with a point of view.

Knowing Your Audience

In almost every case, a writer creates written material so that others can read it. The writer and audience are partners in this process. Knowing who your audience is will help you communicate successfully.

Key Questions About Your Audience

In school, your primary audience is your instructors. For many assignments, instructors will want you to assume that they are typical readers. Writing for "typical readers" usually means that you should be as complete as possible in your explanations. You may also write for "informed readers" who know a great deal about your topic. In every case, ask yourself some or all of the following questions to help you define your readers' needs:

- What are my readers' ages, cultural backgrounds, interests, and experiences?
- What are their roles? Are they instructors, students, employers, or customers?
- How much do they know about my topic? Are they experts in the field or beginners?
- Are they interested, or do I have to convince them to read what I write?
- Can I expect my audience to have open or closed minds?

After you answer the questions about your audience, take what you have discovered into consideration as you write.

Your Commitment to Your Audience

Your goal is to communicate—to organize your ideas so that readers can follow them. Suppose, for example, you are writing an informative research paper for a nonexpert audience on using Internet job banks to get a job.

One way to accomplish your goal is first to explain what these employment services are and the kinds of help they offer, then to describe each
service in detail, and finally to conclude with how these services will
change job hunting in the twenty-first century.

Effective and successful writing involves following the steps of the
writing process.

W HAT IS THE WRITING PROCESS?

The writing process provides an opportunity for you to state and
refine your thoughts until you have expressed yourself as clearly as possible. Critical thinking plays an important role every step of the
way. The four main parts of the process are planning, drafting, revising,
and editing.

Planning

Planning gives you a chance to think about what to write and how to write
it. Planning involves brainstorming for ideas, defining and narrowing your
topic by using *prewriting strategies,* conducting research if necessary, writing a thesis statement, and writing a working outline. Although these steps
are listed in sequence, in real life the steps overlap one another as you plan
your document.

Open Your Mind Through Brainstorming

Whether your instructor assigns a partially defined topic (novelist
Amy Tan) or a general category within which you make your own
choice (women authors), you should brainstorm to develop ideas
about what you want to write. Brainstorming is a creative technique
that involves generating ideas about a subject without making judgments (see page 139).

First, let your mind wander. Write down anything on the assigned subject that comes to mind, in no particular order. Then, organize that list
into an outline or think link that helps you see the possibilities more clearly. To make the outline or think link, separate list items into general ideas
or categories and subideas or examples. Then associate the subideas or
examples with the ideas they support or fit. Figure 8.6 shows a portion of
an outline that student Michael B. Jackson constructed from his brainstorming list. The assignment is a five-paragraph essay on a life-changing
event. Here, only the subject that Michael eventually chose is shown broken down into different ideas.

Part of a brainstorming outline.

A life-changing event...
  – Family
  – Childhood
  → Military
    – travel
    → boot camp
      – physical conditioning
        ◦ swim tests
        ◦ intensive training
        ◦ ENDLESS push-ups!
      – Chief who was our commander
      – mental discipline
        ◦ military lifestyle
        ◦ perfecting our appearance
      – self-confidence
        ◦ walk like you're in control
        ◦ don't blindly accept anything

Narrow Your Topic Through Prewriting Strategies

When your brainstorming has generated some possibilities, narrow your topic. Focus on the subideas and examples from your brainstorming session. Because they are relatively specific, they will be more likely to point you toward possible topics. Choose one or more subideas or examples that you like and explore them by using prewriting strategies such as brainstorming, freewriting, and asking journalists' questions.[2] Prewriting strategies will help you decide which of your possible topics you would most like to pursue.

Brainstorming. The same process you used to generate ideas will also help you narrow your topic further. Generate thoughts about the possibility you have chosen and write them down. Then, organize them into categories, noticing any patterns that appear. See if any of the subideas or examples seem as if they might make good topics.

Freewriting. Another technique that encourages you to put ideas on paper as they occur to you is called *freewriting*. When you freewrite, you write whatever comes to mind without censoring ideas or worrying about grammar, spelling, punctuation, or organization. Freewriting helps you think creatively and gives you an opportunity to begin weaving in information you know. Freewrite on the subideas or examples you have created to see if you want to pursue any of them. Here is a sample of freewriting:

> Boot camp for the Coast Guard really changed my life. First of all, I really got in shape. We had to get up every morning at 5 A.M., eat breakfast, and go right into training. We had to do endless military-style push-ups—but we later found out that these have a purpose, to prepare us to hit the deck in the event of enemy fire. We had a lot of aquatic tests, once we were awakened at 3 A.M. to do one in full uniform! Boot camp also helped me to feel confident about myself and be disciplined. Chief Marzloff was the main person who made that happen. He was tough but there was always a reason. He got angry when I used to nod my head whenever he would speak to me, he said that made it seem like I was blindly accepting whatever he said, which was a weakness. From him I have learned to keep an eye on my body's movements when I communicate. I learned a lot more from him too.

Asking journalists' questions. When journalists begin work on a story, they ask themselves: Who? What? Where? When? Why? and How? You can use these *journalists' questions* to focus your thinking. Ask these questions about any subidea or example to discover what you may want to discuss.

Who?	Who was at boot camp? Who influenced me the most?
What?	What about boot camp changed my life? What did we do?
When?	When in my life did I go to boot camp, and for how long?
Where?	Where was camp located? Where did we spend our day-to-day time?
Why?	Why was it such an important experience?
How?	How did we train in the camp? How were we treated?

As you prewrite, keep an eye on paper length, assignment due date, and any other requirements (such as topic area or purpose). These requirements influence your choice of a final topic. For example, if you have a month to write an informative 20-page paper on a learning disability, you might discuss the symptoms, effects, and treatment of attention deficit hyperactivity disorder (ADHD). If you have a week to write a five-page persuasive essay, you might write about how elementary students with ADHD need special training.

Prewriting will help you develop a topic broad enough to give you something with which to work but narrow enough to be manageable. Prewriting also helps you see what you know and what you don't know. If your assignment requires more than you already know, you may need to do research.

Conduct Research

Some college writing, such as an opinion essay or exam essay, will rely on what you already know about a subject. In these cases, prewriting strategies may generate all the ideas and information you need. In other writing situations, outside sources are necessary. Try doing your research in stages. In the first stage, look for a basic overview that can lead to a thesis statement. In the second stage, go into more depth, tracking down information that will help you fill in gaps and complete your thoughts.

Write a Thesis Statement

Your work up until this point has prepared you to write a thesis statement, the central message you want to communicate. The thesis statement states your subject and point of view, reflects your writing purpose and audience, and acts as the organizing principle of your paper. It tells your readers what they should expect to read. Here is an example from Michael's paper:

Topic	Coast Guard boot camp
Purpose	To inform
Audience	Instructor with unknown knowledge about the topic
Thesis statement	Chief Marzloff, our Basic Training Company Commander at the U. S. Coast Guard Basic Training Facility, shaped our lives through physical conditioning, developing our self-confidence, and instilling strong mental discipline.

A thesis statement is just as important in a short document, such as a letter, as it is in a long paper. For example, when you write a job application letter, a clear thesis statement will help you tell the recruiter why you deserve the job.

Write a Working Outline

The final step in the preparation process is writing a working outline. Use this outline as a loose guide instead of a final structure. As you draft your paper, your ideas and structure may change many times. Only by allowing changes and refinements to occur can you get closer to what you really want to say. Some students prefer a more formal outline structure, while others like to use a think link. Choose whatever form suits you best.

Create a Checklist

Use the checklist in Table 8.1 to make sure your preparation is complete. Under "Date Due," create your own writing schedule, giving each task an intended completion date. Work backward from the date the assignment is due and estimate how long it will take to complete each step. Refer to Chapter 5 for time-management skills that will help you schedule your writing process.

As you develop your schedule, remember that you'll probably move back and forth between tasks. You might find yourself doing two and even three things on the same day. Stick to the schedule as best you can—while balancing the other demands of your busy life—and check off your accomplishments on the list as you complete them.

Drafting

Some people aim for perfection when they write a first draft. They want to get everything right—from word choice to tone to sentence structure to paragraph organization to spelling, punctuation, and grammar. Try to

TABLE 8.1 Preparation checklist.

DATE DUE	TASK	IS IT COMPLETE?
	Brainstorm	
	Define and narrow	
	Use prewriting strategies	
	Conduct research if necessary	
	Write thesis statement	
	Write working outline	
	Complete research	

resist this tendency because it may lead you to shut the door on ideas before you even know they are there.

A *first draft* involves putting ideas down on paper for the first time—but not the last. You may write many different versions of the assignment until you create one you like. Each version moves you closer to communicating exactly what you want to say in the way you want to say it. It is as if you started with a muddy pond and gradually cleared the mud away until your last version became a clear body of water, showing the rocks and the fish beneath the surface. Think of your first draft as a way of establishing the pond before you start clearing it up.

The process of writing a first draft includes freewriting, crafting an introduction, organizing the ideas in the body of the paper, formulating a conclusion, and citing sources.

Freewriting Your Draft

Envision the introduction, body, and conclusion as three parts of a sandwich: freewriting, then, is the process of searching the refrigerator for the ingredients and laying them all on the table. Taking everything that you have developed in the planning stages, freewrite a very rough draft. Don't censor yourself. For now, don't consciously think about your introduction, conclusion, or structure within the paper's body. Focus on getting your ideas out of the realm of thought and onto the paper in whatever form they prefer to be at the moment.

When you have the beginnings of a paper in your hands, you can start to shape it into something with a more definite form. First, work on how you want to begin.

Writing an Introduction

The introduction tells your readers what the rest of the paper will contain. A thesis statement is essential. Here, for example, is a draft of an introduction for Michael's paper about the Coast Guard. The thesis statement is underlined at the end of the paragraph:

> Chief Marzloff took on the task of shaping the lives and careers of the youngest, newest members of the U. S. Coast Guard. During my eight weeks in training, he was my father, my instructor, my leader, and my worst enemy. He took his job very seriously and demanded that we do the same. <u>The Chief was instrumental in conditioning our bodies, developing our self-confidence, and instilling mental discipline within us.</u>

When you write an introduction, you might try to draw the reader in with an anecdote—a story that is related to the thesis. You can try other hooks, including a relevant quotation, dramatic statistics, and questions

REAL WORLD PERSPECTIVE

Jonathan Fish, *Claremont McKenna College, 1991, Major: International relations, Minor: Literature*

I graduated from Claremont McKenna College in 1991 with a major in international relations and a minor in literature. I completed a law degree at California Western School of Law in 1996. I was an on-campus representative for Teach For America for two years as a college student and a resident advisor. This gave me an opportunity to do something for the country. I taught English for Teach for America during the two years immediately after CMC. The idea was that by starting your working life as a teacher, you would always have the issues of education on your mind.

I taught at a junior high school in Houston. This was serious inner-city teaching, taking weapons away from 12-year-olds and everything that went with it. I realized after two years that this was not for me.

Entering the legal field gave me an opportunity to provide service in a different area. There's something about my generation. Everyone thinks they have to go to law school.

I am presently a Deputy District Attorney for the Orange County, California, District Attorney's Office. I always wanted to become a prosecutor, to wear the "white hat" and decide what is right. I'm also a wannabe cop. I am thinking of going to the police academy and becoming a reserve officer.

(continued)

that encourage critical thinking. Whatever strategy you choose, link it to your thesis statement. In addition, try to state your purpose without referring to its identity as a purpose. For example, in your introductory paragraph, state "Computer technology is infiltrating every aspect of business" instead of "In this paper, my purpose is to prove that computer technology is infiltrating every aspect of business."

After you have an introduction that seems to set up the purpose of your paper, make sure the body fulfills that purpose.

I was impressed with how much Claremont taught me about the importance of writing. Every single class at CMC (accounting and math excepted) is writing intensive.

I can think of a particular professor who was neurotic about excessive words, going through a paper, looking for mistakes, lining things out. That is what good legal writing is about. You have to learn to write appropriately or it's not going to get read—juries, judges, *everyone* evaluates your writing. You also have to write to be an advocate, making your points quickly and cogently. My classes at CMC stressed that.

My writing was initially too flowery. I had to learn to get down to the nitty-gritty, make my points clearly and concisely.

I CAN THINK OF A PARTICULAR PROFESSOR WHO WAS NEUROTIC ABOUT EXCESSIVE WORDS GOING THROUGH A PAPER, LINING THINGS OUT.

I also credit liberal education with giving me strong and broad learning skills. Liberal arts is for the long-term in your career, not the immediate; it teaches you to think and analyze. You can always pick up the specifics of any job.

What is the meaning of liberal education? I would liken it to getting a car for one's family. You wouldn't get a two-seater without four-wheel drive; you would want the car to be able to go anywhere, do anything. With a liberal education, the entire territory of work and life is available to you.

Creating the Body of a Paper

The body of the paper contains your central ideas and supporting evidence. *Evidence*—proof that informs or persuades—consists of the facts, statistics, examples, and expert opinions that you know or have gathered during research.

Look at the array of ideas and evidence in your draft in its current state. Think about how you might group certain items of evidence with the particular ideas they support. Then, try to find a structure that helps you to organize such evidence groups into a clear pattern. Here are some strategies to consider:

Arrange ideas by time. Describe events in order or in reverse order.

Arrange ideas according to importance. You can start with the most important idea and move to the least important, or vice versa.

Arrange ideas by problem and solution. Start with a specific problem; then discuss one or more solutions.

Writing the Conclusion

Your conclusion is a statement or paragraph that communicates that your paper is complete. Summarize the information that is in the body of your paper and critically evaluate what is important about it. Try one of the following strategies:

- Summarize main points (if material is longer than three pages).
- Relate a story, statistic, quote, or question that makes the reader think.
- Call the reader to action.
- Look to the future.

As you work on your conclusion, try not to introduce new facts or restate what you feel you have proved ("I have successfully proven that violent cartoons are related to increased violence in children"). Let your ideas as they are presented in the body of the paper speak for themselves. Readers should feel that they have reached a natural point of completion.

Crediting Authors and Sources

When you write a paper using any materials other than your own thoughts and recollections, the ideas you gathered in your research become part of your own writing. This does not mean that you can claim these ideas as your own or fail to attribute them to someone. To avoid plagiarism, you need to credit authors for their ideas and words.

To avoid plagiarism, learn the difference between a quotation and a paraphrase. A *quotation* refers to a source's exact words, which you should set off from the rest of the text by quotation marks. A *paraphrase* is a restatement of the quotation in your own words, using your own sentence structure. Restatement means to completely rewrite the idea, not just to remove or replace a few words. A paraphrase may not be acceptable if it is too close to the original.

Even an acceptable paraphrase requires a citation of the source of the ideas within it. Take care to credit any source that you quote, paraphrase, or use as evidence. To credit a source, write a footnote or endnote that describes it. Use the format preferred by your instructor. Writing hand-books, such as Modern Language Association's *MLA Style Manual and Guide to Scholarly Publishing* (1998) contain acceptable formats.

See revision as 'envisioning again.' If there are areas in your work where there is a blur or vagueness, you can simply see the picture again and add the details that will bring your work closer to your mind's picture.

NATALIE GOLDBERG

Revising

When you revise, you critically evaluate the word choice, paragraph structure, and style of your first draft. Any draft, no matter how good, can always be improved. Be thorough as you add, delete, replace, and reorganize words, sentences, and paragraphs. You may want to print out your draft and then make notes and corrections on the hard copy before you make changes on a typewritten or computer-printed version. Figure 8.7 shows a paragraph from Michael's first draft with revision comments added.

In addition to revising on your own, some classes may include peer review (having students read one another's work and offer suggestions). A peer reviewer can tell you what comes across well and what seems confusing. Having a different perspective on your writing is extremely valuable. Even if you don't have an organized peer review system, you may want to ask a classmate to review your work as a favor.

The elements of revision include being a critical writer, evaluating paragraph structure, and checking for clarity and conciseness.

Being a Critical Writer

Critical thinking is as important in writing as it is in reading. Thinking critically when writing will help you move beyond restating what you have researched and learned. Of course, your knowledge is an important part of your writing. What will make your writing even more important and unique, however, is how you use critical thinking to construct your own new ideas and knowledge from what you have learned.

One key to critical writing is asking the question "So what?" For example, if you were writing a paper on nutrition, you might discuss a variety of good eating habits. Asking "So what?" could lead into a discussion of why these habits are helpful or what positive effects they have. If you were writing a paper on egg imagery in the novel *All the King's Men* by Robert Penn Warren, you might list all the examples of it that you

8.7 Sample first draft with revision comments.

Of the changes that ~~happened to us,~~ the physical *[military recruits undergo]*

transformation is the ~~biggest.~~ *most evident* ~~When we arrived at the~~

~~training facility, it was January, cold and cloudy. At the~~ *Too much ↗*

~~time,~~ I was a little thin, but I had been working out and *Maybe— upon my January arrival at the training facility,*

thought that I could physically do anything. Oh boy, was

I wrong! The Chief said to us right away: "Get down, *✓ his trademark phrase*

maggots!" Upon this command, we ~~all~~ *were* to drop to the

ground and do *endless* military-style push-ups. Water survival

tactics were also part of the training ~~that we had to~~

~~complete.~~ *unnecessary* Occasionally, my dreams of home were

interrupted at 3 a.m. when we had a surprise aquatic

test. Although we ~~didn't feel too happy about~~ *resented* this *mention how chief was involved*

sub-human treatment at the time, we learned to

appreciate how the conditioning was turning our bodies

into fine-tuned machines. *say more about this (swimming in uniform incident?)*

noticed. Then, asking "So what?" could lead you to evaluate why that imagery is so strong and what idea you think those examples convey.

Use mind actions to guide your revision. As you revise, ask yourself questions that can help you think through ideas and examples, come up with your own original insights about the material, and be as complete and clear as possible. Here are some examples of questions you may ask:

- Are these examples clearly connected to the idea?
- Are there any similar concepts or facts I know of that can add to how I support this?
- What else can I recall that can help to support this idea?

  In evaluating any event or situation, have I clearly indicated the causes and effects?
- What new idea comes to mind when I think about these examples or facts?
- How do I evaluate any effect, fact, or situation? Is it good or bad, useful or not?
- What different arguments might a reader think of that I should address here?

Finally, critical thinking can help you evaluate the content and form of your paper. As you start your revision, ask yourself the following questions:

- Will my audience understand my thesis and how I've supported it?
- Does the introduction prepare the reader and capture attention?
- Is the body of the paper organized effectively?
- Is each idea fully developed, explained, and supported by examples?
- Are my ideas connected to one another through logical transitions?
- Do I have a clear, concise, simple writing style?
- Does the paper fulfill the requirements of the assignment?
- Does the conclusion provide a natural ending to the paper?

Checking for Clarity and Conciseness

Aim to say what you want to say as clearly and concisely as you can. Try to eliminate extra words and phrases. Rewrite wordy phrases in a more straightforward, conversational way. For example, you can write "if" instead of "in the event that," or "now" instead of "at this point in time." "Capriciously, I sauntered forth to the entryway and pummeled the door that loomed so majestically before me" might become "I skipped to the door and knocked loudly."

Editing

In contrast to the critical thinking of revising, *editing* involves correcting technical mistakes in spelling, grammar, and punctuation, as well as checking style consistency for such elements as abbreviations and capitalizations.

REAL WORLD PERSPECTIVE

Erin Lardner Lee, *University of California at Davis, 1997, Major: Rhetoric, Minor: English*

I graduated from the University of California at Davis in 1997 with a major in rhetoric and a minor in English. I completed my first two years of college at Sierra Community College, where I majored in liberal arts.

After graduation I was hired by Prima Publishing in Rocklin, California, as a publicity assistant. Prima is a fast-growing medium-sized publisher in a rural area of northern California.

I wanted to try publishing but I did not want to move to a big city, so Prima was perfect. I stayed there two years and was senior publicist by the time I left. I got the job initially because I had been a student intern at Prima and they knew I could do the job.

My other two internships were at KCRA Channel Three in Sacramento and in the office of the Governor of California. I recommend internships as a way to get work experience and help you decide what fields of work you like.

I learned on the job at Prima Publishing and gradually developed expertise in marketing. My liberal arts skills of writing, speaking, and analyzing were always coming into play.

In 1999, I joined The Audio Partners, a small company based in Auburn, California, to work as a marketing specialist. The company publishes books on audiotape. By this time, following my experience at Prima, I had a good handle on marketing, promotion, and publicity.

I left Audio Partners in 2000 to join Intel, the major computer chip manufacturer. I was hired because of my marketing skills and experience. I am a communications specialist in the Information Technology Division of Intel.

(continued)

My job involves internal marketing, which means marketing to Intel employees. I work with Information Technology Global Engineering. This group develops and implements standards that can be used across the various enterprise applications. We have approximately 80,000 employees overall worldwide.

I use liberal arts skills in my job. I use my communication skills every day. Writing is prominent, in terms of reports, memos, and marketing materials. Speaking skills are especially crucial. I am required on a regular basis to make presentations and I have to do them well. Presentations force me to learn much more than if I simply worked on my own.

MANY COMMUNICATIONS ISSUES ARE LIKE MYSTERIES TO BE SOLVED.

Also, liberal arts taught me problem solving, and we have many communications issues to solve. I often have to analyze how different groups communicate. This involves researching them, their products, and so forth.

Many communications issues are like investigative reporting, or mysteries to be solved. My Shakespeare courses taught me to think about plots and the twists and turns they take.

A lot of the departments I market to are filled with engineers. Communication is often not their major strength, so I have to figure out how to reach them and help them.

I took a course at UCD called "Freedom of Speech." It was very much a law course and I did not like it. However, lately I have come to appreciate that course because it taught me how to look at several sides of a discussion or argument.

In liberal arts you're deliberately not trained to do anything, and that is good. Liberal arts frees you to do many kinds of work after you graduate.

Editing comes last, after you are satisfied with your ideas, organization, and style of writing. If you use a computer, you might want to use the grammar-check and spell-check functions to find mistakes. A spell checker helps, but you still need to check your work on your own. Although a spell checker won't pick up the mistake in the following sentence, someone who is reading for sense will:

They are not hear on Tuesdays.

Look also for *sexist language,* which characterizes people according to their gender. Sexist language often involves the male pronoun *he* or *his.* For example, "An executive often spends hours each day going through his electronic mail" implies that executives are always men. A simple change will eliminate the sexist language: "Executives often spend hours each day going through their electronic mail." Try to be sensitive to words that leave out or slight women; for example, *mail carrier* is preferable to *mailman.*

Proofreading is the last editing stage and happens after your paper is in its final form. Proofreading means reading every word and sentence to make sure they are accurate. Look for technical mistakes, run-on sentences, and sentence fragments. Look for incorrect word usage and unclear references.

Teamwork can be a big help as you edit and proofread because another pair of eyes may see errors that you didn't notice on your own. If possible, have someone look over your work. Ask for feedback on what is clear and what is confusing. Then ask the reader to edit and proofread for errors.

A Final Checklist

You are now ready to complete your revising and editing checklist. All the tasks listed in Table 8.2 should be complete when you submit your final paper.

Your final paper reflects all the hard work you put in during the writing process. Figure 8.8 shows the final version of Michael's paper.

JOURNAL ENTRY

To record your thoughts, use a separate sheet or journal.

What piece of powerful writing have you read most recently? Did it make you feel something, think something, or do something? If so, why? What can you learn about writing from this piece?

Revising and editing checklist.

DATE DUE	TASK	IS IT COMPLETE?
	Check the body of the paper for clear thinking and adequate support of ideas	
	Finalize introduction and conclusion	
	Check word spelling, usage, and grammar	
	Check paragraph structure	
	Make sure language is familiar and concise	
	Check punctuation and capitalization	
	Check transitions	
	Eliminate sexist language	
	Get feedback from peers and/or instructor	

FIGURE

8.8 Final version of paper.

Michael B. Jackson
BOYS TO MEN

His stature was one of confidence, often misinterpreted by others as cockiness. His small frame was lean and agile, yet stiff and upright, as though every move were a calculated formula. For the longest eight weeks of my life, he was my father, my instructor, my leader, and my worst enemy. His name is Chief Marzloff, and he had the task of shaping the lives and careers of the youngest, newest members of the U. S. Coast Guard. As our Basic Training Company Commander, he took his job very seriously and demanded that we do the same. Within a limited time span, he conditioned our bodies, developed our self-confidence, and instilled within us a strong mental discipline.

Of the changes that recruits in military basic training undergo, the physical transformation is the most immediately evident. Upon my January arrival at the training facility, I was a little thin, but I had been working out and thought that I could physically do anything. Oh boy, was I wrong! The Chief wasted no time in introducing me to one of his trademark phrases: "Get down, maggots!" Upon this command, we were all to drop to the ground and produce endless counts of military-style push-ups. Later, we found out that this exercise prepared us for hitting the deck in the event of enemy fire. Water survival tactics were also part of the training. Occasionally, my dreams of home were interrupted at about 3 a.m. when our company was selected for a surprise aquatic test. I recall one such test that required us to swim laps around the perimeter of a pool while in full uniform. I felt like a salmon swimming upstream, fueled only by natural instinct. Although we resented this sub-human treatment at the time, we learned to appreciate how the strict guidance of the Chief was turning our bodies into fine-tuned machines.

Beyond physical ability, Chief Marzloff also played an integral role in the development of our self-confidence. He would often declare in his raspy voice, "Look me in the eyes when you speak to me! Show me that you believe what you're saying!" He taught us that anything less was an expression of disrespect. Furthermore, he appeared to attack a personal habit of my own. It seemed that whenever he would speak to me individually, I would nervously nod my head in response. I was trying to demonstrate that I understood, but

Continued.

FIGURE 8.8

to him, I was blindly accepting anything that he said. He would roar, "That is a sign of weakness!" Needless to say, I am now conscious of all bodily motions when communicating with others. The Chief also reinforced self-confidence through his own example. He walked with his square chin up and chest out, like the proud parent of a newborn baby. He always gave the appearance that he had something to do, and that he was in complete control. Collectively, the methods that the Chief used were all successful in developing our self-confidence.

Perhaps the Chief's greatest contribution was the mental discipline that he instilled in his recruits. He taught us that physical ability and self-confidence were nothing without the mental discipline required to obtain any worthwhile goal. For us, this discipline began with adapting to the military lifestyle. Our day began promptly at 0500 hours, early enough to awaken the oversleeping roosters. By 0515 hours, we had to have showered, shaved, and perfectly donned our uniforms. At that point, we were marched to the galley for chow, where we learned to take only what is necessary, rather than indulging. Before each meal, the Chief would warn, "Get what you want, but you will eat all that you get!" After making good on his threat a few times, we all got the point. Throughout our stay, the Chief repeatedly stressed the significance of self-discipline. He would calmly utter, "Give a little now, get a lot later." I guess that meant different things to all of us. For me, it was a simple phrase that would later become my personal philosophy on life. The Chief went to great lengths to ensure that everyone under his direction possessed the mental discipline required to be successful in boot camp or in any of life's challenges.

Chief Marzloff was a remarkable role model and a positive influence on many lives. I never saw him smile, but it was evident that he genuinely cared a great deal about his job and all the lives that he touched. This man single-handedly conditioned our bodies, developed our self-confidence, and instilled a strong mental discipline that remains in me to this day. I have not seen the Chief since March 28, 1992, graduation day. Over the years, however, I have incorporated many of his ideals into my life. Above all, he taught us the true meaning of the U. S. Coast Guard slogan, "Semper Peratus" (Always Ready).

Listening, Memory, and Test Taking

TAKING IN, RETAINING, & DEMONSTRATING KNOWLEDGE

This chapter relates to Chapter 10, "Advantages for Liberal Arts Graduates," in that retaining and demonstrating knowledge contribute greatly to the liberal arts graduate's effectiveness on the job. Graduates should be able to absorb new areas of knowledge and demonstrate their knowledge on projects that cover a wide range of content. When achieved, this versatility of learning makes the liberal arts graduate highly valued in the marketplace.

College exposes you daily to facts, opinions, and ideas—your job is to make use of them. Listening helps you take in information, and memory skills enable you to retain it. Then, through test preparation and test taking, you demonstrate knowledge and mastery of what you learn. Compare your skills to using a camera: You start by locating an image through the viewfinder, then you carefully focus the lens (listening), record the image on film (remembering), and produce a print (test taking). Mastery also involves the ability to apply your new knowledge to new situations. In this chapter, you will learn strategies to improve your ability to take in, remember, and show knowledge of what you have learned.

In this chapter, you will explore answers to the following questions:

- How can you become a better listener?
- How does memory work?
- How can you improve your memory?
- What types of preparation can improve test performance?
- What strategies can help you succeed on tests?
- How can you learn from test mistakes?

HOW CAN YOU BECOME A BETTER LISTENER?

The act of hearing isn't quite the same as the act of listening. Although *hearing* refers to sensing spoken messages from their source, *listening* involves a complex process of communication. Successful *listening* results in the speaker's intended message reaching the listener. In school and at home, poor listening may cause communication breakdowns and mistakes, whereas skilled listening promotes mutual understanding. Listening is a teachable—and learnable—skill.

Ralph G. Nichols, a pioneer in listening research, studied 200 students at the University of Minnesota over a nine-month period. His findings, summarized in Table 9.1, demonstrate that effective listening depends as much on a positive attitude as on specific skills.[1]

Listening is made up of four stages that build on one another: sensing (hearing the message), interpreting (understanding the message), evaluating (deciding what you feel about the message), and reacting (giving feedback). These stages take the message from the speaker to the listener and back to the speaker. Improving your learning skills involves managing listening challenges and becoming an active listener. Although good listening will help in every class, it is crucial in subject areas you find difficult.

What helps and hinders listening.

LISTENING IS HELPED BY	LISTENING IS HINDERED BY
. . . making a conscious decision to work at listening; viewing difficult material as a listening challenge.	. . . caring little about the listening process; tuning out difficult material.
. . . fighting distractions through intense concentration.	. . . refusing to listen at the first distraction.
. . . continuing to listen when a subject is difficult or dry, in the hope that one might learn something interesting.	. . . giving up as soon as one loses interest.
. . . withholding judgment until hearing everything.	. . . becoming preoccupied with a response as soon as a speaker makes a controversial statement.

Manage Listening Challenges

Classic studies have shown that immediately after listening, students are likely to recall only half of what was said. This is partly due to particular listening challenges, including divided attention and distractions, the tendency to shut out the message, the inclination to rush to judgment, and partial hearing loss or learning disabilities.[2] To help create a positive listening environment in both your mind and your surroundings, explore how to manage these challenges.

Divided Attention and Distractions

Internal and external distractions often divide your attention. *Internal distractions* include anything from hunger to headache to personal worries. Something the speaker says may also trigger a recollection that causes your mind to drift. In contrast, *external distractions* include noises (e.g., whispering or sirens) and excessive heat or cold. It can be hard to listen in an overheated room in which you are falling asleep.

Your goal is to reduce distractions so that you can focus on what you're hearing. Sitting where you can clearly see and hear will help you to listen. To avoid distracting activity, you may want to sit away from people who might chat or make noise. Dress comfortably, paying attention to the temperature of the classroom, and try not to go to class hungry or thirsty.

REAL WORLD PERSPECTIVE

O'Keeya Singleton, *Claremont McKenna College, 1999, Major: Psychology*

I graduated in 1999 from Claremont McKenna College. I am not kidding when I say, "I really do miss final exams." I'm serious. I loved the pressure of cramming at the end of the term. You have absolutely no idea what's going to be on each exam. Now THAT's pressure! By comparison, outside of school there is not nearly as much pressure.

Contrary to what you may think, I did not study all the time during college. I was a coach for the high school football team in Claremont, wrote for two college newspapers, and was a member of the Debate Team and Judiciary Board.

My first job after graduation was as an assistant project manager for an import/export company. My second job was as a multimedia litigation consultant: We prepared materials for courtroom presentations. Graphics, charts, videos, and diagrams. The two jobs were unrelated to each other or anything I ever studied in a classroom in college.

Most of the work I have done in my jobs since college, I never studied or learned during my academic career. I learned on the job by doing. When I graduated CMC, I felt I was qualified to do everything, and not qualified to do anything. Now, I know that I can go into any job area, learn it, and do it. However, convincing employers of this, especially major corporate entities, is the tough part. That's what college prepared us to do.

(continued)

Shutting Out the Message

Instead of paying attention to everything the speaker says, many students fall into the trap of focusing on specific points and shutting out the rest of the message. If you perceive that a subject is too difficult or uninteresting, you may tune out.

Creating a positive listening environment includes accepting responsibility for listening. Although the instructor is responsible for communicating information to you, she cannot force you to listen. You are responsible for

The assistant project manager and multimedia litigation jobs became boring and mundane. Now, I have a job I really love. I am the multimedia analyst at the National Health Foundation in downtown Los Angeles, a small nonprofit organization. I started here as a Web developer, but in a short time I became the go-to person for any questions, problems, or projects involving new media or Internet technology. I get to use my creativity, problem-solving skills, and other talents, which is a major reason I enjoy my job as much as I do. If you have the smarts, the desire to learn, and access to the information you need, you can do almost anything. CMC gave me confidence in my ability to learn any job and compete with anyone. It was not until after I graduated that I truly appreciated my educational and college experience. Education is not something I have to do anymore. Now, I learn things because they interest me or are necessary. I read much more on my own than I did in college.

I REALLY MISS FINAL EXAMS.

I had no idea what I wanted to do when I was at Claremont. I took psychology courses because they're what I enjoyed. My view of that now is that because I developed such a wide variety of skills from all the studying and reading in college, I believe I can now do anything I want to do.

I plan to be at NHF for at least two years. After that, perhaps the FBI; or I may continue in Web development at another company or just stay here.

---

taking in that information. Instructors often cover material from outside the textbook during class and then test on that material. If you work to take in the whole message in class, you will be able to read over your notes later and think critically about what is most important.

The Rush to Judgment

People tend to stop listening when they hear something they don't like. If you rush to judge what you've heard, making a quick uncritical assumption about it, your focus turns to your personal reaction rather than the content of the message. Judgments also involve reactions to the speakers themselves. If you do not like your instructors or if you have preconceived notions about their ideas or background, you may assume that their words have little value.

> No one cares to speak to an unwilling listener. An arrow never lodges in a stone; often it recoils upon the sender of it.
>
> **ST. JEROME**

Work to recognize and control your judgments by making an effort to listen first without jumping to any conclusions. Stay aware of what you tend to judge so that you can avoid rejecting messages that clash with your opinions. Consider education as a continuing search for evidence, regardless of whether that evidence supports or negates your perspective.

Partial Hearing Loss and Learning Disabilities

Good listening techniques don't solve every listening problem. Students who have a partial hearing loss have a physical explanation for listening difficulty. If you have some level of hearing loss, seek out special services that can help you listen in class. You may require special equipment, or you might benefit from tutoring. You may be able to arrange to meet with your instructor outside of class to clarify your notes.

Other disabilities, such as attention deficit hyperactivity disorder (ADHD) or a problem with processing spoken language, can make it hard to focus on and understand oral messages. If you have one of these disabilities, don't blame yourself for your difficulty. Visit your school's counseling or student health center, or talk with your advisor or instructors about getting the help you need to meet your challenges.

Become an Active Listener

Effective listening is an active process that involves setting a purpose for listening, asking questions, and paying attention to *verbal signposts.*

Set purposes for listening. Active listening is possible only if you know (and care) why you are listening. In any situation, establish what you want to achieve through listening, such as greater understanding of the material.

Ask questions. A willingness to ask questions shows a desire to learn and is the mark of a critical thinker. Some questions are *informational*—seeking information. Other *clarifying* questions ask if your understanding of something you just heard is correct.

Paying attention to verbal signposts.

TABLE 9.2

SIGNALS POINTING TO KEY CONCEPTS	SIGNALS OF SUPPORT
There are two reasons for this . . .	For example, . . .
A critical point in the process involves . . .	Specifically, . . .
Most importantly, . . .	For instance, . . .

SIGNALS POINTING TO DIFFERENCES	SIGNALS THAT SUMMARIZE
On the other hand, . . .	Finally, . . .
In contrast, . . .	In conclusion, . . .
However, . . .	As a result, . . .

Source: Adapted from George M. Usova, *Efficient Study Strategies: Skills for Successful Learning.* Pacific Grove, CA: Brooks/Cole Publishing, 1989, p. 69.

Pay attention to verbal signposts. You can identify important facts and ideas and predict test questions by paying attention to the speaker's specific choice of words. Let phrases like those in Table 9.2 direct your attention to the material that follows them.

Listening in order to acquire knowledge is only the first step. The next goal is to remember what you hear, read, and take in through your other senses.

HOW DOES MEMORY WORK?

Your memory enables you to use the knowledge you take in. Human memory works like a computer. Both have essentially the same purpose: to encode, store, and retrieve information.

- During the *encoding stage,* information is changed into usable form. On a computer, this occurs when keyboard entries are transformed into electronic symbols and stored on a disk. In the brain, sensory information becomes impulses that the central nervous system reads and codes. You are encoding, for example, when you study a list of chemistry formulas.

- During the *storage stage,* information is held in memory (the mind's version of a computer hard drive) for later use. In this example, after you complete your studying of the formulas, your mind stores them until you need to use them.

- During the *retrieval stage,* memories are recovered from storage by recall, just as a saved computer program is called up by name and used again. In this example, your mind would retrieve the chemistry formulas when you had to take a test or solve a problem.

Memories are stored in three different storage banks. The first, called *sensory memory,* is an exact copy of what you see and hear and lasts for a second or less. Certain information is then selected from sensory memory and moves into *short-term memory,* a temporary information storehouse that lasts no more than 10 to 20 seconds. You are consciously aware of material in your short-term memory. Whereas unimportant information is quickly dumped, important information is transferred to *long-term memory*—the mind's more permanent information storehouse.

Having information in long-term memory does not necessarily mean that you will be able to recall it when needed. Particular techniques can help you improve your recall.

OW CAN YOU IMPROVE YOUR MEMORY?

Most forgetting occurs within minutes after memorization. In a classic study conducted in 1885, researcher Herman Ebbinghaus memorized a list of meaningless three-letter words such as CEF and LAZ. Within one hour he measured that he had forgotten more than 50 percent of what he learned. After two days, he knew fewer than 30 percent. Although his recall of the syllables remained fairly stable after that, the experiment shows how fragile memory can be—even when you take the time and energy to memorize information.[3]

People with superior memories may have an inborn talent for remembering. More often, though, they have mastered techniques for improving recall. Remember that techniques aren't a cure-all for memory difficulties, especially for those with learning disabilities. If you have a disability, the following strategies may help but may not be enough. Seek specific assistance if you consistently have trouble remembering.

Use Memory Improvement Strategies

As a student, your job is to understand, learn, and remember information—everything from general concepts to specific details. The following suggestions will help improve your recall.

Have Purpose and Intention

Why can you remember the lyrics to dozens of popular songs but not the functions of the pancreas? Perhaps this is because you want to remember the lyrics, you connect them to a visual image, or you have an emotional tie to them. To achieve the same results at school or on the job, make sure you have a purpose for what you are trying to remember. When you know why it is important, you will be able to strengthen your intention to remember it.

Understand What You Memorize

Something that has meaning is easier to recall than something that is gibberish. This basic principle applies to everything you study—from biology to English literature. If something you need to memorize makes no sense, consult textbooks, fellow students, or an instructor for an explanation.

> The true art of memory is the art of attention.
>
> **SAMUEL JOHNSON**

Recite, Rehearse, and Write

When you *recite* material, you repeat it aloud to remember it. Reciting helps you retrieve information as you learn it and is a crucial step in studying (see Chapter 7). *Rehearsing* is similar to reciting but is done silently. It is the process of repeating, summarizing, and associating information with other information. *Writing* is rehearsing on paper. The act of writing solidifies the information in your memory.

Separate Main Points from Unimportant Details

Use critical-thinking skills to select and focus on the most important information. Asking questions about what is most crucial to remember, highlight only the most important information in your texts and write notes in the margins about central ideas. When you review your lecture notes, highlight or rewrite the most important information to remember.

Study During Short but Frequent Sessions

Research shows that you can improve your chances of remembering material if you learn it more than once. Study in short sessions followed by brief rest periods rather than studying continually with little or no rest. Even though studying for an hour straight may feel productive, you'll probably remember more from three 20-minute sessions. Try studying between classes or during other breaks in your schedule.

Separate Material into Manageable Sections

When material is short and easy to understand, studying it from start to finish may work. With longer material, however, you may benefit from dividing it into logical sections, mastering each section, putting all the sections together, and then testing your memory of all the material.

Use Visual Aids

Any kind of visual representation of study material can help you remember. Try converting material into a think link or outline. Use any visual that helps you recall it and link it to other information.

Flash cards (easily made from index cards) are a great visual memory tool. They give you short repetitive review sessions that provide immediate feedback. Use the front of each card to write a word, idea, or phrase you want to remember. Use the back side for a definition, explanation, and other key facts. Figure 9.1 shows two flash cards for studying psychology.

FIGURE **9.1** Sample flash cards.

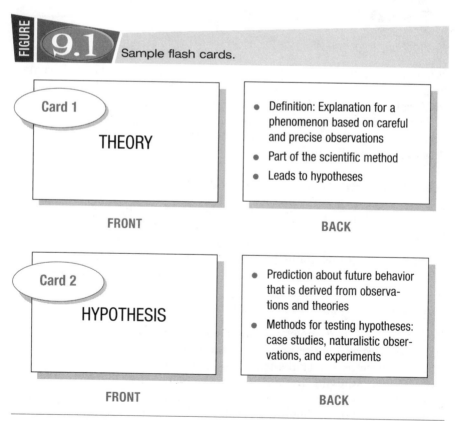

Card 1

THEORY

FRONT

- Definition: Explanation for a phenomenon based on careful and precise observations
- Part of the scientific method
- Leads to hypotheses

BACK

Card 2

HYPOTHESIS

FRONT

- Prediction about future behavior that is derived from observations and theories
- Methods for testing hypotheses: case studies, naturalistic observations, and experiments

BACK

Here are some additional suggestions for making the most of your flash cards:

- Carry the cards with you and review them frequently.
- Shuffle the cards and learn the information in various orders.
- Test yourself in both directions (e.g., first look at the terms and provide the definitions or explanations; then turn the cards over and reverse the process).

Use Mnemonic Devices

Mnemonic (pronounced neh MAHN ick) *devices* work by connecting information you are trying to learn with simpler information or information that is familiar. Instead of learning new facts by rote (repetitive practice), associations give you a hook on which to hang and retrieve these facts. Mnemonic devices make information familiar and meaningful through unusual, unforgettable mental associations and visual pictures.

Here's an example of the power of mnemonics. Suppose you want to remember the names of the first six presidents of the United States. The first letters of their last names—Washington, Adams, Jefferson, Madison, Monroe, and Adams—together are W A J M M A. To remember them, you might add an E after the J and create a short nonsense word: *wajemma*.

Visual images, idea chains, and acronyms are a few of the more widely used kinds of mnemonic devices. Apply them to your own memory challenges.

Create Visual Images and Associations

Visual images are often easier to remember than images that rely on words alone. The best mental images often involve bright colors, three dimensions, action scenes, inanimate objects with human traits, ridiculousness, and humor.

Turning information into mental pictures helps improve memory, especially for visual learners. To remember that the Spanish artist Picasso painted *The Three Women,* you might imagine the women in a circle dancing to a Spanish song with a pig and a donkey (pig-asso). Don't reject outlandish images—as long as they help you.

Create Acronyms

Another helpful association method involves the use of the *acronym.* In history, you can remember the "big-three" Allies during World War II— Britain, America, and Russia—with the acronym BAR.

You can also create an acronym from an entire sentence in which the first letter of each word in the sentence stands for the first letter of each memorized term. When science students want to remember the list of planets in order of their distance from the sun, they learn the sentence: My very elegant mother just served us nine pickles (Mercury, Venus, Earth, Mars, Jupiter, Saturn, Uranus, Neptune, and Pluto).

All of the study skills you have read about up to this point—reading, studying, note taking, writing, listening, and memory—will help you to succeed in the final skill discussed in this chapter: test taking.

WHAT TYPES OF PREPARATION CAN IMPROVE TEST PERFORMANCE?

Exams are preparation for life. For example, when you get a job or work on your budget, you'll have to put your knowledge to work. This is exactly what you do when you take a test. Exams are also part of life; you may encounter them when you apply for a driver's license, interview for a job, or qualify to practice in a particular career (e.g., a state nursing exam).

You can take steps to improve your test-taking skills. Your two goals are to know the material and to convey that knowledge to others.

Identify Test Type and Material Covered

Before you begin studying, find out what you can about the test. Try to identify:

- the type of questions on the test (short-answer, essay, or a combination)
- what the test will cover (class lectures and/or readings)
- whether the test deals with material from the whole semester or a more limited topic

Your instructors may answer these questions for you. Even though they may not reveal specific test questions, they might let you know the question format or information covered. Beyond the information they give you, here are a few other strategies for predicting what may be on a test:

Use SQ3R (see Chapter 7) to identify important ideas and facts. Often, the questions you write and ask yourself when you read assigned materials may be part of the test. Textbook study questions are also good candidates.

Examine old tests, if instructors make them available in class or on reserve in the library. If you can't get copies of old tests, use clues from the class to predict test questions. After taking the first exam in the course, you will have a lot more information about what to expect in the future.

Talk to people who took the instructor's course before. Try to find out how difficult the tests are and whether they focus more on assigned readings or class notes. Ask about instructors' preferences—one instructor may emphasize the repetition of facts, another may prioritize applying knowledge, and so on—and study accordingly.

> A little knowledge that acts is worth infinitely more than much knowledge that is idle.
>
> **KAHLIL GIBRAN**

Use Specific Study Strategies

Before you do anything, choose the materials that contain the information you need to study. Go through your notes, texts, and any related readings or handouts. Set aside materials you don't need. Once you are sure you aren't studying anything you don't need to, implement the following strategies:

Make a study plan. Consider the materials you need to study, how many days or weeks until the test, and how much time you can study each day. For example, if the test is in three days and you have no other obligations during that time, you might set two 2-hour sessions each day. If you have two weeks before a test, classes during the day, and work three nights a week, you might spread study sessions over your nights off during those two weeks.

Prepare through critical thinking. Using techniques from Chapter 6, approach your preparation critically, working to understand rather than just repeat facts. As you study, try to connect ideas to examples, analyze causes and effects, examine assumptions, and look at issues from different perspectives. Critical thinking is especially important for essay tests. Prepare by writing responses to potential essay questions.

Review carefully. Use SQ3R (see pages 152–157) and study techniques from Chapter 8 (page 176) to comprehensively review your materials.

Take a pretest. Use textbook study questions to create your own pretest. Choose questions that are likely to appear on the test and answer them under testlike conditions—in quiet, with no books or notes to help you, and with a clock to determine when time is up. If your course doesn't have an assigned text, develop questions from your notes and from assigned readings.

Prepare Physically

When taking a test, you often need to work efficiently under time pressure. If your body is tired or under stress, you will probably not think as clearly or perform as well as you usually do. If you can, get some sleep so that you can be rested and alert. If you tend to press the snooze button in your sleep, try setting two alarm clocks and placing them across the room from your bed.

Eating right is also important. Sugary snacks will bring up your energy, only to send you crashing back down much too soon. Also, too much caffeine can add to your tension and make it difficult to focus. Eating nothing will leave you drained, but too much food can make you sleepy. The best advice is to eat a light, well-balanced meal before a test. When time is short, grab a quick-energy snack such as a banana, some orange juice, or a granola bar.

Work Through Test Anxiety

A certain amount of stress can be a good thing. Your body is alert, and your energy motivates you to do your best. For some students, however, the time before and during an exam brings test anxiety. A bad case of nerves that makes it hard to think or remember, test anxiety can also cause physical symptoms such as sweating, nausea, dizziness, headaches, and extreme fatigue. Defend yourself against test anxiety with two primary strategies: preparation and attitude.

Preparation

Preparation is the basic defense against anxiety. The more confident you feel about your knowledge of the material, the more you'll feel able to perform on test day. In this way, you can consider all of the preparation and study information in this chapter as test anxiety assistance. Also, finding out what to expect on the exam will help you feel more in control.

Making and following a detailed study plan will help you build the kind of knowledge that can help you fight off anxiety. Divide the plan into a series of small tasks. As you finish each one, you will build your sense of accomplishment, confidence, and control. Preparation is all about action. Instead of sitting and worrying about the test, put your energy toward concrete, active steps that will help you succeed.

Attitude

Although good preparation will help build your confidence, maintaining a positive *attitude* toward testing is as important as studying. Here are some key ways to maintain an attitude that will help you:

See the test as an opportunity to learn. Focus on learning instead of failure. See that a test is an opportunity to show what you have learned, as well as to learn something new about the material and about test taking itself.

See the test as a signpost. It's easy to see a test as a contest. If you pass, or "win" the contest, you might feel no need to retain what you've learned. If you fail, or "lose" the contest, you might feel no need to try again. However, if you see the test as a signpost along the way to a greater goal, you may be more likely to try your best, learn from the experience, and move on.

Give your instructor a positive role. Your instructors test you to give you an opportunity to grow and to demonstrate what you have accomplished. They test you so that, in rising to this challenge, you will become better prepared for challenges outside of school.

Practice relaxation. When you feel test anxiety coming on, take some deep breaths, close your eyes, and visualize positive mental images related to the test, such as getting a good grade and finishing confidently, with time to spare. Do whatever you have to do to ease muscle tension—stretch your neck, tighten and then release your muscles, or take a trip to the rest room to do a couple of forward bends.

Test Anxiety and the Returning Student

If you're returning to school after 5, 10, or even 20 years, you may wonder if you can compete with younger students or if your mind is still able to learn new material. To counteract these feelings of inadequacy, focus on how your life experiences have given you useful skills. For example, managing work and a family requires strong time-management, planning, and communication skills, which can help you plan your study time, juggle school responsibilities, and interact with students and instructors.

In addition, life experiences give you examples through which you can understand ideas in your courses. For example, your relationships may help you understand psychology concepts; managing your finances may help you understand economics or accounting practices; and work experience may give you a context for what you learn in a business management course. If you let yourself feel positive about your knowledge and skills, you may improve your ability to achieve your goals.

When you have prepared using the strategies that work for you, you are ready to take your exam. Focus on methods that can help you succeed when the test begins.

HAT STRATEGIES CAN HELP YOU SUCCEED ON TESTS?

Even though every test is different, there are general strategies that will help you handle almost all tests, including short-answer and essay exams.

Write Down Key Facts

Before you even look at the test, write down any key information—including formulas, rules, and definitions—that you studied recently or even just before you entered the test room. Use the back of the question sheet or a piece of scrap paper for your notes (be sure it is clear to your instructor that this scrap paper didn't come into the test room already filled in). Recording this information right at the start will make forgetting less likely.

Begin with an Overview of the Exam

Take a few minutes at the start of the test to examine the kinds of questions you'll be answering, what kind of thinking they require, the number of questions in each section, and their point values. Use this information to schedule your time. For example, if a two-hour test is divided into two sections of equal point value—an essay section with 4 questions and a short-answer section with 60 questions—you can spend an hour on the essays and an hour on the short-answer section.

As you make your calculations, think about the level of difficulty of each section. If you think you can handle the short-answer questions in less than an hour and that you'll need more time for the essays, rebudget your time that way.

Know the Ground Rules

A few basic rules apply to any test. Following them will give you an advantage.

Read test directions. Although a test of 100 true-or-false questions and one essay question may look straightforward, the directions may tell you to answer only 80 or that the essay is an optional bonus question. Some questions or sections may be weighted more heavily than others. Try circling or underlining key words and numbers that remind you of the directions.

Begin with the parts or questions that seem easiest to you. Starting with what you know best can boost your confidence and help you save time to spend on the harder parts.

Watch the clock. Keep track of how much time is left and how you are progressing. You may want to plan your time on a piece of scrap paper, especially if you have one or more essays to write. Wear a watch or bring a small clock with you to the test room. Also, take your time. Rushing is almost always a mistake, even if you feel you've done well. Stay until the end so that you can refine and check your work.

Master the art of intelligent guessing. When you are unsure of an answer, you can leave it blank or you can guess. In most cases, guessing will help you. First eliminate all the answers you know—or believe—are wrong. Try to narrow your choices to two possible answers; then choose the one that makes more sense to you. When you recheck your work, decide if you would make the same guesses again, making sure there isn't a qualifier or fact that you hadn't noticed before.

Use Critical Thinking to Avoid Errors

Critical thinking can help you work through each question thoroughly and avoid errors. Use these critical-thinking strategies during a test:

Recall facts, procedures, rules, and formulas. Base your answers on the information you recall. Make sure you recall it accurately.

Think about similarities. If you don't know how to attack a question or problem, consider any similar questions or problems that you have worked on in class or while studying.

Notice differences. Especially with objective questions, items that seem different from the material you have studied may indicate answers you can eliminate.

Think through causes and effects. For a numerical problem, think about how you plan to solve it and see if the answer—the effect of your plan—makes sense. For an essay question that asks you to analyze a condition or situation, consider both what caused it and what effects it has.

Find the best idea to match the example or examples given. For a numerical problem, decide what formula (idea) best applies to the example or examples (the data of the problem). For an essay question, decide what idea applies to, or links, the examples given.

Support ideas with examples. When you put forth an idea in an answer to an essay question, be sure to back up your idea with an adequate number of examples that fit.

Evaluate each test question. In your initial approach to any question, decide what kinds of thinking will best help you solve it.

For example, essay questions frequently require cause-and-effect and idea-to-example thinking, and objective questions often benefit from thinking about similarities and differences.

These general strategies also can help you address specific types of test questions.

Master Different Types of Test Questions

Using different approaches, all test questions try to discover how much you know about a subject. *Objective questions,* such as multiple-choice or true-or-false, test your ability to recall, compare, and contrast information and to choose the right answer from among several choices. *Subjective questions,* usually essay questions, demand the same information recall, but they require you to use the mind actions to formulate a response and then to organize, draft, and refine it in writing. The following guidelines will help you choose the best answers to both types of questions.

Multiple-Choice Questions

Multiple-choice questions are the most popular type on standardized tests. The following strategies can help you answer them:

Read the directions carefully. Although most test items ask for a single correct answer, some give you the option of marking several choices that are correct.

First, read each question thoroughly. Then, look at the choices and try to answer the question.

Underline key words and phrases in the question. If the question is complicated, try to break it down into small sections that are easy to understand.

Pay special attention to qualifiers such as *only, except,* **and so on.** For example, negative words in a question can confuse your understanding of what the question asks ("Which of the following is *not . . .* ").

If you don't know the answer, eliminate those answers that you know or suspect are wrong. Your goal is to narrow down your choices. Ask yourself these questions:

- Is the choice accurate in its own terms? If there is an error in the choice—for example, a term that is incorrectly defined—the answer is wrong.
- Is the choice relevant? An answer may be accurate, but it may not relate to the essence of the question.

- Are there any qualifiers, such as *always, never, all, none,* or *every?* Qualifiers make it easy to find an exception that makes a choice incorrect. For example, the statement that "children *always* begin talking before the age of two" can be eliminated as an answer to the question "When do children generally start to talk?" because some children start later. Choices containing conservative qualifiers (*often, most,* or *rarely*) are often correct.

- Do the choices give clues? Does a puzzling word remind you of a word you know? If you don't know a word, does any part of the word (prefix, suffix, or root) seem familiar to you?

Look for patterns that may lead to the right answer; then use intelligent guessing. Particular patterns in multiple-choice questions, such as the following, may help you.

- Consider the possibility that a choice that is more *general* than the others is the right answer.

- Look for a choice that has a *middle value in a range* (the range can be from small to large or from old to recent). This choice may be the right answer.

- Look for two choices with *similar meanings.* One of these answers is probably correct.

Make sure you read every word of every answer. Instructors have been known to include answers that are right except for a single word.

When questions are keyed to a long reading passage, read the questions first. This will help you to focus your reading efforts on the information you need to answer the questions.

Here are some examples of the kinds of multiple-choice questions you might encounter in an Introduction to Psychology course[4] (the correct answer follows each question).

1. Which of the following has not been shown to be a probable cause of or influence in the development of alcoholism in our society?

    A. intelligence   C. personality

    B. culture   D. genetic vulnerability   *(The correct answer is A.)*

2. Geraldine is a heavy coffee drinker who has become addicted to caffeine. If she completely ceases her intake of caffeine over the next few days, she is likely to experience each of the following EXCEPT _____.

    A. depression   C. insomnia

    B. lethargy   D. headaches   *(The correct answer is C.)*

True-or-False Questions

True-or-false questions test your knowledge of facts and concepts. Read them carefully to evaluate what they truly say. If you're stumped, guess (unless you're penalized for wrong answers).

Look for qualifiers in true-or-false questions, such as *all, only, always, generally, usually,* and *sometimes,* that can turn a statement that would otherwise be true into one that is false or vice versa. For example: "The grammar rule 'I before E except after C' is always true" is false, whereas "The grammar rule 'I before E except after C' is usually true" is true. The qualifier makes the difference.

Here are some examples of true-or-false questions you might encounter in an Introduction to Psychology course.

1. Alcohol use is always related to increases in hostility, aggression, violence, and abusive behavior. *(False)*

2. Marijuana is harmless. *(False)*

3. Simply expecting a drug to produce an effect is often enough to produce the effect. *(True)*

Essay Questions

An essay question allows you to express your knowledge and views on a topic in a much more extensive manner than any short answer can provide. With the freedom to express your views, though, comes the challenge to both exhibit knowledge and show you have command of how to organize and express that knowledge clearly.

1. Start by reading the essay questions. Decide which to tackle (if there's a choice). Then focus on what each question is asking and the mind actions you will need to use. Read directions carefully—some essay questions may contain more than one part.

2. Watch for action verbs. Certain verbs can help you figure out how to think. Figure 9.2 explains some words commonly used in essay questions. Underline these words as you read the question, clarify what they mean, and use them to guide your writing.

3. Budget your time and begin to plan. Create an informal outline or think link to map your ideas, indicating examples you plan to cite in support. Avoid spending too much time on introductions or flowery language.

Common action verbs on essay tests.

Analyze—Break into parts and discuss each part separately.

Compare—Explain similarities and differences.

Contrast—Distinguish between items being compared by focusing on differences.

Criticize—Evaluate the positive and negative effects of what is being discussed.

Define—State the essential quality or meaning. Give the common idea.

Describe—Visualize and give information that paints a complete picture.

Discuss—Examine in a complete and detailed way, usually by connecting ideas to examples.

Enumerate/List/Identify—Recall and specify items in the form of a list.

Evaluate—Give your opinion about the value or worth of something, usually by weighing positive and negative effects, and justify your conclusion.

Explain—Make the meaning of something clear, often by making analogies or giving examples.

Illustrate—Supply examples.

Interpret—Explain your personal view of facts and ideas and how they relate to one another.

Outline—Organize and present the main examples of an idea or subideas.

Prove—Use evidence and argument to show that something is true, usually by showing cause and effect or giving examples that fit the idea to be proven.

Review—Provide an overview of ideas and establish their merits and features.

State—Explain clearly, simply, and concisely, being sure that each word gives the image you want.

Summarize—Give the important ideas in brief.

Trace—Present a history of the way something developed, often by showing cause and effect.

4. Write your essay. Start with an idea that states your topic and premise. In the first paragraph, introduce key points (subideas, causes, effects, or even examples). Use simple, clear language. Carefully establish your ideas and support them with examples, and look back at your outline or think link to make sure you are covering everything. Wrap it up with a conclusion that is short and to the point. Try to write legibly; if your instructor can't read your ideas, it doesn't matter how good they are.

5. Reread and revise your essay. Look for ideas you left out, ideas you didn't support with enough examples, and sentences that might confuse the reader. Check for mistakes in grammar, spelling, punctuation, and usage. No matter what you are writing about, having a command of these factors will make your work more complete and impressive.

HOW CAN YOU LEARN FROM TEST MISTAKES?

The purpose of a test is to see how much you know, not merely to achieve a grade. Making mistakes, or even failing a test, is human. Rather than ignoring mistakes, examine them and learn from them just as you learn from mistakes on the job and in your relationships. Working through your mistakes will help you avoid repeating them again on another test—or outside of school life.

Try to identify patterns in your mistakes by looking for the following:

- *Careless errors.* In your rush to complete the exam, did you misread the question or directions, blacken the wrong box, skip a question, or use illegible handwriting?

- *Conceptual or factual errors.* Did you misunderstand a concept or never learn it in the first place? Did you fail to master certain facts? Did you skip part of the assigned text or miss important classes in which ideas were covered?

If you have time, rework the questions you got wrong. Based on the feedback from your instructor, try rewriting an essay, recalculating a math problem, or reanswering the questions that follow a reading selection. If you see patterns of careless errors, plan to double-check your work next time. If you pick up conceptual and factual errors, rededicate yourself to better preparation.

When you fail a test, don't throw it away. First, know that a lot of students have been in your shoes and that you have room to grow and improve. Then recommit to the process by seeking a true understanding of why you failed. You may want to ask for an explanation from your instructor. Finally, develop a plan to really learn the material if you didn't understand it in the first place.

Here are some examples of essay questions you might encounter in an Introduction to Psychology course. In each case, notice the action verbs from Figure 9.2.

1. Summarize the theories and research on the causes and effects of daydreaming. Discuss the possible uses for daydreaming in a healthy individual.

2. Describe the physical and psychological effects of alcohol and the problems associated with its use.

3. Explain what sleep terrors are, what appears to cause them, and who is most likely to suffer from them.

OURNAL ENTRY

To record your thoughts, use a separate sheet or journal.

Do you experience test anxiety? Describe how tests generally make you feel (you might include an example of a specific test situation and what happened). Identify your specific test-taking fears, and write out your plan to overcome fears and self-defeating behaviors.

Advantages for Liberal Arts Graduates

SUCCEEDING IN THE JOB MARKET

Because liberal education is definitely not "vocational training," you must wonder what your employment possibilities are compared to those who study business and other "vocational" fields of study. The purpose of this chapter is to address your prospects in the job market as a liberal arts graduate and advise you how you can take fullest advantage of your liberal arts background.

In this chapter, you will explore answers to the following questions:

- What are the most important skills that employers are looking for?
- How wide is the range of jobs that liberal arts graduates can apply for with a good chance of being hired?

- What do you say to employers who ask: "Why didn't you major in business?"

- What are some reasons that "floundering" during your job hunting may actually have benefits for you?

- In what ways does liberal arts apply to "the real world" of jobs?

- For what reasons are liberal arts graduates strong candidates for leadership roles in the world of work?

D O I HAVE THE SKILLS NECESSARY TO COMPETE?

Liberal arts graduates have more to offer in a constantly shifting marketplace because their broad learning skills are called into play again and again. As technologies grow and configurations of workers change rapidly, the job-seeker is continually faced with situations in which he is given new information and told to absorb it quickly and take action on it. Liberal arts graduates are most comfortable when a new body of knowledge is thrown on their desk and someone says, "Here. Learn it."

In most cases, being "trained" for a single occupation won't be enough because new areas of knowledge come into being each year. Every problem in the world of work has many dimensions—political, scientific, cultural, mathematical, even religious—and the person who is uncomfortable with any of these areas is easily left behind.

This chapter will give you good reasons to be optimistic about your job and career future. It will describe the features of liberally educated graduates that are desirable to employers and will encourage you to get the most out of your education so that you can have the skills and qualities that employers are looking for. *Graduates must sell their skills, not grades or course titles.*

Grades and transcripts are nice, but they are impossible to translate into what you can do for an employer. If you're wondering whether your college education will have any meaning for a corporation or other employer, think in terms of skills—"What can I *do* that will be useful to them?"

If I could choose one degree for the people I hire it would be English. . . .

You can teach a pack of Cub Scouts how to do portfolio analysis.

SENIOR VICE-PRESIDENT, FIRST ATLANTA CORPORATION

The people I work for told me they had no intention of hiring anybody when I first walked through the door, but after talking to me and reading my writing, they felt they would be making a mistake not to hire me.

COMMUNICATIONS EXECUTIVE, HISTORY MAJOR

The skills that you offer in the marketplace are not limited to those that can be directly observed, such as writing and speaking. More abstract skills, such as critical judgment, integrity, and maturity, are in great demand. Liberal arts fosters these kinds of skills. Also, when thinking about skills, do not overlook your ability to discuss a wide range of subjects with most everyone.

It is a fantastic advantage to be able to carry on a conversation on almost any topic with almost any person. In my career, personal contact is vitally important.

COMMODITIES BROKER, UNIVERSITY OF TEXAS GRADUATE

WHAT ARE THE TEN HOTTEST MARKETABLE SKILLS?

This will be a review of skills discussed in previous chapters, but it's important to draw them into one place, so you can recognize the cards you have in your hand that will prove to your advantage. There are 10 particular skill areas that are notably present in liberal arts students, and these skill areas are almost always considered in short supply by the job market. Simply put, employers can't get enough of these skills; they always want more. They do their best to recruit for these skills, and they are delighted when they find graduates who have them.

That you will have a liberal arts degree is no guarantee that you have acquired these skills. You can use your ingenuity or laziness to slide through or avoid courses you dislike, and miss out developing some of these skills. For example, some professors will challenge your writing skills. You may start a course kicking and screaming, but eventually you'll see your writing grow into something you enjoy reading. Many professors will make you think harder than you want to and, of course, you'll thank them later.

Thinking is the hardest work there is, which is probably the reason why so few engage in it.

HENRY FORD II

Employers look for certain skills in potential employees, and it is your responsibility to develop them. The following is a list of the 10 skills employers demand.

1. *Writing*—the ability to write memos, reports, letters, position statements, e-mails, and other communications clearly and persuasively, and hold the reader's interest.

2. *Speaking*—the ability to talk comfortably to groups ranging in size from 3 to 300, and get your point across in a way that is clear and enjoyable for the "audience." This includes committee meetings, board meetings, informal discussions, and formal speaking occasions.

3. *Listening*—the ability to focus on another person's words and non-verbal cues, be empathic with their thoughts and feelings, and respond in ways that demonstrate you "hear" them.

4. *Public relations*—the ability to effectively represent an organization to the public, including a wide variety of potential customers, clients, or constituents. This includes handling complaints, giving talks to community groups, and educating the public about your organization's activities.

5. *Risk taking*—the ability to risk failure in the pursuit of an important goal. Few ventures can be guaranteed successful because no one can predict how things will work out. Your talent for trying new things and being resilient in the face of the results is a measure of risk taking.

6. *Adaptability*—the ability to move from one project to another, from one problem to another, from one situation to another, and from one group of people to another—all done smoothly, with little friction. The ability to accommodate changing conditions in your job and adapt to whatever your employer asks of you.

It really doesn't matter how smart you are, how much education you have or how well you understand technology if you don't know how to work effectively with others.

DICK LYLES[1]

---

7. *Leadership*—the ability to take responsibility for the progress being made toward a particular goal. This does not necessarily mean being the person "in charge." It means deciding that you will exercise initiative by investigating and trying to solve a certain problem and you'll work with whoever is necessary to move toward that end.

8. *Problem solving*—the ability to focus your energies, resources, and the efforts of others toward solving a particular problem; being

resourceful in the face of obstacles; not taking "no" for an answer; and being both imaginative and persistent in the pursuit of solutions to a complicated problem.

9. *Researching*—the ability to identify both the information and the knowledge that contribute to moving an organization toward a goal. This includes library research, computer research, first-hand data gathering, and synthesizing information into a coherent, usable whole.

10. *Coping with pressure*—the ability to produce good work when you're governed by external deadlines, and being capable of functioning on other people's schedules, even when the time frame is hurried.

You won't necessarily have all of these skills in great abundance, but the more you cultivate each of them, especially a balance between all of them, the more effective you'll be in developing your career. Most jobs, businesses, and careers require some measure of all 10 of these skills. You have opportunities here in college to develop all of them, both in and out of class.

WHAT TYPE OF JOBS ARE AVAILABLE AND HOW DO YOU FIND THEM?

Look around towns and cities. Talk with your neighbors. Talk to people in the workplace. Interview alumni of your college. There are thousands of liberal arts graduates in successful business roles, in the arts, in government, in nonprofits, and everywhere else in the world of work. You name any job or field of work (outside of the most arcane and highly technical fields), and you will find liberal arts graduates in it.

Look through the *Occupational Outlook Handbook*.[2] Outside of the highly technical occupations, you will find liberal arts graduates in every field that requires a bachelor's degree. Why? Because the employers are looking for the general ability to learn and the skills listed previously.

But, you might protest, wouldn't the graduate having a journalism major have a better chance at jobs in journalism? Not necessarily. Wouldn't a graduate with a business major have a leg up for jobs in the business world? Not necessarily. These "vocational" majors do not necessarily get the advantage in hiring because employers know that courses on a transcript always mean less than the skills that the graduate brings to the job.

An employer may ask you, "Well, why did you major in liberal arts when you could have studied business?" Although this is leaping ahead to job hunting, a few years away for you, suffice it to say that you can answer that question by saying, "I preferred to develop my learning, thinking, and communication skills in liberal arts, knowing that I can learn about your business soon enough, and my analytical abilities will help me to be a productive member of your team."

There are plenty of good reasons for you to choose liberal arts rather than a vocational major, and by the time you're near graduation, you can coordinate your skills and aspirations with your career objectives. You can also have internships, summer jobs, or volunteer experiences that will give you exposure to fields of work where you may want to be employed.

For highly technical jobs that require a bachelor's degree (e.g., engineering and certain scientific jobs), liberal arts graduates cannot apply. However, recognize that such "technical" jobs represent only about 5–10 percent of the job market for college graduates. Most jobs, including the vast proportion of computer jobs, will be available to you.

> I have observed time and time again those who are able to express themselves clearly and simply—either spoken or written word—move ahead more rapidly.
>
> **HAMLINE UNIVERSITY GRADUATE**

Don't let the graduates of other colleges intimidate you with their "vocational" majors. Their transcripts don't mean much unless they can show they have the skills employers want the most. You may well have more of those skills than they do, especially if you wade into the liberal arts curriculum and take the courses that really build the skills you're going to need.

If you're concerned about not having enough exposure to business during college, take a few business courses at your college or elsewhere, and get some exposure to business through internships, volunteer work, or part-time jobs during the school year or summer.

Explore Potential Careers

Career possibilities extend far beyond what you can imagine. Brainstorm about career areas. Ask instructors, relatives, and fellow students about their own careers and ones they know about. Check your library for books on careers or biographies of people who worked in fields that interest you. Explore careers you discover through reading the newspaper, novels, or nonfiction. If a character in your favorite movie has a job you think you'd like, see what you can find out about it.

Your school's career center is an important resource in your investigation. The career center may offer job listings, occupation lists, assessments of skills and personality types, questionnaires to help you pinpoint career areas that may suit you, informational material about different career

Critical-thinking questions for career investigation.

What can I do in this area that I like/am good at?	Do I respect the company and/or the industry?
What are the educational requirements (certificates or degrees, courses)?	Do companies in this industry generally accommodate special needs (child care, sick days, flex time, or working at home)?
What skills are necessary?	Do I need to belong to a union?
What wage or salary is normal for an entry-level position, and what benefits can I expect?	Are there opportunities in this industry within a reasonable distance from where I live?
What kinds of personalities are best suited to this kind of work?	What other expectations are there beyond the regular workday (travel, overtime, etc.)?
What are the prospects for moving up to higher-level positions?	Do I prefer a service or manufacturing industry?

areas, and material about various companies. The people who work at the center can help you sort through the material.

Use your critical-thinking skills to determine what questions you should ask in addition to inquiring what tasks you would perform for any given job. Many other factors will be important to you. Look at Figure 10.1 for some of the kinds of questions you might ask as you talk to people or investigate materials.

Within every career field, a wide array of job possibilities exists that you might not see right away. For example, the medical world involves more than just doctors and nurses. Emergency medical technicians respond to emergencies, administrators run hospitals, researchers test new drugs, lab technicians administer specific procedures such as X-rays, pharmacists administer prescriptions, retirement community employees work with the elderly, and more.

Within each job, there is also a variety of tasks and skills that often go beyond what you know. You may know that an instructor teaches, but you may not see that instructors also often write, research, study, create course outlines, create strategy with other instructors, give presentations, and counsel. Push past your first impression of any career and explore what else it entails. Expand your choices as much as you can using thorough investigation and an open mind.

Career Planning and Placement Offices

Generally, the career planning and placement office deals with post-graduation job placements, while the student employment office, along with the financial aid office, has more information about working while in school. At either location you might find general workplace information, listings of job opportunities, sign-ups for interviews, and contact information for companies. The career office may hold frequent informational sessions on different topics. Your school may also sponsor job or career fairs that give you a chance to explore job opportunities.

Many students, because they don't seek job information until they're about to graduate, miss out on much of what the career office can do. Don't wait until the last minute. Start exploring your school's career office early in your university life. The people and resources there can help you at every stage of your career and job exploration process.

Networking

Networking is one of the most important job-hunting strategies. With each person you get to know, you build your network and tap into someone else's. Imagine a giant think link connecting you to a web of people just a couple of phone calls away. Of course, not everyone with whom you network will come through for you. Keep in contact with as many people as possible in the hope that someone will. You never know who that person might be.

With whom can you network? Friends and family members may know of jobs or other people who can help you. At your school, instructors, administrators, or counselors may give you job or contact information. People at school employment or career offices can help you locate work. Some schools even have opportunities for students to interact with alumni. Look to your present and past work experience for more leads. Employers or coworkers may know someone who needs new employees. A former employer might even hire you back with similar or adjusted hours, if you left on good terms.

The contacts with whom you network aren't just sources of job opportunities. They are people with whom you can develop lasting, valuable relationships. They may be willing to talk to you about how to get established, the challenges on the job, what they do each day, how much you can expect to make, or any other questions you have similar to those in Figure 10.1. Thank your contacts for their help and don't forget them. Networking is a two-way street. Even as you receive help, be ready to extend yourself to others who may need help and advice from you.

WHAT IS ENTRY-LEVEL PSYCHOSIS?

You may be skeptical about the ability of liberal arts graduates to be hired. After all, you may know some who graduated with liberal arts degrees and they are driving taxicabs, flipping burgers, or doing menial kinds of work. You might wonder, "What good were their liberal arts studies?"

Well, yes, the "first jobs" of liberal arts graduates are sometimes menial and certainly not reflective of their abilities. This is a well-known phenomenon. It represents the "slow start" that sometimes (not always) characterizes the career progress of a liberal arts graduate. Usually the slow start is because the graduate is trying to figure out what she wants to do. Warming up to the world of business after you've been studying the great problems of humanity takes a little adjusting. Sometimes the graduate takes off for a while to see what China is like, sometimes she hangs around a computer start-up business just to get her feet on the ground, and sometimes he hides out in graduate school not knowing what else to do.

All of these are not necessarily bad things to do. They allow you time to develop your focus, decide what kinds of work are worth doing, get your personal philosophy in shape, or see parts of the world before you get committed to a work role.

This is called "entry-level psychosis" because when a liberal arts graduate starts his career, it may look as though he's out of touch with the reality of the working world, and that maybe he will never join it. Not to worry. Your best days lie ahead.

Who will society turn to in the next century to ponder the impact of technological change on the human condition? Computer scientists? Who will we rely upon to explain this change to the average citizen? Engineers? Obviously not. Only those people with a solid foundation in the humanities will be able to cope with the changes which we will see in the upcoming decades.

HENRY CAMPBELL, *PRESIDENT, WADSWORTH PUBLISHERS OF CANADA, LTD.*

The "slow start" is misleading. The liberal arts graduate is gathering herself for the road ahead. Her abundant skills will make themselves known soon enough. Research has shown that, after a year or two in a corporation or other organization, the liberal arts graduates "catch up" to the rest of the college graduates and often pass them on the way to positions of higher responsibility.

The first jobs of liberal arts graduates often send their parents into apoplectic fits. "Your education cost thousands of dollars and you're doing *what?*" The initial jobs—cab drivers, bank clerks, river rafting

REAL WORLD PERSPECTIVE

Shonda Buchanan, *Loyola Marymount University, 1997, Major: English*

I am presently associate editor of *Turning Point Magazine,* an African American publication that is issue oriented. It has a circulation of 50,000 in Southern California and Washington, DC. I manage the production of the magazine.

I decided to invest $30,000 in myself by attending LMU for a liberal education. I could have attended a public university for very little money. I had to pay for college on my own. I decided instead to get the best education I could get for myself by going there. I felt that a good liberal education would help me to become a better writer and a better thinker.

It was worth it to me to spend $30,000 for a liberal education because, as a poet and writer, I do not feel pigeon-holed by any career changes I want to make. For instance, I'm finishing up my first novel with a goal of selling this novel and beginning my life as a full-time writer.

I am also a performance poet, and do readings across the country. My novel is pretty much consuming all my time now, and after I finish this, I'll begin a memoir. See what a liberal arts education has done for me?

I'm thinking of going back to school next year to obtain my MA in English so that I can teach. There are no limits to career choice or redirecting your career with a liberal arts education.

(continued)

guides, restaurant servers—are not accurate indicators of what is to come. The adjustment from liberal education to the world of work—Kierkegaard one day, market share the next—can be a shocking transition.

Entry-Level Psychosis Is Good for You

In most cases, the menial jobs are "interim jobs," ways of earning money and staying loose while getting oneself together, deciding what to do, and developing future opportunities. No one said you were going to become King or Queen of The World immediately.

Everything that I learn is fodder for writing. Literature helped me to understand how to relate to people who are not like me. For example, reading the book *The House on Mango Street* helped me to better understand Latina people. The entire class on literature from different cultures opened up those other cultures for me.

Liberal arts taught me to be interested in everything. This broad foundation helps me in any job or career. You'll know more, you'll understand more.

If a person doesn't know what he wants to do, and he comes to college, liberal arts is the area to get into because eventually he'll find something.

I DECIDED TO INVEST $30,000 IN MYSELF BY ATTENDING LMU

FOR A LIBERAL EDUCATION.

I credit my mother with stirring my initial responsiveness to learning. The best thing my mom did for me was that she would bring me a box filled with books and I would choose what I wanted to read. I knew I was going to become a writer. I used to walk around the neighborhood when I was a little girl and take notes on everything that happened. Liberal arts gave me more breadth as a writer than studying journalism would have.

Many liberal arts graduates go through entry-level psychosis. It is a useful rite of passage. Why miss the chance to suffer? Why bypass the bouts of uncertainty and existential woe? If you get a cushy first job, you would likely envy your friends who lived in the pits for a while. A dose of despair and a bleak outlook is good for you. It sharpens your personal philosophy. What is "The Good Life" anyway? Barbara Ehrenreich says

> The problem is that our educated young people have never heard of anyone—outside of certain monastic orders—subsisting voluntarily on less than $50,000 per year. The result . . . is that middle-class youth have come to expect to leap directly from a college dorm to a condominium,

eliminating that entire stage of the human life cycle known as "finding yourself." And that phase, now as in Kerouac's day, is best conducted in a sixth-floor walkup apartment and on a diet of peanut butter and day-old bread.[3]

You're looking forward to entry-level psychosis already, aren't you? This will be your chance to keep conventional success at arm's length, to step back and be skeptical about the consumerist culture for a while before deciding where or whether to set foot in it.

The first year out you need to dwell a bit on how you define "success," or if you even like the word at all. You can do anything you want with the first year or two after graduation. Don't let it bother you if people say, "Well, how about getting your career rolling?" There'll be plenty of time for that. For now, drive the cab, observe, muse about things, explore, see what's going on, and only when you're ready, jump in.

Some may ridicule the idea of "finding oneself," but they're just caught in their own washing machines. The straight-ahead type gets one idea, tumbles it on spin cycle, and comes up with the same thing. You, by contrast, are willing to take off the blinders and look around. Every thoughtful person seeks to find who they are. A liberal education gives you the foundation for considering where on the playing field you want to leave your footprint.

LIBERAL ARTS GRADUATE IN THE REAL WORLD: CASE 3

Devlin stumbled away from graduation with $20,000 of debt and a sick feeling that he'd take forever to pay it off. Yet, he refused to compete for job offers from the on-campus recruiters of Corporate America, and he resisted looking for a job on his own because he wanted to travel, fool around, stay a kid for a while. Why not? No chance to do it later. He worked on a farm to get free of the scholarly life, did retreats in a Buddhist monastery to develop his "mindfulness," and sold a little publication he created about dirt bike trails in Pennsylvania.

Devlin was in the persistent mode of "I don't know who I am, what I want, or where I'm going." This is not necessarily a bad thing! In fact, it may be very useful to be bewildered for a period of time. With his economics major and business/marketing courses firmly in hand, Devlin could easily have landed jobs in marketing or advertising departments or agencies. But he had no drive or energy for these pursuits. He needed time. Travel, odd jobs, and wandering afforded him the chance to look around and reflect. As long as he didn't commit any crimes or incur massive debt, Dev's "wandering" was constructive.

After a year and a half, Devlin realized that his work in a youth agency as a volunteer gave him the clue—he really wanted to apply his business-type skills to helping nonprofit organizations obtain government grants. This way he could be "entrepreneurial" and be helpful to agencies in need. Two years after graduation, his career began by helping a Youth Service Center obtain a federal grant for drug and alcohol prevention. From there he became a program director and grants administrator for a large youth services agency.

WHAT IS FLOUNDERING?

When new college graduates lack focus in their job hunting, and instead they travel, or spend their time in menial employment, they are usually accused by those around them (or themselves) of "floundering." This is a derisive term that conjures up the image of a flopping fish that can barely keep its head up and most definitely knows not where it's going.

If you listen the critics, you would imagine that those who "flounder" are destined for oblivion. Yet, floundering can be good for you.

What does floundering do for you? It broadens your exposure to the working world. It allows you to develop skills you would otherwise have ignored. It makes you more a citizen of the world because you know a little of what's going on. It helps you get a firmer grip on what you *don't* want to do. Perhaps most importantly, it encourages you to be creative about your career. You see more possibilities and tend to want to create your own future.

> Whatever you do in this world, somebody helps you.
>
> **ALTHEA GIBSON**

Floundering gives you a chance to laugh at people who think "floundering" is bad for you. They just looked at one option and went for it. How silly. How narrow. College keeps you hidden from work possibilities, so a little time is needed to investigate before settling into a career.

You undoubtedly have something great in you. You don't think so? If you give yourself freedom and explore patiently, you'll find something interesting and important to do. But, if you get obsessed about having a job, *any* job, you'll head for the nearest job opening and fail to use your imagination.

Having a readily available job doesn't mean you're necessarily "making it." You may be just feeding your insecurities. People who do great things usually flounder for a while first because they are letting their unconscious intuition lead them to where they really want to be.

REAL WORLD PERSPECTIVE

Elsa Rousseau, *Loyola Marymount University, 1995,*
Major: Sociology, Minor: History

I graduated from Loyola Marymount University in 1995 with a sociology major and a history minor. Today, I work for a real estate and investment banking firm as head of the marketing department. I manage a staff of 15 people, do all the graphic design, and plan the special events. I started as a database coordinator and was office manager until my recent promotion to marketing manager.

We act as financial advisors in the sale of commercial properties. Our customers are banks, life insurance companies, and so on.

They hired me because there was energy and compatibility between us. I was very detail oriented and very organized. It wouldn't have mattered if I were a dance major.

I knew nothing about that financial stuff when I started . . . absolutely nothing. I learned everything on the job. I taught myself everything by playing around with the computer, and reading trade magazines and journals, instructional manuals, and books. I talk to people. If they mention a book or an Internet site, I read that. In my company, if you want to learn it, then learn it.

I didn't take any courses at all involving numbers or math during my years at LMU. I'm getting those now in an MBA program at Pepperdine.

How necessary is an advanced degree in business for the work that you do? In my specific area, I don't think an advanced degree is necessary. I think the experience counts more.

Not too many people at my company have advanced degrees in business. Of the six owners, only two have such degrees. At my company, your performance is what's important. At the beginning, it was hard to establish myself because I was a woman in a male-dominated industry and I was young. Now that I have been here for five years, I am well respected. I like

(continued)

this work because it's so exciting. I like the energy, the stress. No two days are alike.

I did not look specifically for a job in the financial field. I was looking for a job after graduation and went to a temp agency. They sent me to this company and I took the job because I needed one and this seemed like a pretty good place.

Many students think, "Well, a lot of liberal arts courses are just prerequisites. It doesn't matter what you take. Just get through them." You're focused on getting to your major as fast as possible. But I realized that the prereqs gave me necessary writing skills, speaking skills, analytical skills, and more.

Standing in front of a group and making a presentation was one of the skills that I had to use right away in my job. When you do this and feel confident, it's really a good feeling.

I had led such a sheltered life before college. Taking a course such as race relations opened me up to the very many and different ideas that everyone else had. It was like this in other required courses too.

I KNEW NOTHING ABOUT THAT FINANCIAL STUFF WHEN I STARTED.
ABSOLUTELY NOTHING.

I would say to a freshman, "A lot of business people want liberal arts grads because they think more creatively than the business major." I'm in management. I'm not looking for the cookie-cutter. Nowadays the buzz is "think outside the box." The courses in liberal arts cover a lot more. There's a broader range of ideas, and that breadth can be applied to business.

You (a liberal arts graduate) can get a job just about anywhere because you know how to research, you know how to speak, you know how to think.

Liberal arts prepares you better to go out into the world, but liberal arts graduates are not exactly sure how to make that jump. They have to put a little more effort into the job search, starting with figuring out what they think they want to do.

WHY DO MANY EMPLOYERS FAVOR LIBERAL ARTS GRADUATES?

Your question may be hanging in the air, "No matter what I say, won't the business major have more to offer?" The answer is that many employers favor liberal arts graduates over business graduates because they think more broadly, they communicate more clearly, they relate better to a wide variety of people, and they are more likely to become leaders.

The well-prepared manager of the next generation will simply need more than the nation's graduate schools of business can provide. These needs can be best addressed in the liberal arts. . . . Managers must understand foreign cultures, languages, politics, and business practices.

PROFESSOR G. C. PARKER, *STANFORD BUSINESS SCHOOL*

Susan graduated with majors in English and religious studies. She got hired by Texas Instruments because she could rewrite the reports and memos of the engineers and technology majors. Susan knew nothing about systems and engineering, but she gradually learned enough to speak to the technicians. She was promoted to manager because of her ability to motivate people. Susan left to work with the Austin Chamber of Commerce, where she was immediately thrust into complicated economic development projects. She knew nothing about them, but the Chamber liked her ability to speak and write and her fearlessness in learning new technical and financial concepts. Susan climbed on the learning curve and eventually talked "rates of return" with the best of them, advancing to vice president for economic development. What did English and religion have to do with her careers? She was used to grappling with big ideas and unafraid of taking on new belief systems. High finance is just another version of religion.

HOW DO LIBERAL ARTS COURSES APPLY TO JOBS IN THE REAL WORLD?

You will see connections between any field of liberal arts study and any field of work. Thus, every course you take has value in the working world. Knowledge does not fall into neat compartments that are unrelated. Knowledge intertwines. That is one of the best-kept secrets of the liberal education. Some people think you have to study business to do business. You know better. Business is economics, sociology, psychology, mathematics, philosophy, and religion all rolled into one.

Let's play a game. It's called "Everything Relates To Everything." Choose a liberal arts field of study and randomly select a field of work. Say biology and stock broker. How does one apply biology to stock brokering? Painstaking research skills, honed in the library and laboratory, can be applied to researching company earnings reports and volumes of data. The careful classification of species might apply to understanding the subtle and complex differences between a variety of investment instruments.

Here's another one to ponder: English literature and banking. Great novels relating to usury and financial mismanagement help the liberal arts graduate appreciate how people feel about their money. Many of today's banks have come to be regarded as faceless, uncaring bureaucracies. A wise English major might think of ways to communicate that could restore the bank customers' faith and confidence.

How about chemistry and a job in an art gallery? The restoration of great art works requires a detailed knowledge of chemistry. How about political science and a job in a railroad museum? Politics is present throughout the railroad movement in America—recruitment of immigrant laborers, competition with the highway lobby, and businesses both helped and hurt by the railroads. What does philosophy have to do with computer jobs? Philosophy includes the study of logic, and computer systems are based on logic. Philosophy also encourages broad and conceptual thinking of a high order, as does computer systems design.

Not only do connections exist between liberal arts fields of study and areas of employment, but also liberal arts graduates can "see" these connections and apply them. Solutions for the problems of the world draw on many areas of knowledge at once. Life is, after all, inter-disciplinary. A plant nursery deals with botany, economics, marketing, sociology, art, and even physics (how do plants affect the acoustics of a concert hall?). Liberal arts graduates are fully aware that once they graduate most of their learning lies ahead of them. They know how to learn what they don't know, apply what they do know, and ask questions to determine what they need to know.

Carolyn graduated with her psychology major and contemplated law school, but before she could enroll, she needed money. She started a little business creating videotapes about Colorado history and selling them to the Colorado public schools. Her knowledge of historical research began the day she arrived in Colorado. Her knowledge of marketing began the day she first thought about how to do it. Her knowledge of education began the first day she walked into a public school.

In starting her enterprise, Carolyn's advantage as a liberal arts graduate was that she knew she would have to learn her business along the way. She accepted her role as a learner and went forward with the confidence that she could learn anything she needed to know. Her business prospered for three years until she was accepted to law school.

HY ARE LIBERAL ARTS GRADUATES STRONG CANDIDATES FOR LEADERSHIP ROLES?

When you've studied political systems, ecosystems, social systems, and philosophies that are more vast than all outdoors, you can tackle business problems without flinching. Liberal arts graduates may take a year or two to show their full capabilities, but employers often recognize and encourage their growth potential. Liberal arts equals leadership.

Many CEOs and a wide range of successful professionals are liberal arts graduates. It's no accident. Welcome to "The Law of Expanding Influence." The higher you go in any organization or career field, the more your liberal arts skills are valued. Your advantage tends to accelerate as your career progresses.

> The major problems encountered in the business world deal with human nature, human error, and human understanding.
>
> **ST. LOUIS UNIVERSITY GRADUATE**

Technical skills—the kinds that liberal arts people have less of—are nice for solving technical problems. However, when it comes to raising the money to fund a project, or building a working team, or navigating the local politics, or educating the public about the necessity for a project, or analyzing how a project will fit into the community, many employers would rather have liberal arts graduates.

Liberal arts graduates are strong candidates for leadership roles in business and elsewhere because they think broadly from day one. They look at a job and ask, "Where is this company heading, where is the industry moving, where is the country heading?" Leaders are not always right, but it takes a leadership attitude to even ask these questions.

> If money is your hope for independence you will never have it. The only real security that a man can have in this world is a reserve of knowledge, experience, and ability.
>
> **HENRY FORD**

You'll have so many choices about what to do with your degree that they may even confuse you. It's a confusion that will cause you to be more creative, to think of combining fields of work. You'll also think of inventing new jobs or careers. Let your heart take over. Ask yourself what kinds of work fit your ideals.

This does not necessarily mean a grand design, a presidency, a cure for a disease, or a "big" mission. But it does mean doing something that reaches beyond yourself and your daily comfort needs. The biggest advantage that liberal arts gives you is the push to do something rewarding and of value. When you do that, the other things you're seeking—prosperity, challenge, personal growth, and enjoyment—will fall into place.

> I'll bet my presence at Dickinson (College) has hardly been missed since my graduation except for the collective sigh of relief from my defeated professors. Good people all but not really up to the challenge, I'm afraid. I've become a blue-collar celebrity of sorts. Imagine a local horseshoer with a B.S. in biology and economics. Rather titillates the fancy of over-educated and under-educated people alike.
>
> I am given to reflections and gentle musings from time to time on the nature of man, the understanding of happiness. How is one to separate one's own talents, interests, ideas, predilections, strengths . . . from the exposure and polish of four years of liberal arts education? Am I not the same person today I was four years ago?
>
> I'll answer that. I'm very much the same person but just as a marathon runner is strengthened by the rigors of training, so have I benefited from the rigors of four years of liberal arts education. That, combined with my natural tenacity, gives me the skills to be successful at anything I put my hand to. Attitude is the one prerequisite for success, and a liberal arts education can give you an attitude of quiet confidence.
>
> I am a successful farrier because I can read, write, and express myself to all levels of understanding. I can communicate with people without condescending or offending them. I can hold my own with a highbrow who has a plunging charger in the back yard. I suspect the skill of communication weaves through the success of people and careers universally.[4]

JOURNAL ENTRY

To record your thoughts, use a separate sheet or journal.

The liberal arts curriculum can provide a breadth of learning and communications skills that are desirable to a wide variety of employers. What are the benefits that you hope to get from liberal arts that will help in your career? What are the skills you will cultivate in liberal arts that will most help you? Liberal arts graduates sometimes have difficulty getting the first job after graduation, but they tend to do better with each succeeding job. How do you expect to fare in the job market in the short run and in the long run?

Liberal Arts Graduates Do "Good Work"

SEEKING BETTERMENT OF COMMUNITY AND SELF

The purpose of this chapter is to consider what satisfactions you hope to get from your career. We will examine the concept of "good work"—work that looks beyond material gain. Liberal education encourages you to look at your career as something more than "making a living." It suggests that you regard career choices as the expression of your personal values.

In this chapter, you will explore answers to the following questions:

- In your view, what is "good work"?
- What role does money play in your consideration of career options?

- Why is it important to look beyond yourself in your choice of career?

- For what reasons is your role in the world of work more than earning a living?

- How can material gain and doing good be compatible?

- Why is "good work" not limited to "save-the-world" types of people?

- How does liberal education encourage graduates to be visionaries?

Work has no meaning at all unless it creates value.

Some people don't observe the idea that they have purposes in life other than the material.

E. F. SCHUMACHER

WHAT DOES "GOOD WORK" MEAN?

There is work, and there is "good work." Liberal arts will encourage you to envision your work in terms of the values it satisfies for you. You decide what the "good" is in good work. The more your work fits your values, the happier you'll be.

You may not even want to read this chapter. You're focused on getting through school, barely able to think about what jobs might lie ahead. Now, we're talking about the "value" of your work. However, there are bills to be paid, and it's all so far away. Let's get the courses completed first, a job in hand, and then maybe we can talk about the "value" of work. Why talk about it now?

Because the life we wish for is often what we get. If you dream of a room filled with money, chances are you'll make that happen. You'll concentrate your energies in that direction. And then, your peak life experience will be diving around in your room filled with bills, whooping and hollering, living it up.

If you fantasize about being famous, becoming a celebrity, there's a pretty good chance you'll figure out a way to do it. And then your peak experience will be seeing your image reflected from a magazine cover, a TV screen, a Web site, or corporate public relations literature. You'll love being recognized on the street and the street will love you right back.

So, the thoughts you have now about the life you want will lead you in certain directions. Liberal arts gives you opportunities to broaden and deepen your perspective on what "desirable" careers are.

HAT IS THE POTENTIAL RETURN ON YOUR INVESTMENT?

With all the money expended for college, and all the income postponed while you are diligently studying, it is tempting to view college as an "investment." You may want to see the "payoff" for your hard work in terms of dollars.

"My dream was to go into psychiatric social work, but I don't think I could live on that, so I'm going into banking instead." When I protested that she should hold onto her ideals and try to get by on the $30,000 or so that psychiatric social workers earn, she looked baffled, as if I were recommending an internship with Mother Teresa.

BARBARA EHRENREICH, *MS. MAGAZINE*

So, when you hear that liberal arts graduates may be a little slow to get started and their initial earnings are a bit lower than other graduates, you get even more anxious to see a satisfactory "return."

A real test for smarts would ask not for the nearest synonym for 'acquisitive,' but Are you doing what you love? . . . Have you figured out what's important?

ADAIR LARA, *SAN FRANCISCO CHRONICLE*

Earnings after graduation are one way to keep score. You can anticipate that a few years after graduation, you'll be earning right up there with many other graduates and you may find opportunities to create entrepreneurial income for yourself. Over the long haul, college will be worth many more dollars to you than what you would earn without any higher education. Employers prefer college graduates and look to them to fill most of their jobs having the greatest responsibility. There is a cachet associated with a college degree and you will benefit from it.

REAL WORLD PERSPECTIVE

William Cowden, *Claremont McKenna College, 1998, Major: Economics*

I'm a 1998 graduate of Claremont McKenna College with an economics major; however, I wish I had studied more literature and other nonbusiness courses. I started as a chemistry major with an interest in the environment, but I believed the job market was not good for environmental jobs, so I switched to economics.

I'm a bit of a tree-hugger at heart. I think someday I'll get back to that. I have been exposed to community service since the seventh grade when it was required. This consciousness has stayed with me. I have valued the spirit of giving since that time. Unfortunately, I leaned more toward the practical degree than I should have. I took too many economics courses.

Currently, I manage portfolio managers at a large investment bank in Minneapolis, Minnesota. For the previous two years, I was a portfolio manager in Long Beach, California, managing trust accounts for wealthy individuals.

Practicum courses helped me to get the job with the bank because I had to go out to get information, and then come back and "teach" the class what I had learned. These presentations definitely help me in my job today.

The recruiter who hired me for the first job after college was looking for community involvement. In taking into account my community service and service to the school, I think he was looking for signs of responsibility and honesty. For over two years, I was co-president of the main community service organization here at CMC called Civitas. I also worked with Pomona College to develop an organization called Food Salvage that takes surplus food out to soup kitchens. I also worked with composting, blood drives, and others.

(continued)

I'm concerned about the role of money in people's lives. The power that money has over people really troubles me. I also worry about the power it could have over me. That's partly why I chose to get a job in this field.

I have a long-range interest in nonprofit concerns. I want to use my financial skills to help charitable organizations. Managing money for huge charities would be a lot more motivating than helping wealthy individuals. My dream job might be managing funds for The Nature Conservancy.

MY DREAM JOB MIGHT BE MANAGING FUNDS FOR
THE NATURE CONSERVANCY.

Many of these charities are much more demanding about how their money is invested than trust fund people are, which would make it a far greater challenge for me.

The breadth of liberal arts learning is something I value highly. One of the advantages of a liberal education is that I was introduced to topics I never would've thought about, and developed a passion for them. It helped me be excited about learning in general. When you develop a love of learning, it's really something to be treasured.

When you have so many interesting classes available in your concentration, and also so many areas to taste, you can't help but wish there was more room for electives or more hours in the day.

Liberal arts people are more likely to read the newspaper and keep up with events that don't necessarily affect them, such as people having troubles in different places in the world.

I am pleased that my liberal arts skills, such as writing and analytical thinking, helped me get the jobs with the banks because I now have a basis of financial knowledge that will help me whatever I do. I've shown that I can succeed in the financial world even though my education is mainly liberal arts.

There are other ways to keep score, to evaluate the benefits that you derive from your college degree. These ways are not as countable as income. These benefits include:

1. Enriching your life through exposure to the arts and involvement with a variety of ideas and people

2. Being elevated to positions of responsibility at work, involving high-level projects and learning new concepts

3. Creating opportunities for graduate or professional study, based on the foundation of a liberal education

4. Passing on your learning to your children, other loved ones, and friends

So, a dollar-for-dollar return on your investment is difficult to measure. Carol Jin Evans, in her insightful poem on pages 6 and 7, makes fun of this notion because she believes that dollars are very much the *least* of what you derive from your liberal education. By viewing dollars as excessively important, you may miss the more lasting benefits as opportunities pass in front of your eyes.

OW DOES LIBERAL ARTS HELP YOU DEVELOP YOUR IDEA OF "GOOD WORK"?

Schumacher spells out three purposes of human work—guidelines to "good work"—in the following fashion: First, to provide necessary and useful goods and services. Second, to enable every one of us to use and thereby perfect our gifts like good stewards. Third, to do so in service to, and in cooperation with, others, so as to liberate ourselves from our inborn egocentricity.[1]

Liberal arts encourages you to consider what "good work" means to you. Your professors don't do this directly. They don't say, "We're going to talk about 'good work' today." But, by introducing the central and compelling topics of humanity, you're encouraged to think, "What is there that's happening in this world where I might want to become involved?"

Perhaps you study earthquakes in geology class and you consider how you might become part of the world of tremors and the prevention of human loss and destruction. Or maybe you become interested in Russian culture through a language class and want to be in that country as a political analyst.

Liberal arts throws the whole human experience on your table and says, "Here it is. What looks good to you?"

The most magnificently trained doctor can actually be injurious to our psychological well-being; technical competence cannot compensate for human indifference.

CHANGE MAGAZINE

No matter what courses you may take in liberal arts, if you find them especially interesting, there are jobs out there that can get you involved in that subject matter. Good work is everywhere. But you say, "There must be some courses that have no connection to 'the real world.'" What about philosophy? Not applicable? Hardly. Philosophy stresses analytical thinking and that skill is highly sought in computer systems, management consulting, artificial intelligence, and many other areas of work. What about religious studies? People seeking to extend that background can work in government agencies that deal with religious cultures, nonprofit organizations that work with religious groups either within or outside the United States, or church-related organizations.

> "One often hears someone say, 'I work to take care of my family and so I don't stop to ask whether I like the work or not.' It may be that we burden our families unnecessarily by making them the excuse or reason why we hate our work."[2]

Perhaps you think that providing for yourself and your future family is "good work" enough without worrying about saving the rest of the world. In fact, "saving the world" is a derisive term that is often applied to people who want their work to extend beyond their immediate circle of loved ones. Why emphasize reaching beyond yourself?

Never doubt that a small group of thoughtful committed citizens can change the world. Indeed it's the only thing that ever has.

MARGARET MEAD

People whose work reaches far beyond themselves tend to be the happiest, most fulfilled people. And they do not necessarily sacrifice earnings either. A recent study of millionaires by Dr. Thomas Stanley points out that most millionaires are exceptionally happy with their work and one of their main sources of happiness is believing that their work provides benefits for humanity.[3] Gail Sheehy reports in her book *Passages* that people who have a sense of purpose in their work described themselves as the happiest of all her respondents.[4] Purpose was more closely linked with happiness than money, status, fame, or any of the usual inducements.

The liberal education lets you know what kind of world we live in, and examines humanity from many different angles. The more differences

REAL WORLD PERSPECTIVE

Greg Stearns, *Claremont McKenna College, 1993, Majors: Government and Russian/Soviet–European Studies*

I graduated from Claremont McKenna College in 1993 with majors in government and Russian/Soviet–European studies. I am presently a detective with the Los Angeles Police Department.

My first job after CMC was as a platoon leader in the Army. My ROTC training at CMC helped me make quick, solid decisions. This experience as an Army officer has helped me in all of my police work since that time.

My next job was as a deputy for the San Diego Sheriff's Department. I joined the LAPD in 1995. My assignments with LAPD have included under-cover narcotics, homicide, and registration of sex offenders. I am one of the youngest detectives on the force. I am currently assigned to the sex crimes unit of the Hollywood detectives.

Only a high school education is required to be a member of the LAPD. It's something that graduates of Claremont McKenna College do not usually do. But my thought is that my CMC background is an advantage in my work. It has allowed me to progress at a much faster rate.

I'm not wasting my education, because I have a leg up on many of my peers. I have an advantage that I might not enjoy in other fields of work or professions. I run into CMC graduates all the time and they're absolutely stunned about what I do for a living.

When I made my initial decision to enter law enforcement, my parents were not happy. They were afraid for my safety. Detective work appears to be somewhat safer to them. They might still like me to become a lawyer, but I'm not interested in that.

CMC has helped me in many ways. One of the things I developed was the ability to make sound decisions quickly. That has helped me greatly in my career.

(continued)

Writing is another important skill that I developed at CMC. I use it every day. My reports are reviewed by supervisors, judges, juries, and so on. This skill quickly sets you apart.

Having had opportunities in college to get up in front of a group of people and make presentations definitely has helped me with my job. I speak with people each day.

My language skills have given me an advantage at work. Taking four years of Russian has helped me to do translating for the Russian population here in LA. I also use these language skills when the LAPD gets involved in Russian organized crime. Suspects use the language barrier as a shield, so I can break through that. Speaking to people in their native language can also break down barriers, generate some trust, and get the information you need.

WHEN I CAN PUT AWAY A CHILD MOLESTER AND HAVE A POSITIVE IMPACT ON SOMEBODY'S LIFE, THEN THAT HAS VALUE FOR ME.

Many liberal arts courses have helped me develop my analytical thinking. Shakespeare and ethics courses have helped me with moral dilemmas both in my life and at work.

Many courses provided me the opportunity to be an independent thinker. My job involves collecting the facts and remaining impartial.

In my own small way, I think that I am doing something positive for my community. When I can put away a child molester who's been abusing a child or a man who's sexually assaulted someone and have a positive impact in somebody's life, then that has value to me.

Other CMC graduates sometimes have a condescending attitude about my line of work. Here's a story:

A few years ago I was having lunch with several college graduates who majored in accounting. All of them were employed by Big Five accounting firms.

(continued)

One woman persisted in asking me: "How much do you make?" It turns out that I make $10,000 more per year than she does. "And you only need a high school diploma to be a cop, right?"

"Yes."

"Well, I think you're overpaid," she said.

"Well, let me ask you something. Ever been shot at before?"—"No."

"Ever been run over by a car?"—"No."

"Ever had to hold in some guy's guts that just got blasted by a shotgun while you're waiting for an ambulance to come?"—"No."

"Ever had to chase somebody down an alley at 2 A.M. who's armed with a gun, not knowing if they're going to turn around and shoot back at you?"—"No."

"Well, I've done all those things in the last couple of years. While you sit up in some office building figuring out how to fire another couple hundred employees to aid the bottom line for the next shareholders' meeting of the corporation, I'm out on the streets doing the things that you certainly don't have the guts to do, and dealing with the situations that you don't want to know about. I hardly think you're in a position to judge what I'm worth."

between people you discover in liberal arts—languages, cultures, physical traits, norms, histories, religions, philosophies—the more likely you may hear about something that really gets you curious.

From this multitude of perspectives, a liberal arts student has a better understanding of what "good work" might be than if he had simply studied a "vocational training" program.

HOW DOES LIBERAL ARTS HELP YOU TO SEE OUTSIDE YOURSELF?

If more college students studied liberal arts, we'd have fewer citizens who believe the world starts and ends at their front door. And fewer who believe that history began the day they were born.

Today's non-liberally educated population is too often characterized by:

- believing that a "current event" is a schedule of tonight's TV programs
- thinking that other countries are populated by poor slobs who must suffer because they had the bad judgment not to be born in the United States
- forgetting that their ancestors made it possible for them and their children to feel "entitled" to everything
- believing that anyone who is different is bad and needs to be corrected
- creating their home, other possessions, and their career as monuments to themselves
- viewing higher education as a union card, rather than a vast cornucopia of learning pleasures

The abundance that is America makes it difficult for its citizens to see beyond themselves. Your parents may want you to get little more from college than the ability to live in the style to which you have become accustomed. When comfort and security become our main goals, we pull inward and forget there are other people who have different values, norms, and priorities. Philip Slater, in *The Pursuit of Loneliness,* wrote that, as our earnings and net worth increase, we tend to build both physical and psychological fences, thus isolating ourselves from neighbors and others.[5] Gated communities are not only about safety. They're about not wanting to have much contact with people who are different.

Liberal arts opens your eyes. You may not like everything you see, but at least you'll know that Indians weren't necessarily born shooting arrows, not all cultures want to do tummy-tucks to look better, and there are societies where marriages are arranged by families.

The heart has its reasons, which reason cannot know.

BLAISE PASCAL

The main thing is that we're all in this together, whether we like it or not. Something besides your bank account can be considered when you're choosing your work. And, when you cast a wider lens upon this world, you find many more exciting things to do than if you simply stared straight ahead or riveted yourself to the TV.

Why would anyone want to "see outside themselves"? There's mostly trouble out there. "Other people" panhandle you and generally threaten your existence. You leave your front door open, even in the country these days, you're asking to be robbed.

Perhaps you're pessimistic about your ability to do anything to help anyone. There is the "look out for number one" philosophy. If your loved ones are ranked 2, 3, and 4, is there a number 28? Who ever said people had to be put in rank order? Are some people to be paid attention to and all others disregarded?

If you want to change the world, first make yourself better. That will have an effect on those around you, who will affect those around them, and so on. Every act of kindness creates a comforting angel in this world, and we control how many of them there will be.

RABBI MARVIN SCHWAB, *SUNRISE JEWISH CONGREGATION, SACRAMENTO, CALIFORNIA*

Liberal arts teaches you that there is a *there* out there, and it has people in it. Democracy gives you the freedom to ignore them, but why do that?

You're still wondering: "What does this have to do with me? I'm just a plain old student, trying to get through." Well, to tell the truth, it's more than just you. It has to do with your place in the world. The problem with focusing on day-to-day survival is that you're backsliding to your hunting and gathering roots. The more you look out and see a jungle, the more you'll act accordingly. You can pretend that passing courses is all you're about, but this narrows your vision and you lose the opportunity to see your career as a role in the world.

WHAT IS YOUR ROLE?

A role may be a less individualistic and a more cosmic way of envisioning our work in the world. Our quest for roles to play in the world is a quest for relationships. Work as a role fits a postmachine cosmology very well. Questions we might ask of our work then are the following: What role does my work have me play in the Great Work and in the work of my community and my species at this time in history? What role am I equipped to play?[6]

Playing a role? Is this a drama we're in? Well, yes. The human drama. And your role indicates that you are part of something much larger than yourself. Marching through college may give you the idea that life is self-centered. Study, study more, and the first thing anyone asks you is about your grade average or what your major is. All very you-oriented stuff. The more you go off by yourself to read or study, the more you feed the beast of self-centeredness.

You may forget that you're already part of a community—the college is a collection of people having common ends. It's a microcosm of other communities you'll be a part of later. You have a role in this college community. There is a place for cooperation among students, no matter how self-centered you think you need to be. Learners learn better from and with each other. And you may often learn better by "teaching" another student.

This is similar to what can happen when two competing businesses open on the same street. They can ignore each other, keep trade secrets, and act as islands unto themselves. Or, if they're smart and community-oriented, they can talk about ways that, cooperatively, they can attract more customers to that part of town, thereby increasing business for both of them.

"What role does my work have me play in The Great Work?" Matthew Fox asks in *The Reinvention of Work*.[7] Everyone has a role. You have a role right now, and you'll have a different one after college. You can either contemplate that role or let it be thrust upon you by default.

WHY GIVE BACK TO THE COMMUNITY AND THE WORLD?

Everyday life is demanding. You can become so caught up in the issues of your own life that you neglect to look outside your immediate needs. However, from time to time you may feel that your mission extends beyond your personal life. With all that you have to offer, you have the power to make positive differences in the lives of others. Every effort you make, no matter how small, improves the world.

Your Imprint on the World

As difficult as your life can sometimes seem, looking outside yourself and into the lives of others can help put everything in perspective. Sometimes you can evaluate your own hardships more reasonably when you look at them in light of what is happening elsewhere in the world. There are always many people in the world in great need. You have something to give to others. Making a lasting difference in the lives of others is something to be proud of.

Your perspective may change after you help build a house for Habitat for Humanity. Your appreciation of those close to you may increase after you spend time with cancer patients at the local hospice. Your perspective on your living situation may change after you help people improve their living conditions.

If you could eavesdrop on someone *talking about you* to another person, what do you think you would hear? How would you like to hear yourself described? What you do for others makes an imprint that can have far more impact than you may imagine. Giving one person hope, comfort, or help can improve his or her ability to cope with life's changes. That person in turn may be able to offer help to someone else.

As each person makes a contribution, a cycle of positive effects is generated. For example, Helen Keller, blind and deaf from the age of two, was educated through the help of her teacher Annie Sullivan, and then spent much of her life lecturing to raise money for the teaching of the blind and deaf. Another example is Betty Ford, who was helped in her struggle with alcoholism and founded the Betty Ford Center to help others with addiction problems.

How can you make a difference? Many schools and companies are realizing the importance of community involvement and have appointed committees to find and organize volunteering opportunities. Make some kind of volunteering activity a priority on your schedule. Organize a group of students to clean, repair, or entertain at a nursing home or shelter. Look for what's available to you or create opportunities on your own.

Volunteerism is also getting a great deal of attention on the national level. The government has made an effort to stress the importance of community service as part of what it means to be a good citizen, and it provides support for that effort through AmeriCorps. AmeriCorps provides financial awards for education in return for community service work. If you work for AmeriCorps, you can use the funds you receive to pay current tuition expenses or repay student loans. You may work either before, during, or after your college education. You can find more information on AmeriCorps by contacting this organization:

The Corporation for National and Community Service
1201 New York Avenue, NW
Washington, DC 20525
1-800-942-2677

Sometimes it's hard to find time to volunteer when so many responsibilities compete for your attention. One solution is to combine other activities with volunteer work. Get exercise while cleaning a park or your yard or bring the whole family to sing at a nursing home on a weekend afternoon. Whatever you do, your actions will have a ripple effect, creating a positive impact for those you help and those they encounter in turn. The strength often found in people surviving difficult circumstances can strengthen you as well.

WHAT DOES IT MEAN TO BE DOING WELL AND DOING GOOD?

A career can be an expression of what you believe is worth doing, an expression of your philosophy about the world and the place you'd like to have in it. An opportunity for you to make a contribution, do something new or better than it's been done before. Let's call this "Doing Good."

However, there's always the matter of survival. Economic survival. You may worry about how you're going to "make it" economically. Where will the jobs be? Will you make "enough" money? Will you and your future family have everything you want and need? Let's call this "Doing Well."

There may be tension between doing well and doing good. You might see an opportunity to help society, but it doesn't pay very well. Or, you might want to start a business that can be a great service to people, but it's risky. Conversely, you might have an opportunity to make "big bucks," but you fail to see its social value.

John Zehring once said that every career choice is a decision about where you stand on the scale of "Giving versus Getting."[8] A good bet is to look for career options that have the potential to satisfy you on both counts—you can make good money and you will feel satisfied that your work gives value to others. Do it in this order. First, look for the "doing good" kinds of work because these are where your heart is. You'll give far more energy to career paths that you feel pumped up about than you will to jobs that are merely there but don't excite you. Second, interview people who are in these fields and ask them how you can do okay financially. For example, you might choose to be a social worker or book editor, two fields not known for their high pay. Talk to people in these jobs and ask how they "make it."

Meaning is not something you stumble across, like the prize in a treasure hunt. Meaning is something you build into your life. You build it out of your affections and loyalties, out of the things you believe in, out of the things and people you love, out of the values for which you are willing to sacrifice something. The ingredients are there. You are the only one who can put them together into that unique pattern that will be your life. Let it be a life that has dignity and meaning for you. If it does, then the particular balance of success and failure is of less account.

JOHN GARDNER, *STANFORD MAGAZINE, MARCH, 1994*

By doing these two things, you will be able to strike a balance between doing good and doing well that will feel comfortable to you. You will be deciding how much of each is important to you. In the final analysis, if you're committed to your work (doing good), you're likely to be doing well because you will devote your full motivation to it.

You can also strike this balance the opposite way: Find a field of work that is likely to produce income, and then create ways of doing the work that have social value. This can include a business you believe in, a profession that serves people well, or a job that has value. Your career is a key step in your search for meaning in your life.

WHY IS GOOD WORK FOR EVERYONE?

Liberal arts students have studied the great human drama. They want to be a part of it. Liberal arts fosters a desire to do socially valuable work. We need all the community-mindedness we can get. Most people want to feel their work is useful to others. Good work allows one to feel connected to humanity. People need this more than they know.

> Your reason to live is being needed.
>
> **VICTOR FRANKL**

Good work is for you; it is for everyone. Regardless whether you want to be an office worker, a doctor, an accountant, a business owner, or a sea otter rehabilitator, you want your work to have a good effect. You don't want to hurt anyone. You want to offer a product or service that makes someone's life better.

Social consciousness is not only for social workers. It is for anyone who wants a successful and satisfying career. Without a concern for others, a salesperson will not make a sale, a political office seeker will not get the votes she wants, an office worker will not stay hired, and a rising executive will not get promoted.

> We make a living by what we get. We make a life by what we give.
>
> **WINSTON CHURCHILL**

Regardless of the work you're involved in, it will have a social impact. Even the most isolated scientist or the most oblivious bureaucrat will do work that affects people. If they do it well, social good will result.

We all complain about some piece of the world we believe is not good enough. A complaint is a latent desire to serve people better. We need better highways, more durable camping equipment, low-cost health insurance, safer bicycles, a Mexican restaurant in this town, recreation centers for young adults, and so on. Each of these needs suggests a profit-making or nonprofit organization that can serve people and provide satisfying careers for individuals in the process.

Profit-making has its virtues besides generating dollars. If a business gives its customers something they want, and they do it on a consistent basis, this is good work. If a business is responsive to its customers' changing needs, this is good work. You can make any job or career into good work if you have the best interests of your customers and clients at heart.

Why think about that now? Because college gives you four years to look around and ask, "What kind of work is worth doing?" This is a part of developing your personal philosophy. You're going to choose to do *something*. Why not have it be a "work" that you feel strongly about? If what you feel most strongly about is making money, then let that be your personal philosophy. You'll still have to serve the needs of many other people in order to make that money. Regardless of what you choose, let it be good work that reflects how you believe life should be lived.

WHY ARE LIBERAL ARTS GRADUATES OFTEN VISIONARIES?

Ideas are vital and liberal arts students have plenty of them. Even if only one idea in a hundred has lasting value, it may be the one that starts a revolutionary business, cures a disease, or creates a new area of knowledge. Liberal arts graduates think not only about ideas, but more importantly, "How will these ideas affect people?" They think about the consequences of their actions.

An invasion of armies can be resisted, but not an idea whose time has come.

VICTOR HUGO

Businesses and nonprofits survive and prosper because they solve tomorrow's problems today. The liberal arts graduate is a broad thinker. Years of reading Joyce, Kant, Darwin, Skinner, Durkheim, Levi-Strauss, Kafka, Dos Passos, and Shaw will do that to you. Liberal arts graduates like to think in visionary terms because after a while it becomes fun.

Furthermore, liberal arts graduates have a unique characteristic. They like to do things better than they have been done before. They like the challenge of inventing, reshaping, reconceiving—reflecting on how a problem can be solved or how can a task be moved closer to perfection.

They make money for themselves and their employers. But the game's the thing, not the money. After four years of the great sweep of history, sociology, science, anthropology, literature, art, and music, the liberal arts graduate looks at any business and instinctively asks, "Where is this thing going? What's going to happen next and how can I be a part of it?"

Education is not filling a bucket but lighting a fire.

WILLIAM BUTLER YEATS

Steve Jobs came back to Apple for the excitement of driving the vision. John Englander created his scuba diving business, the Underwater Explorer Society, in the Bahamas because the vision was compelling. Gloria Steinem lived a meager existence to become a journalist because she had a vision of what was to become *Ms. Magazine.* Carl Sagan envisioned the heavens while classmates laughed at him for being a stargazer. Barbara Walters went to secretarial school after college, but kept her spirits alive with visions of a future in television work.

Liberal education develops a sense of right, duty, and honor; and more and more in the modern world large business rests on rectitude and honor as well as on good judgment.

EDUCATOR CHARLES WILLIAM ELIOT

Good work begins and ends with integrity. Defined as "moral uprightness and honesty," integrity is the heartbeat of all the work you do. Sooner or later people will find out who you are, and they will decide how much they can trust you. It's a good idea to make a decision right now that you will be one they can trust and that you will work for organizations or enterprises that can be trusted.

Is integrity even possible in a world of sharpies, where "con game" activity has been prevalent since the Industrial Revolution, when people moved to the cities and began dealing increasingly with strangers? How do you know who you're dealing with anymore?

The potential for cheating on college tests and papers gives you ample opportunity to make a decision about where you stand on integrity. The decisions you make to compete and get ahead in college will parallel decisions you'll make later in the world of employment or running your own business.

Good work is only truly good when you know you have a moral base for how you get the job done. Ethics and morality don't get enough attention these days; yet, they're the bread and butter of a good life. So, check your integrity index in whatever career choices you make. There are plenty of people who succeed with their integrity intact. And you'll be happy that you're one of them.

For of those to whom much is given, much is required. And when at some future date the high court of history sits in judgment on each of us [we] will be measured by the answer to four questions: First, were we truly men of courage? Second, were we truly men of judgment? Third, were we truly men of integrity? Finally, were we truly men of dedication?

JOHN F. KENNEDY

JOURNAL ENTRY

To record your thoughts, use a separate sheet or journal.

Values play a central role in the most satisfying career choices. If your strongest values are part of your career, you will feel a sense of purpose in your work. How important is it to you that you feel your work has a purpose? Have you thought about what you might like your purpose to be? How does "making a difference to others" (doing good) weigh with your desire for material gain (doing well)? What will the role of money be in your career choices?

Endnotes

Introduction

1. Lance Robertson, "Liberal arts graduates' stock rising in a fast-changing economy," *The Register-Guard*, October 9, 1999, 1.

Chapter 1

1. Ann Landers column, *San Francisco Chronicle*, December 20, 1997.

2. *Chronicle of Higher Education*, August 27, 1999.

3. Lance Robertson, "Liberal arts graduates' stock rising in a fast-changing economy," *The Register-Guard*, October 9, 1999, 1.

4. Carol Jin Evans, "I tell them I'm a liberal arts major," *Chronicle of Higher Education*, June 9, 1980, Volume 20, Number 15, 48.

5. Gary Hamel, "Life, liberty, and the pursuit of cheap stuff," *The Sacramento Bee*, reprinted from *The Los Angeles Times*, April 2, 2000.

6. Tom Jackson, "Wake Up, Corporate America," *Business Week's Guide to Careers*, March–April, 1984, 43–44.

7. Robert Treadway, "E-mail alert from Treadway and Associates," April 20, 2000.

8. Daniel Goleman, *Emotional Intelligence: Why it can matter more than IQ* (New York: Bantam Books, 1995).

9. Chad Roedemeier, "Book probes the minds of millionaires," *The Sacramento Bee*, February 7, 2000.

10. Thomas J. Stanley, Ph.D., *The Millionaire Mind* (Kansas City, MO: Andrews McMeel Publishing, 2000) 34.

11. Dan K. Thomasson, "Brainpower isn't everything in the presidency," *The Sacramento Bee*, March 23, 2000.

12. Joseph W. Meeker, *The Comedy of Survival* (New York: Scribner's, 1974).

13. Carl T. Hall, "Scientist says early hominids had to walk on two legs before they could laugh," *San Francisco Chronicle*, January 10, 2000.

Chapter 2

1. Roger E. Axtell, *The Do's and Taboos of Body Language Around the World* (New York: Wiley & Sons, 1991).

2. Jennifer F. Taylor, "Bite the Wax Tadpole," e-mail correspondence, September 2, 1997.

3. Lou Marinoff, *Plato, Not Prozac! Applying Philosophy to Everyday Life* (New York: HarperCollins, 1999), 5.

Chapter 3

1. Reprinted with permission from *HIGH-TECH CAREERS FOR LOW-TECH PEOPLE,* Second Edition, by William A. Schaffer. Copyright © 1999 by William A. Schaffer, Ten Speed Press, Berkeley, CA. Available from your local bookseller, by calling 800-841-2665, or by visiting www.tenspeed.com.

2. Lou Marinoff, Ph.D., *Plato, Not Prozac! Applying Philosophy to Everyday Life* (New York: HarperCollins, 1999), 5–6.

3. Gary Belsky and Thomas Gilovich, *Why Smart People Make Big Money Mistakes* (New York: Simon & Schuster, 1999).

4. Herbert A. Chesler, "Tell them that a 'pure' liberal arts degree is marketable," *Journal of Career Planning and Employment*, Spring, 1994, 50–51.

Chapter 4

1. Howard Gardner, *Multiple Intelligences: The Theory in Practice* (New York: HarperCollins, 1993), 5–49.

2. Developed by Joyce Bishop, Ph.D., Psychology faculty, Golden West College, Huntington Beach, California. Based on Howard Gardner, *Frames of Mind: The Theory of Multiple Intelligences* (New York: HarperCollins, 1993).

Chapter 5

1. Paul R. Timm, *Successful Self-Management: A Psychologically Sound Approach to Personal Effectiveness* (Los Altos, CA: Crisp Publications, 1987), 22–41.

2. Stephen Covey, *The Seven Habits of Highly Effective People* (New York: Simon & Schuster, 1989), 108.

3. Timm, *Successful Self-Management*, 22–41.

4. Jane B. Burka and Lenora M. Yuen, *Procrastination: Why Do You Do It and What to Do About It* (Reading, MA: Perseus Books, 1983), 21–22.

Chapter 6

1. Frank T. Lyman Jr., "Think-Pair-Share, Thinktrix, Thinklinks, and Weird Facts: An Interactive System for Cooperative Thinking," in *Enhancing Thinking Through Cooperative Learning*, ed. Neil Davidson and Toni Worsham (New York: Teachers College Press, 1992), 169–181.

2. Roger von Oech, *A Kick in the Seat of the Pants* (New York: Harper & Row Publishers, 1986), 7.

3. J. R. Hayes, *Cognitive Psychology: Thinking and Creating* (Homewood, IL: Dorsey, 1978).

4. Roger von Oech, *A Whack on the Side of the Head* (New York: Warner Books, 1990), 11–168.

5. Dennis Coon, *Introduction to Psychology: Exploration and Application*, 6th ed. (St. Paul: West Publishing, 1992), 295.

6. "What Everyone Should Know About Media" (Los Angeles, CA: Center for Media Literacy, 1998).

Chapter 7

1. Steve Moidel, *Speed Reading* (Hauppauge, NY: Barron's Educational Series, 1994), 18.

2. George M. Usova, *Efficient Study Strategies: Skills for Successful Learning* (Pacific Grove, CA: Brooks/Cole Publishing, 1989), 45.

3. Francis P. Robinson, *Effective Behavior* (New York: Harper & Row, 1941).

4. Sylvan Barnet and Hugo Bedau, *Critical Thinking, Reading, and Writing: A Brief Guide to Argument*, 2nd ed. (Boston: Bedford Books of St. Martin's Press, 1996), 15–21.

Chapter 8

1. Walter Pauk, *How to Study in College*, 5th ed. (Boston: Houghton Mifflin, 1993), 110–114.

2. Analysis based on Lynn Quitman Troyka, *Simon & Schuster Handbook for Writers* (Upper Saddle River, NJ: Prentice Hall, 1996), 22–23.

Chapter 9

1. Ralph G. Nichols, "Do We Know How to Listen? Practical Help in a Modern Age," *Speech Teacher* (March 1961): 118–124.

2. Ibid.

3. Herman Ebbinghaus, *Memory: A Contribution to Experimental Psychology,* trans. H. A. Ruger and C. E. Bussenius (New York: New York Teacher's College, Columbia University, 1885).

4. Many of the examples of objective questions used in this section are from Gary W. Piggrem, "Test Item File" for Charles G. Morris, *Understanding Psychology,* 3rd ed. (Upper Saddle River, NJ: Prentice Hall, 1996).

Chapter 10

1. Michael Kinsman, "Dot com generation can't figure out how to share knowledge with others," *The Sacramento Bee,* May 7, 2000, quoting Dick Lyles, author of *Winning Ways.*

2. *Occupational Outlook Handbook, 2000–2001.* Washington, DC: U.S. Department of Labor, Bureau of Labor Statistics.

3. Barbara Ehrenreich, "Hope I die before I get rich," *Mother Jones,* September, 1986, 64.

4. Steve Parker, response to Dickinson College, Carlisle, PA, alumni survey.

Chapter 11

1. Matthew Fox, *The Reinvention of Work* (San Francisco, CA: HarperCollins, 1994, 31–32.

2. Ibid., 32.

3. Thomas J. Stanley, Ph.D., *The Millionaire Mind* (Kansas City, MO: Andrews McMeel Publishing, 2000), 186.

4. Gail Sheehy, *Passages* (New York: Bantam Books, 1984).

5. Philip Slater, *The Pursuit of Loneliness,* 3rd ed. (Boston, MA: Beacon Press, 1990).

6. Matthew Fox, *The Reinvention of Work* (San Francisco, CA: HarperCollins, 1994, 105.

7. Ibid.

8. John Zehring, personal communication, 1975.

Index